ECOLOGICAL VULNERABILITY

Humans are responsible for biodiversity loss in many related and sometimes conflicting ways. Human–wildlife conflict, commonly defined as any negative interaction between people and wildlife, is a primary contributor to wildlife extinction and a manifestation of the destructive relationship that people have with wildlife. The author presents this 'wicked' problem in a social and legal context and demonstrates that legal institutions structurally deny human–wildlife conflict, while exacerbating conflict, promoting values consistent with individual autonomy, and ignoring the interconnected vulnerabilities shared by human and non-human species alike. It is the use of international and state law that sheds light on existing conflicts, including dingo conflict on K'Gari (Fraser) Island in Australia, elephant conflict in Northern Botswana, and the global wildlife trade contributing to COVID-19. This book presents a critical analysis of human–wildlife conflict and its governance, to guide lawyers, scientists and conservations alike in the transformation of the management of human–wildlife conflict.

Katie Woolaston is an award-winning writer, interdisciplinary researcher, lawyer and senior lecturer in the QUT Law School. She works in the fields of wildlife law and conservation conflicts. She was an expert on the Intergovernmental Science-Policy Platform on Biodiversity and Ecosystem Services (IPBES) panel concerning biodiversity and pandemics, is an associate editor of the *Asia-Pacific Journal of Environmental Law*, and is a board member of Australia's National Environmental Law Association.

Ecological Vulnerability

THE LAW AND GOVERNANCE OF HUMAN–WILDLIFE RELATIONSHIPS

KATIE WOOLASTON
Queensland University of Technology

CAMBRIDGE
UNIVERSITY PRESS

CAMBRIDGE
UNIVERSITY PRESS

Shaftesbury Road, Cambridge CB2 8EA, United Kingdom

One Liberty Plaza, 20th Floor, New York, NY 10006, USA

477 Williamstown Road, Port Melbourne, VIC 3207, Australia

314–321, 3rd Floor, Plot 3, Splendor Forum, Jasola District Centre, New Delhi – 110025, India

103 Penang Road, #05–06/07, Visioncrest Commercial, Singapore 238467

Cambridge University Press is part of Cambridge University Press & Assessment, a department of the University of Cambridge.

We share the University's mission to contribute to society through the pursuit of education, learning and research at the highest international levels of excellence.

www.cambridge.org
Information on this title: www.cambridge.org/9781009054881

DOI: 10.1017/9781009051958

First published 2022
First paperback edition 2026

A catalogue record for this publication is available from the British Library

Library of Congress Cataloging-in-Publication data
NAMES: Woolaston, Katie, 1983– author.
TITLE: Ecological vulnerability : the law and governance of human–wildlife relationships / Katie Woolaston, Queensland University of Technology.
DESCRIPTION: Cambridge, United Kingdom; New York, NY: Cambridge University Press, 2021. | Based on author's thesis (doctoral - Griffith University, 2020) issued under title: Legal responses to human-wildlife conflict : individual autonomy vs ecological vulnerability. | Includes bibliographical references and index.
IDENTIFIERS: LCCN 2021057196 (print) | LCCN 2021057197 (ebook) | ISBN 9781316511992 (hardback) | ISBN 9781009054881 (paperback) | ISBN 9781009051958 (epub)
SUBJECTS: LCSH: Wildlife conservation–Law and legislation. | Animals–Law and legislation. | Human-animal relationships.
CLASSIFICATION: LCC K3525 .W66 2021 (print) | LCC K3525 (ebook) | DDC 346.04/69516–dc23/eng/20220331
LC record available at https://lccn.loc.gov/2021057196
LC ebook record available at https://lccn.loc.gov/2021057197

ISBN 978-1-316-51199-2 Hardback
ISBN 978-1-009-05488-1 Paperback

Contents

Abbreviations

AIDS	acquired immune deficiency syndrome
CAMPFIRE	Communal Areas Management Programme for Indigenous Resources
CBD	Convention on Biological Diversity
CBNRM	community-based natural resource management
CHA	controlled hunting area
CI	Conservation International
CITES	Convention on the International Trade of Endangered Species
CMS	Convention on Migratory Species
CoP	Conference of the Parties
DWNP	Department of Wildlife and National Parks (Botswana)
EEZ	exclusive economic zone
FIDMS	Fraser Island Dingo Management Strategy
FIDO	Fraser Island Defenders Organisation
FINIA	Fraser Island Natural Integrity Alliance
GEF	Global Environment Facility
HEC	human–elephant conflict
HWC	human–wildlife conflict
ICRW	International Convention on the Regulation of Whaling
IHR	International Health Regulations
IIED	International Institute on Environment and Development
IPBES	Intergovernmental Science-Policy Platform on Biodiversity and Ecosystem Services
IUCN	International Union for the Conservation of Nature
IUCN SSC	International Union for the Conservation of Nature, Species Survival Commission
KAZA TFC	Kavango–Zambezi Transfrontier Conservation Area

MEA	Multilateral Environmental Agreement
NAMWC	North American Model of Wildlife Conservation
NGO	non-governmental organisation
ODRS	Okavango Delta Ramsar Site
QPWS	Queensland Parks and Wildlife Service
RNTBC	Registered Native Title Body Corporate
UN	United Nations
UNDHR	United Nations Declaration of Human Rights
UNESCO	United Nations Educational, Scientific and Cultural Organisation
UNFPA	United Nations Population Fund
WCN	World Charter for Nature
WHC	World Heritage Convention
WHO	World Health Organisation
WMA	wildlife management area
WTO	World Trade Organisation
WWF	World Wildlife Fund

1

Introduction

The story of how this book came to be starts on one Christmas day when I was 16. I grew up on the Far North Coast of New South Wales in Australia, in a little surfing town called Cabarita Beach. On that now notorious day, I was surfing (or attempting to) in big surf on my home beach. I was not a natural surfer but my deep love and respect for the ocean, fostered over many years of it being my haven, along with my imagined teenage invincibility, made me believe that this would be the day I would conquer the surf. The waves were grey, rough and looming, difficult even for me to paddle over. It didn't take long for me to be wiped out. I was pushed onto my board's fin, it digging into my thigh, and then onto the sand below. I had a distinct thought that I was going to drown, the ocean had conquered me, not the other way around. After what felt like minutes, I was eventually carried to the surface, although not without a substantial injury requiring 11 stitches to my thigh and even more substantial damage to my pride. I haven't really surfed since but have remained connected to the ocean. It has cared for me over many years, embracing my thoughts, pain and stress as I became an adult and carried children. Perhaps because of my relationship with this place, my awareness and my connection to the ocean, I have always felt that it was worthy of illumination, awe and, most importantly, protection.

This protective mechanism was probably why I came to be aware of the phenomenon called 'human–wildlife conflict'. I have always been aware of the presence of sharks and the potential conflict they represent when we are in the water, their home. This conflict has been represented and recreated many times over in my home state of New South Wales and elsewhere around the coast of Australia. In early 2014, I was at the start of my research career. At the same time, there had been several fatal shark attacks in Western Australia and my research interest was piqued. The Western Australian government sought to implement a drum line programme and targeted killing of White Sharks off its coast. I have been continually disturbed by the social and legal response to surfers being injured or killed by sharks around the coast of Australia, this being just one example. The response, typically dictated by what is effectively a 'hunt' for the criminalised shark or, worse, a wide-reaching cull or the deployment of destructive drum lines, was being very aptly demonstrated by the Western Australian Government.

I was not the only one to question this institutional response. The proposal was hotly contested. Media and scientific articles disputed the effectiveness of a drum-line programme in reducing negative interactions with sharks and numerous community petitions and protests took place. In one instance, over 5,500 Western Australians were polled by a local paper about the shark cull, with 86 per cent of participants voting against the programme and only 13 per cent favouring the shark culls to begin again. A petition opposing the shark culls had over 32,000 signatures. Another petition received over 38,000 signatures. Despite all this societal resistance, the programme went ahead. I was confused and disheartened. In a situation where most local people, scientists, academics and others were against a cull and the drum-line and had evidence to show it would not be effective, how was this allowed to go ahead? If science and a wide-reaching social movement against the proposal were not enough to discard it, then what was?

Since then I've become aware that these seemingly isolated conflicts we have with nature are evident in a million little, less obvious examples. Not long after the implementation of the drum-line programme in Western Australia, I revisited my hometown and was struck by a very specific oddity. There were no bugs on my windscreen when driving at night. Where were they? As a teenager with my first car, bugs on my windscreen were a fact of life. Now my windscreen is clean. I felt, and continue to feel, distinct grief surrounding the loss of those bugs. I have also since been emotionally struck by the treatment of wildlife and our wider relationship with nature in numerous other ways; melancholy elephants used and abused by tourists and their handlers in Asia; dingoes euthanised on K'gari (formerly known as Fraser Island) because they have conflicts with tourists and locals; the sheer number of wildlife deaths in the Australian Black Summer fires of 2019/2020, numbering in the billions; and the plight of 'endlings' – animals that are the last of their species, to name just a few examples.

My environment-related distress was heightened during March 2020, when I, like many people around the world, could not sleep. All around me people, governments and other institutions were escalating their strategies to minimise the spread of COVID-19 and reduce its devastating impact on communities, individuals and the economy. I was also deeply anxious about these things, but at a deeper level, I couldn't sleep because I was grappling with the complete fiction-like state that the world had found itself in, while also recognising its absolute inevitability. I could not believe that we, as a collective, had arrived at this place, while simultaneously knowing that this disaster, like many others, was predicted and likely entirely avoidable. Yet, the social change required to avoid this and other disasters had not gained any significant traction.

What struck me during those sleepless nights was that it was distinct, modern consumer and pro-development type behaviour (wildlife consumption, individual and business travel as examples) that had led the collective to suffer in such a universal way as a result of the lightning spread of COVID-19.

This book is my exploration of my longstanding love of the ocean and nature more generally, concern for sharks, grief for an increasingly shrinking natural environment and how all of these feelings (and those in between) can be reconciled with the way humanity treats nature. It is an exploration of the behaviour that led to pandemics such as COVID-19, in many instances the very same behaviour that has also magnified climate change, biodiversity loss, land-clearing, income-inequality, racism, sexism and other social inequalities. It is an exploration of the interconnected dominations associated with all these events and our relationship with nature, through a legal lens.

1.1 THE BROKEN HUMAN–WILDLIFE RELATIONSHIP

As a lawyer, I am trained to believe that law has a purpose and is inherently good. It structures society, guides behaviour (both individual and collective) and ensures fair and just transactions and relationships. Naturally, I thought there must be a rational legal approach to resolving specific conflicts with wildlife so that humanity did not respond to shark attacks (and other instances of conflict) through indiscriminate killing. Of course, any social scientist, philosopher or conservationist (or any other number of people) could have told me that my perspective and trained ideology was fundamentally flawed. Humanity's relationship with wildlife is broken and beyond a quick legal fix.

In this book, the primary demonstration of such a proposition is the ubiquitous and intense nature of negative wildlife encounters around the world, such as shark attacks, and the human/social response to those encounters. They are often called 'human–wildlife conflicts', and that is the phrase I will use throughout this book, but I note there are difficulties with the semantics of this phrase and they will be discussed in Chapter 3.

Human–wildlife conflicts vary from physical attacks to crop damage and farm animal predation to vehicle–animal collisions. They evoke certain negative emotions, and affect the way that we think about wildlife and our relationship with them. We need to be concerned about human–wildlife conflict because the cumulative impacts of a world of myriad individual conflicts can have long-term serious consequences that extend further than any isolated conflict situation. We have seen these long-term serious consequences in recent months, as humanity's consumption of wildlife caused a global pandemic. Beyond this, the ramifications can extend to an ecosystem if the species involved in the conflict has a strong ecological role and if the conflict leads to mass killings, severe population reduction or the setting of minimal conservation goals. Ineffective responses to conflict can lead to public antagonism and that can affect the ability to cultivate a conservation or environmental ethic. Ineffective state responses to human–wildlife conflict can also have immediate effects for the wildlife that is the subject of the conflict. Illegal and retaliatory killings are very common where people perceive that the state is not prioritising their needs and interests. Further, ineffective responses can create further social conflict. Often it is not the conflict itself that creates tension but the conservation response, so that conservation becomes the conflict and the conservation process becomes futile.

Human–wildlife conflict is also one of the largest contributors to biodiversity loss and thus a primary cause of the current extinction crisis. More than one in eight species are currently threatened with global extinction. We can literally see species going extinct within one lifetime. Overall, humanity ought to be more concerned about the loss of biodiversity. The loss of a species can have large and devastating consequences on an ecosystem and the environment more generally, particularly if that species is a keystone species. Wildlife has a direct effect on the make-up of their habitats, habitats which people also use to survive and flourish. For example, the loss of large herbivores, such as the elephant, will mean their habitats eventually turn into forests, which can cause the disappearance of habitat for grassland species and also can affect the ability to sustain crops and farm domesticated animals. Various species can interact with the evolutionary adaptions of flora and play a vital role in seed dispersal and pollination. Global food security is at risk, as is the safety of agricultural systems. These interactions are only some of the known positive influences wildlife have on their habitat and there is still much we do not know about the role that species play in ensuring the survival of their surrounding environment and indeed about the species themselves.

Naturally, some of the effects of the loss of a species may be beneficial to humans, at least in the short-term. For example, there is some indication that the elimination of mosquitos would be desirable from a human health perspective. However, there remain to be unknown effects of extinction. For example, the genetic information held in wild species, even a species viewed as a threat to humans, represents 'future opportunity' from an anthropological perspective. The drug 'captopril', used to treat heart failure, is derived from snake venom. Treatments for nerve disorders have been developed from spider venoms. There are many potential hidden benefits (medicinal and others) within wild animal species. We simply do not know what the overall effect of eliminating mosquitos would be on the health of the environment and the security of humanity. We do not know if eliminating mosquitos from existence would have a net benefit or net cost to humankind and the world as a whole. Further, we have not yet settled on the morality of eliminating an entire species in this way. The science around sentience is underdeveloped and so we make assumptions about the consciousness of species like mosquitos that might not be accurate. We have only just learnt of the intelligence and sentience of the octopus for example. There are of course arguments around the immorality of killing animals and removing species that have nothing to do with their level of intelligence and centre instead on the intrinsic value of each animal. Each of these arguments has merit and, therefore, we need to be very careful when balancing the costs and benefits of these kinds of actions.

Similarly, there are unlimited associated benefits in maintaining biodiversity and curbing the human-induced extinction rate, many of which we have only recently discovered. There are undoubtedly countless more that we are yet to discover. The 'spirit' and physical well-being of people is directly related to nature and this emotional response is biological. Manfredo discusses the emotional connection that people have with animals and wildlife and how the emotional benefits of experiencing wildlife in a positive way can decrease early morbidity.[1] We also know that we experience real feelings of grief and loss as a result of species death and environmental change. As a result, the 'value' of wildlife and biodiversity as a whole is a factor that remains unknown, an idea in itself that warrants the ongoing care and protection of the natural environment and a more structured and considered response to instances of human–wildlife conflict.

1.2 THE NATURE OF THE PROBLEM

Human–wildlife conflict is a social problem, as well as an environmental one. Often, conflicts evolve and mutate into distinct social issues because different stakeholders have different views over how 'problem wildlife' should be managed. We have seen too, post the onset of COVID-19, that the problem

[1] Michael J. Manfredo, *Who Cares about Wildlife?: Social Science Concepts for Exploring Human–Wildlife Relationships and Conservation Issues* (Springer, 2008).

can also be economic, technological, medical and political. This is because the complexity of the relationships between stakeholders and wildlife is not limited to individuals or groups of people. Institutions add another dimension to the conflict. For example, religious practice can have a very large impact on held values and attitudes towards wildlife. The presence of environmental values in education can shape future values. Importantly for this book, the law also has a very large role that feeds into the conflict. Traditionally, the law and lawmakers have played an end role within the process of addressing human–wildlife conflict. Law most often takes on a punishment/enforcement role when the conflict escalates to the point that conservation or other types of laws are broken. For example, penalties are imposed when a threatened or endangered species are killed in retaliation against crop-raiding or farm animal predation. Policies around fencing and separation are implemented when an animal kills or injures a person. The law is an afterthought in the process of responding to human–wildlife conflict and is used to achieve a goal after the conflict has been assessed. However, human–wildlife conflict is a legal problem that extends beyond using law as a product of an earlier non-legal process. Law, as a set of rules governing society and social behaviour, clearly has a larger role to play. However, even beyond that, the role of law plays deep into the heart of human–wildlife conflicts around the world. Law is an institution and, like all other institutions, has a two-way relationship with the people it seeks to govern. Law is made and shaped by people, but also people are shaped by the laws around them. The way that law is conceived, formulated, written, monitored and enforced can shape people's relationship with the environment and their values and attitudes towards wildlife. It can cause or exacerbate conflict or help to resolve it. The law as an institution is vulnerable to people and people are vulnerable to the influence of the law. Neither one is autonomous from the other. As a result, we must also examine the role of all institutions in shaping the values that feed into the relationship that people have with wildlife, including all levels of law.

However, to date, we have been unable to simultaneously engage all necessary levels of society for governance purposes to address the complex and numerous relationships that operate around any particular conflict scenario. Researchers and activists have connected with individuals, businesses, companies, institutions and states at different times for different purposes, but rarely (if at all) to solve a specific environmental problem. The conflict itself is institutionalised, and this is rarely acknowledged. The problem is greater than the manifested conflict and encompasses many different facets of society – laws being just one of them. However, as a governance tool, laws need to account for all of those facets and facilitate a response that addresses all respective vulnerabilities. The law cannot do this when it focuses on a particular conservation ethic or prioritises a hierarchy that leads to disaffection and rebellion against conservation, wildlife and nature as a whole.

1.3 A THEORY OF ECOLOGICAL VULNERABILITY

In this book, I suggest that there is a central influence that is ever-present in the problematic relationship between people, wildlife and the greater environment as it is represented in law – the push for autonomy. Autonomy shapes the hierarchy that defines the relationship between wildlife and people and has a symbiotic relationship with the liberal hierarchy evident in environmental laws and policies. This is important because, although liberalism is normally associated with the removal of previous forms of hierarchy and seeks to make all people free and equal, throughout this book I argue that liberalism's promotion of an autonomous liberal being as the ideal actually perpetuates hierarchical and unequal structures. In this sense, autonomy is not defined as 'freedom' or the ability to make one's own choices but the separation of people from each other, the environment and the institutions they have created that continue to define behaviour and society as a whole. It is the belief that individuals operate independently from all those things. It is in the actions of people when they ignore the greater social and environmental consequences of those actions. It is the falsely advertised certainty that continued economic growth does not extend an already existing inequality gap. It is evident by the continued domination of nature even where science is certain of the negative consequences of that domination.

Despite my initial ideological training, it is evident that law is a societal institution that promotes this type of autonomy, instead of responding to collective vulnerabilities and promoting justice and equity. Martha Fineman suggests that western conceptions of law and legal systems have been formulated to promote a sense of autonomy, an understanding that one is independent or immune from intervention by the state and other people.[2] Legal systems work to have people operating independently from societal connection. However, this form of autonomy is a myth. People cannot operate independently from each other, the institutions they have created and the environment. Similarly, societal institutions are not autonomous. The law does not operate in a vacuum and neither does religion, science, the family, systems of education or political institutions. All human institutions have interconnections and

[2] Martha Fineman, *The Autonomy Myth: A Theory of Dependency* (New Press, 2004), 28.

relationships that build and sustain them and so promotion of their autonomy too is a fallacy. Notwithstanding, most of society's institutions continue to promote themselves as independent and free from the influence of other institutions, or at least certain institutions. This perceived autonomy of institutions themselves means that they are not responding appropriately to the needs of people and wildlife, but they are also reducing their resilience by ignoring the very relationships that promote cooperation and synchronicity between themselves.

The answer, then, is to temper the law's promotion of autonomy and balance it with something else – something that is reflective of all the interconnections and relationships that are necessary to live with safety and security, now and into the future. In this book, this 'something' is vulnerability. Vulnerability is universal, while autonomy is not (and nor is it even truly possible). Vulnerability is a concept that can be applied to everyone and everything in the world. People are vulnerable, the environment is vulnerable, wildlife is vulnerable and even society's institutions are vulnerable. To respond to this vulnerability while promoting the necessary relationships that maintain equality and security, the law should be focused on improving resilience to vulnerability, instead of promoting disconnect via individual liberal autonomy.

Fineman and other vulnerability scholars recognise that people have various kinds of vulnerability, including those related to their physical bodies (embodied vulnerability) and those related to their socially, politically and culturally constructed place in society (embedded vulnerability). In this book, I suggest that people have a third type of vulnerability, a type that cannot be separated from the preceding types; ecological vulnerability. Because all three types of vulnerability are interconnected through webs of relationships, the most appropriate course of action is to respond to all three simultaneously by seeking to build resilience in the entire web of connections with reliance on the environment placed squarely in the middle. Throughout this book, this interconnected web of vulnerability and the process of placing the environment at the centre of it will be referred to as eco-vulnerability.

1.4 SOME HOUSEKEEPING

1.4.1 *What Is 'Wildlife'?*

The definition of 'wildlife' can vary vastly between different groups of people. It can mean any living organism, ranging from single-celled bacteria to fish to large primates. Generally, to address human–wildlife conflict, wildlife managers and biologists/ecologists differentiate between terrestrial vertebrates and all other organisms, such that only the former are defined as 'wildlife'.[3] Such a definition is very narrow when one considers the breadth of living organisms on the planet and also suggests that organisms other than terrestrial vertebrates are incapable of being involved in human–wildlife conflict. It excludes spiders that can cause injury by way of a bite; nematodes, worms and snails that can cause losses to crops; termites that can destroy homes; and a vast array of species within the ocean that are also capable of being involved in conflict with humans, for example with the fisheries industry.[4] Some wildlife managers also exclude reptiles, such that the definition is limited to 'free-ranging birds and mammals'.[5]

From a legal perspective, the definition is not based on biology but on whether the animal is 'wild' in the sense of ownership.[6] An animal is 'wild' if it is not under direct human control, thereby excluding domesticated pets and farm animals.[7] This 'legal' definition is preferable for several reasons. First, and as noted above, the current definition used by managers excludes many forms of conflict that also require direct attention and analysis. Second, the biological definition does not accord with the cultural and everyday use of the word. Of course, biology is important to the definition but to be relevant it must be consistent with how society views the term. Third, and in a similar vein, wildlife managers, applied ecologists and people working at the ground level in human–wildlife conflict must operate within the barriers of the law. For there to be consistency between the law and the practice of management at the ground level, there needs to be common ground at a semantic level.

In this book, the legal definition will be utilised, such that domesticated animals, which are subject to individual 'ownership' and hold different legal

3 See for example Michael R. Conover, *Resolving Human–Wildlife Conflicts: The Science of Wildlife Damage Management* (Lewis Publishers, 2002) 4.

4 For some examples see Fabricia Barbieri et al., 'Interactions between the Neotropical Otter (Lontra longicaudis) and Gillnet Fishery in the Southern Brazilian Coast' (2012) 63 *Ocean and Coastal Management* 16; Taylor C. Cook, Kira James and Maddalena Bearzi, 'Angler Perceptions of California Sea Lion (Zalophus californianus) Depredation and Marine Policy in Southern California' (2015) 51 *Marine Policy* 573; Aliki Panagopoulou et al., 'Caught in the Same Net? Small-Scale Fishermen's Perceptions of Fisheries Interactions with Sea Turtles and Other Protected Species' (2017) 4 *Frontiers in Marine Science* 1–15.

5 A. R. E. Sinclair, John M. Fryxell and Graeme Caughley, *Wildlife Ecology, Conservation, and Management* (Blackwell Science, 2005) 2.

6 Although note that this is one among many possible legal definitions. For example, under common law liability rules, 'wild' may refer to the dangerous propensity of an animal, whether it is 'owned' by people or not.

7 David S. Favre, 'Wildlife Jurisprudence' (2010) 25 *Journal of Environmental Law and Litigation* 459–510, 462.

protections, are not included in the scope of the term 'wildlife' and are not subject to state management to the same extent.[8] There is a practical problem with this expanded definition, in that much of the wildlife governance and ecological literature concerns only wildlife that are terrestrial vertebrates and occasionally ocean mammals.[9] It is also the case that the effects are more severe and well documented when it comes to large mammals.[10] Notwithstanding, I assert that the principles discussed in this book are equally applicable to the expanded definition of wildlife.

1.4.2 *Law, Governance and Policy*

To those outside the field of law, the term 'law' may be easily definable. A dictionary definition might suggest that law is 'a set of rules of societal conduct' created by a State or State-authorised body and that are enforceable. However, legal theorists view this type of definition as too simplistic and it is not accurate for all types of legal systems, such as that of international law. Classical writers of legal theory, such as John Austin, H. L. A. Hart and Ronald Dworkin have long debated the existence of a definition of law and whether one is even necessary. One major point of contention is whether law has natural or positivist foundations, that is, whether law is derived from a 'higher' source and is based on an inherent, universal morality or whether law is a social construction that is only loosely associated with morality. It will become clear in Chapter 2 that, in this book, law is very much a social construction, designed to support the 'liberal autonomous agent' to the exclusion of the environment, wildlife and many groups of people.

Yet 'law' is not the only term referred to in this book to discuss sets of socially constructed rules. 'Governance' is referred to herein to mean something greater than law, which often refers only to specified and documented rules. Governance, on the other hand, refers to a larger system surrounding lawmakers and the other processes a State undertakes to wield power and authority, such as political and economic processes and policy. Governance refers to individual actions (such as law-making), but also the nature of

8 It should be noted though that even such a distinction between domesticated and non-domesticated species is sometimes blurred. See Ph Chardonnet et al., 'The Value of Wildlife' (2002) 21(1) *OIE Revue Scientifique et Technique* 15–51, 18–19.

9 Nimmi Seoraj-Pillai and Neville Pillay, 'A Meta-Analysis of Human–Wildlife Conflict: South African and Global Perspectives' (2017) 9(1) *Sustainability* 34.

10 Rosie Woodroffe, S. J. Thirgood and Alan Rabinowitz (eds.), *People and Wildlife: Conflict or Co-existence?* (Cambridge University Press, 2005) 2.

interactions between the State and other social actors such as corporations, individuals and other political actors.

Finally, 'policy' is a term also often referred to in this book and it is evident that lawyers have a very different understanding of policy than compared to say, conservation scientists. Policy is again different to law and governance, and in this book is used to refer to a specific, non-legally binding document that directs behaviour (such as the *Fraser Island Dingo Management Policy*) or a specific, non-binding principle or course of action undertaken by a governing body, institution, corporation or another group.

1.4.3 *The Structure of this Book*

The book begins with a deep exploration of eco-vulnerability as it relates to the human–wildlife relationship through two core theoretical paradigms; vulnerability theory and ecological feminism. Thereafter, Chapter 3 further analyses the concepts of human–wildlife conflict and coexistence and includes a non-legal analysis of specific conflict management models, showing that many of them are not equipped to deal with the value conflicts that surround instances of human–wildlife conflict. Instead, the governance of wildlife at the ground level most often seeks to promote individual autonomy and, as demonstrated in Chapter 2, such an emphasis is not conducive to an appropriate response to human–wildlife conflict.

The later chapters in this book deal with several specific case studies. They are divided into an exploration of a system of governance, exploration of two particular instances of human–wildlife conflict and then exploration of a larger bound problem (a pandemic). The case studies were selected to demonstrate the use of vulnerability theory across legal institutions and specific problems. Each case study draws upon recent and historical documented research, laws and policy documents in environmental wildlife governance, combining critical analysis of the legal structures and assumptions inherent in each scenario.

The first case study presents international wildlife law as an institutional governance system relevant to local responses to human–wildlife conflict. Wildlife governance is an international matter and international environmental law has normative value for environmental governance as a whole, including matters of human–wildlife conflict. The case study includes a critique of the use of autonomy in international wildlife law and in particular the 'rights' paradigm that it presents, before describing various eco-vulnerability principles designed to solve human–wildlife conflicts.

The following two case studies are conflict-specific: human–dingo conflict on K'gari; and human–elephant conflict in Northern Botswana. As they are conflict-specific they incorporate various legal systems and rules and so international law, domestic laws and regional/local laws are all analysed. The final case study is a situational one and centres on the wildlife trade and its relationship with pandemics (in particular COVID-19). The case studies demonstrate the current over-reliance on the promotion of autonomy and the effect that has and show that an eco-vulnerability response to human–wildlife conflict is possible, without necessarily having to experience a worldwide social and cultural revolution. We have the basic principles necessary already in our governance systems and, as the case studies will show, there has been some attempt to implement them to respond to human–wildlife conflict. However, to give them greater effect in building resilience to human–wildlife conflict, we need to expose the dichotomies that underlie the principles and so dictate their continued implementation, especially that of autonomy/vulnerability, so that we can neutrally use the principles. The book concludes with several further research areas and legal and policy reform recommendations to achieve this end.

Overall, this book is my response to the unease I have felt around culls of animals that interfere with human interests in some way (or in some cases are just in the wrong place at the wrong time), the neglect of animal welfare, the continued legal and illegal wildlife trades and the continuing hierarchy that suggests humans are above animals and nature and not an integrated whole. To improve the human–wildlife relationship through law, we first need a deep sociological analysis of the ways that law and other institutional structures define that relationship. And so, we begin.

2

The Human–Wildlife Relationship

An Ecofeminist Approach to Vulnerability Theory

2.1 INTRODUCTION

The study of human–wildlife conflict is more than a study of 'problem wildlife' and necessarily involves a study of the human relationship with nature. It is increasingly recognised that responses to the conflict must manage both wildlife *and* people. Governance techniques that do not include consideration of the human side result in ineffective conservation and often prolong or worsen conflict with wildlife and between stakeholders.

I often find myself having conversations with conservation scientists and wildlife managers on one particular topic: philosophy. This conversation usually centres on the philosophy that drives conservation and/or wildlife damage management or, more specifically, the relevance of philosophy in these fields (or lack thereof) when conservationists and managers know what they know to be true; that their practice is based on science, not philosophy. I have found that these professionals often (although not always)[1] are not aware that their own practice is based on values towards the environment, people and society, that are informed by and theorised within philosophy. This appears to be a problem with the way that conservationists and managers are taught but also holds broader consequences for the study of the human–wildlife relationship, as it is these practitioners that build and negotiate the relationship at the ground level.

Yet, and despite practitioners' lack of knowledge/engagement with this, the fields of wildlife conservation and human–wildlife conflict governance are still deeply rooted in ecological theory and philosophy. Aldo Leopold's theories

[1] As an example of the exception, I note Adrian Treves' description of his journey along this path of discovery in Adrian Treves and Francisco J. Santiago-Ávila, 'Myths and Assumptions about Human–Wildlife Conflict and Coexistence' (2020) 34(4) *Conservation Biology* 811, 813–14.

form *the* basis for ecological study in the field.[2] Other relevant and perhaps more worthy theories, such as those based on care/compassion, deep ecology, and critical theories such as feminist and race theories, are not usually within the realm of consideration. It is my contention that Leopold's theoretical basis is not sufficient for consideration of the human–wildlife relationship or solely appropriate when planning conservation and wildlife interventions.

While many wildlife managers and ecologists are conducting studies on differing human values and attitudes towards wildlife and management practices and are moving towards interdisciplinary collaboration, researchers conduct studies often without an adequate understanding of the philosophy surrounding human relationships with each other, society and the greater environment.[3] We cannot expect to promote a more positive relationship with wildlife and minimise situations of conflict without an adequate conceptual framework that discusses and theorises the different dimensions of the human side of the conflict. A theoretical understanding of the role that society and relationships play in the conflict is necessary to formulate an effective model of action that addresses the greater societal influence over human attitudes to wildlife.

In this chapter, I formulate a theoretical framework needed for responding to conflict through effective law and policy in the wildlife governance arena. The framework is built on heterodox ideas taken from feminist theory, especially those central to the analytical approaches of ecofeminism and vulnerability. I will use these ideas to put forth a new and refined approach to vulnerability theory to help surmount the troubled human–wildlife relationship. First, though, I will outline the unsuitable nature of existing theories on the subject, namely Leopold's ecological holism and the animal liberationist theories of Peter Singer and Tom Regan.

2.2 THE PHILOSOPHICAL DILEMMA OF CONFLICT

The philosophical idea of human domination over wildlife has been ubiquitous for centuries in western culture and has often run alongside and in direct

[2] Note that budding ecologists are also taught animal welfare and animal rights theory, but it appears to be contextualised against the 'superior' land ethic. See, for example, M. Nils Peterson and Shari L. Rodriguez, 'Human Dimensions of Wildlife Management', in Nova J. Silvy (ed.), *The Wildlife Techniques Manual: Management*, 7th ed. (The John Hopkins University Press, 2012) vol. 2, 13–14.

[3] Current research trends in values and attitudes towards wildlife are further addressed in Chapter 3.

opposition to the idea that animals should not be used for human purposes.[4] This idea can be traced to at least the book of Genesis, which described man's dominion over every living thing; 'Then God said, "Let Us make man in Our image, according to Our likeness; and let them rule over the fish of the sea and over the birds of the sky and over the cattle and over all the earth, and over every creeping thing that creeps on the earth".'[5] These ideas are supported by our continued use and abuse of wildlife. Wild animals are hunted, captured and sold, dissected for the use of their parts, culled and fenced, and have had their habitat systematically eliminated. We have taken pride in 'taming the wilderness' and sought to eliminate entire species.[6] Our governments continue to take pride in actions that are detrimental to wildlife, such as the creation of coal mines.[7] We do so with little, if any, consideration of the needs and interests of the wildlife impacted by the action. Such an attitude of domination results in feelings of animosity when wildlife disrupts the usual hierarchy. This animosity often leads to retaliation and prolongs instances of human–wildlife conflict.[8] Our apparent continued domination of wildlife not only creates instances of human–wildlife conflict but also makes it near impossible for appropriate long-term responses to situations of conflict.

Various philosophical positions are based on a critique of the human-centredness of a westernised, capitalist form of liberalism, which results in the domination of wildlife. Many of them have been applied to the environment and wildlife specifically. These include the theories commonly called upon to answer questions of ecology, wildlife and human behaviour,

4 For example, in 400 BC, Socrates stated that animals are produced and nourished for the sake of mankind. See Alastair Harden, *Animals in the Classical World: Ethical Perspectives from Greek and Roman Texts* (Springer, 2013) 28; E. Szucs et al., 'Animal Welfare in Different Human Cultures, Traditions and Religious Faiths' (2012) 25(11) *Asian–Australasian Journal of Animal Sciences* 1499.

5 The Bible, King James Version (KJV), Genesis 1:26–28.

6 Maureen G. Frank and Michael R. Conover, 'Thank Goodness They Got All the Dragons: Wildlife Damage Management through the Ages' (2015) 9(2) *Human–Wildlife Interactions* 156, 158.

7 See, for example, the support provided by the Queensland Government in establishing a coal mine in the Galilee Basin; Joshua Robertson, 'Carmichael Mine to be Given "Essential" Status in Sign of Palaszczuk Support', *The Guardian Australia* (Online), 9 October 2016. Available at: www.theguardian.com/environment/2016/oct/09/carmichael-mine-to-be-given-essential-status-in-sign-of-palaszczuksupport (last accessed 3 December 2021).

8 For example, see the way that individual sharks are persecuted and hunted after 'attacks on humans'; Katie Woolaston and Evan Hamman, 'The Operation of the Precautionary Principle in Australian Environmental Law: An Examination of the Western Australian White Shark Drum Line Program' (2015) 32(4) *Environmental and Planning Law Journal* 327.

including Aldo Leopold's 'land ethic' and theories concerning animal rights and liberation.[9] However, both of these sets of theories are idealistic as to what the relationship with nature/wildlife/animals should be, rather than accounting for why it is the way it is and how it can be improved.

In 1925, Aldo Leopold, a scientist, environmentalist and expert on wildlife management, published his seminal article 'Wilderness as a Form of Land Use'.[10] He expressed the social issue surrounding wildlife management and, more generally, environmental management at that time: 'But because the conquest of wilderness has produced beneficial reactions on social, political, and economic development, we have set up, more or less unconsciously, the converse assumption that the ultimate social, political, and economic development will be produced by conquering the wilderness entirely – that is, by eliminating it from our environment.'[11] Leopold set out to challenge that assumption and came to develop what is now known as his 'land ethic'. He was amongst the first in modern western society to advocate for habitat preservation and management, for the 'wilderness', including land, and the ecology and interrelationships among the land, flora, wildlife and humans.[12] He demonstrated that there was a need for 'land health' and that reckless indifference to wilderness destruction was unsustainable and would ultimately be destructive to humans as well. The most oft-quoted explanation of Leopold's approach summarises his land ethic: 'A thing is right when it tends to preserve the integrity, stability, and beauty of the biotic community. It is wrong when it tends otherwise.'[13] Leopold's approach is considered an example of ecological holism because it views the environment as the primary source of morality. That is to say, human beings are not the only moral consideration. Leopold argued for a world view where humans are acknowledged as only one part of an environmental society and wherein existing theories on human behaviour had to be supplemented with a moral consideration for the greater ecosystem. He viewed the ecosystem as an organism (which was not common scientific thought at the time) so that each

9 See Aldo Leopold, *A Sand County Almanac: And Sketches Here and There* (Oxford University Press, 1969); Steven White, 'Exploring Different Philosophical Approaches to Animal Protection in Law', in Peter Sankoff, Steven White and Celeste Black (eds.), *Animal Law in Australasia; Continuing the Dialogue* (The Federation Press, 2015) 79.

10 Aldo Leopold, 'Wilderness as a Form of Land Use' (1925) 1 *The Journal of Land and Public Utility Economics* 398.

11 Leopold, 'Wilderness as a Form of Land Use', 398.

12 See Aldo Leopold, 'The Conservation Ethic' (1933) 31 *Journal of Forestry* 634.

13 Leopold, *Sand County Almanac*, 262.

relationship in a specific ecosystem added to its overall health.[14] Leopold describes the premise as such:

> The land ethic simply enlarges the boundaries of the community to include soils, waters, plants, and animals, or collectively: the land – and it affirms the right of all to continued existence. The extension of ethics to land and to the animals and plants which is an evolutionary possibility and an ecological necessity. In short, a land ethic changes the role of Homo sapiens from conqueror of the land community to plain member and citizen of it.[15]

A common point of contention with the land ethic approach is that it excludes concern for the individual animal; the pain and suffering of an individual animal were not of moral concern when that suffering benefits the ecosystem as a whole.[16] This can be contrasted with animal liberationist theories, which includes both animal rights advocates and animal welfare advocates (noting that there is an inherent distinction between the two and that distinction in itself is the cause of much conflict in academic writing and practice).[17] It is not my intention to suggest the acceptance of the model results in equality between humans and animals, and indeed not many animal rights and welfare philosophies advocate for equality as we know it in the traditional sense. Instead, they are concerned with the concept that individual animals deserve some moral consideration that is equal to the moral consideration given to humans, where those animals demonstrate a likeness to humans in some way (again, noting that animal liberationist theorists disagree on the extent that likeness is required). It must also be noted that the theories discussed in this section are concerned with the welfare/liberation of all animals, not just wildlife. In fact, most arguments are directed at domesticated animals, farm animals and animals used in research and entertainment. That said, the theories apply to the human–wildlife conflict scenario, especially where governance of the conflict involves a violation of the animals' interests. The theories of Peter Singer and Tom Regan are particularly relevant as they continue to inform most arguments concerning the promotion of animal rights and animal welfare.

14 See Ben Dixon, 'Deriving Moral Considerability from Leopold's "A Sand County Almanac"' (2016) 19(2) *Ethics, Policy & Environment* 196.

15 Leopold, *Sand County Almanac*, 204.

16 See, for example, Lisa H. Sideris, *Environmental Ethics, Ecological Theology, and Natural Selection* (Columbia University Press, 2003) 7–8.

17 See Sideris, Environmental Ethics, chapter 4; J. Baird Callicott, 'Animal Liberation: A Triangular Affair' (1980) 2(4) *Environmental Ethics* 311; Gary L. Francione, 'Animal Rights and Animal Welfare' (1996) 48(2) *Rutgers Law Review* 397.

Singer's theory on the ethics of animal interests was outlined in his influential publication, *Animal Liberation*, and was seen to be drawn from Jeremy Bentham's principle of utility, that is, 'the greatest happiness of the greatest number'.[18] Bentham suggested that happiness was an entitlement of not only the white male elite, but any who could suffer, including women, slaves and animals.[19] The core of Singer's philosophy expands on this proposition and is based on the finding that animals are sentient beings and so have an interest in avoiding pain and suffering. However, instead of recognising that animals' sentience has equal value with ours, most humans who come into conflict with animals assume that the interests of animals are to be viewed in a lesser manner than their own. This is evident from our relationship with animals and the way that they are bred for food and used in research, circuses and zoos. In that way, humans can undertake such activities believing that the enjoyment or use they derive outweighs the little interest that the animal may have.

To the contrary, Singer argues that there is no moral justification for not giving the interests of animals 'equal consideration'.[20] Only 'speciesists' would give greater weight to the pain of their own kind over that of other species.[21] As a result, failure to give equal consideration to the suffering of animals is akin to racism or sexism.

To convince his audience that the interests of animals are worthy of consideration, Singer uses reason to demonstrate the principle of equality and that like cases should be treated alike. He uses the analogy of humans that are not capable of reason, but are capable of pain and suffering, such as infants and the severely mentally disabled, and asks his audience to consider whether they would subject that group of humans to the same treatment that animals receive (a principle known as the 'argument from marginal cases').[22]

Notwithstanding the equal consideration principle, Singer notes this does not mean that animals are necessarily entitled to equal treatment.[23] Instead, equal consideration of interests ought to result in a more egalitarian outcome, even if unequal treatment is the result. For example, you may smack a horse

[18] Peter Singer, *Animal Liberation: A New Ethics for Our Treatment of Animals* (New York review: distributed by Random House, 1975).

[19] Jeremy Bentham, *A Fragment on Government* (Clarendon Press, 1891).

[20] Singer, *Animal Liberation.*

[21] Singer, *Animal Liberation*, 6.

[22] Singer, *Animal Liberation*, 16–17.

[23] Singer, *Animal Liberation*, 2–3.

harder than you would smack your child (if you would do either at all), as a horse is larger and so will not feel the same sensation.[24]

Tom Regan's 'subjects of a life' theory is more commonly described as a rights-based approach, suggesting that animals have certain rights, such as the right to life, and those rights cannot be compromised in any circumstance.[25] Tom Regan borrows basic deontological theory from eighteenth-century philosopher Immanuel Kant, who suggested that every human has moral rights and duties.[26] Regan differs from Kant though in one important respect; Kant suggests that only beings capable of reason are to be included in the moral community, formally ruling out the inclusion of animals based on the science of the time.[27] Regan dismisses this suggestion and again uses the 'argument from marginal cases' or the analogy posited by Singer concerning the inherent value of human life with no ability to reason (for example infants and the severely mentally disabled).[28]

To understand Regan's approach, it is important to understand the distinction between 'moral agents' and 'moral patients', as he terms them.[29] Moral agents are 'individuals' who can consider moral principles in the determination of what ought to be done and freely choose to act (or not act) following those moral principles. They can reason. On the other hand, moral patients cannot control their behaviour based on moral principles and cannot choose between right and wrong. Moral patients include the 'marginal cases' of humans, such as infants and the severely mentally disabled. Although moral patients cannot choose to act in a way that is either morally right or morally wrong, they can be the subject of morally right or morally wrong behaviour. They have an inherent value that is not dependent on their usefulness as an individual. Regan argues that this category includes animals.[30] He states that we must look to the similarities between those humans who are moral agents, and animals as moral patients, instead of the differences. The most significant similarity held is that we are all the subject of a life and that our welfare is important to us, no matter the importance to others.

[24] Singer, *Animal Liberation*.
[25] Tom Regan, *The Case for Animal Rights* (University of California Press, 1983), chapter 8.
[26] Immanuel Kant, Mary J. Gregor and Christine M. Korsgaard, *Groundwork of the Metaphysics of Morals* (Cambridge University Press, 1998).
[27] It is now clear that some animals are capable of rational decision-making. See Cameron Buckner, 'Rational Inference: The Lowest Bounds' (2019) 98(3) *Philosophy and Phenomenological Research* 697.
[28] Tom Regan, 'An Examination and Defense of One Argument Concerning Animal Rights' (1979) 22(1–4) *Inquiry* 189.
[29] Regan, *Case for Animal Rights*, 151–56.
[30] Tom Regan, 'The Rights of Humans and Other Animals' (1997) 7(2) *Ethics & Behavior* 103.

To adduce similarities, Regan analyses the basis for human rights. What characteristics do humans hold, either as moral agents or moral patients, that entitle us to rights? One argument is that we have certain cognitive abilities and that we are rational autonomous agents. Regan argues that we know that some animals have those cognitive abilities as well, such as the great apes, and so it follows that they must have the same moral rights as humans.[31] Also, some humans do not have rational autonomy (the 'marginal cases') but they too have rights. They, like rational humans and animals, are the 'subject of a life' that has 'individual welfare that has importance to us whatever our usefulness to others'.[32] As a result, not only do animals have interests, as theorised by Singer, but they also have rights, and humans have a duty to uphold those rights, no matter what their own interests dictate. This theory, in practice, would lead to the abolition of most forms of human use and abuse of animals.

Each of the theories fails to account for the way that the nature of human–wildlife conflict is understood. There are two primary reasons as to why these theories are not suited to inform law and policy concerning the human–wildlife relationship and the conflicts it involves. First, human–wildlife conflict is usually not only conflict between humans and wildlife but is also conflict between different stakeholder groups over how 'problem' wildlife should be dealt with.[33] Landowners and farmers can have opposing views to ecologists or animal liberationists, and all can clash with governmental involvement and policy.[34] The underlying value position of each stakeholder group is linked to a variety of philosophical and political persuasions, which are often diametrically opposed and not capable of compromise. For example,

[31] Regan, *Case for Animal Rights*, 283–84.

[32] Tom Regan, 'The Case for Animal Rights', in M. W. Fox and Linda D. Mickley (eds.), *Advances in Animal Welfare Science 1986/87* (Springer, 1987) 179, 186.

[33] See, for example, Steve M. Redpath et al., 'Understanding and Managing Conservation Conflicts' (2013) 28(2) *Trends in Ecology & Evolution* 100; Francine Madden and Brian McQuinn, 'Conservation's Blind Spot: The Case for Conflict Transformation in Wildlife Conservation' (2014) 178 *Biological Conservation* 97; Keith Marshall, Rehema White and Anke Fischer, 'Conflicts between Humans over Wildlife Management: On the Diversity of Stakeholder Attitudes and Implications for Conflict Management' (2007) 16(11) *Biodiversity and Conservation* 3129.

[34] For example, Gutierrez et al. discuss research suggesting that ineffective governmental consultation mechanisms led to increased resentment towards the governmental agencies. Goodale et al. suggests that this can lead to individuals bypassing government conflict policies. See R. J. Gutiérrez et al., 'Conservation Conflicts: Future Research Challenges', in Rafael Mateo, Beatriz Arroyo and Jesus T. Garcia (eds.), *Current Trends in Wildlife Research* (Springer, 2016) 267, 268; Kate Goodale, Glen J. Parsons and Kate Sherren, 'The Nature of the Nuisance – Damage or Threat – Determines How Perceived Monetary Costs and Cultural Benefits Influence Farmer Tolerance of Wildlife' (2015) 7(3) *Diversity* 318, 321.

ecological holists that base their ethos on the good of an ecosystem as a whole often clash with the politics of anthropocentric capitalism and economic drivers of environmental policy. Similarly, they disagree with animal liberationists, who see value in the individual instead of the whole. These differences in ontology are not reconcilable, as various theorists have suggested.[35] They involve alternate versions of a hierarchy, where the interests at the top of the respective hierarchy are not negotiable. Whilst they may have the ability to give a perspective on the human–wildlife relationship, they are ill-suited to form the basis of a framework responding to the conflict where accommodation of multiple value positions is required. The issue is not only a moral and philosophical one but also, and perhaps more so, a social and political one. One pure philosophical position will therefore not assist in the practicality of responding to human–wildlife conflict.

This leads to the second point. Accommodation of alternative value positions is often required in human–wildlife conflict because stakeholders see the issue from differing perspectives that are not based solely on intellectual rationality or an agreed theoretical approach. The human–wildlife conflicts stem from differences in ecological and economic perspectives that might be justified on reasoned facts, but which are predicated on far more complex factors such as psychological reactance and social identity.[36] Opposing parties often cannot be 'talked around' through the use of rationality but, instead, need to be engaged on a social, emotional and cultural level, so their non-material social and psychological needs can be met.[37] The issue within the realm of human–wildlife conflict is a divergence in human values, attitudes and emotional response to situations of conflict; subjective states that traditional philosophical thought based on reasoned argument does not accommodate. As a result, the underlying philosophical premise of human–wildlife conflict law and policy must be something that can accommodate subjective

[35] J. Baird Callicott argues, for example, that the animal liberationist theories, ecological holists and classical conservative theories form a triangular opposition. See Callicott, 'Animal Liberation'. Note though that there are authors who argue that an animal liberation perspective is also an earth perspective. See, for example, Dale Jamieson, 'Animal Liberation Is an Environmental Ethic' (1998) 7(1) *Environmental Values* 41.

[36] Marshall, White and Fischer, 'Conflicts between Humans', 3130.

[37] Emotional dispositions and responses are consistently found to be influential in the human–wildlife conflict landscape, and so need to be considered in resolution practices. See Madden and McQuinn, 'Conservation's Blind Spot', 98; Camilla H. Fox and Marc Bekoff, 'Integrating Values and Ethics into Wildlife Policy and Management-Lessons from North America' (2011) 1 (1) *Animals* 126, 126; Ronit Amit and Susan K. Jacobson, 'Understanding Rancher Coexistence with Jaguars and Pumas: A Typology for Conservation Practice' (2017) 26(6) *Biodiversity and Conservation* 1353–74.

values and emotions, allows for compromise and seeks to alter negative feelings towards wildlife over the long term. Theories that discount emotion and emotive motivations at the outset are thus not appropriate, nor will they be able to give a coherent outlook on any conflict that involves sentiment, attitudes and opinions.

In Section 2.3, I will argue that many feminist theories can be considered theories that concern social hierarchy and responses to conflict. In particular, ecofeminism is beneficial as it 'avoids the preclusive closures of a hierarchical stance on knowledge and acquisition'.[38] It also allows the search for a fuller and more complete understanding of the issues surrounding human–wildlife conflict.[39] Together with vulnerability theory, they allow us to see conflict and domination from their social, legal, political and gendered contexts, rather than being caught in the positions of moral philosophical absolutism. The following discussion will demonstrate how ecological feminism (ecofeminism) can provide a theoretical base for our relationship with wildlife and the conflicts that arise.

2.3 WILDLIFE AND HUMANITY'S SHARED OPPRESSIONS

2.3.1 *Defining Ecofeminism*

Just as there are many types of feminism, there are many types of ecofeminism. The concept is more than the assertion that women are closer to nature and so can offer a unique perspective on the human relationship with the environment. Whilst some women are undoubtedly closer to nature than some men are (the vice versa could also be stated), this is not the factor that makes a theory an ecofeminist theory. Instead, the broader commonality that links theories to ecofeminism is the assertion that feminine oppression and environmental degradation are inherently connected and have the same causality. Karen J. Warren explains: '"Ecological Feminism" is an umbrella term which captures a variety of multicultural perspectives on the nature of the connections within social systems of domination between those humans in subdominant or subordinate positions, particularly women, and the domination of nonhuman nature.'[40] The nature of the connections between women's

[38] Karen Morrow, 'Ecofeminist Approaches to the Construction of Knowledge and Coalition Building – Offering a Way Forward for International Environmental Law and Policy', in Andreas Philippopoulos-Mihalopoulos and Victoria Brooks (eds.), *Research Methods in Environmental Law* (Edward Elgar, 2017) 289, 291.

[39] Morrow, 'Ecofeminist Approaches'.

[40] Karen Warren and Barbara Wells-Howe (eds.), *Ecological Feminism* (Routledge, 1994) 1.

oppression and environmental domination differs between theorists. Ecofeminists often describe the shared domination of women and the environment in theoretical terms. Val Plumwood posits ecofeminism as a series of shared oppressions, where the views that support those oppressions are culturally and socially constructed, rather than a result of pure biology.[41] Warren describes the subordination of women and the environment as the 'twin dominations'.[42] In exploring these, feminist theorists have elicited a series of dichotomies that are evident in legal and political institutions and other societal structures, that lead to the domination of both women and the environment. Marti Kheel refers to these dichotomies as 'western dualistic thinking', and they include the static polarities of 'us and them', 'subject and object', 'superior and inferior', 'mind and body', 'animate and inanimate', 'reason and emotion', 'culture and nature', 'public and private', amongst others.[43] These dualities or dichotomies are another commonality in different categories of feminist theory, wherein the first half of the duality is seen as having more value and is associated with men and the latter half is seen as having less value and is associated with women. The environment, it is argued, clearly also fits into the latter, subordinate categories.

Some ecofeminists suggest that the shared nature of our oppressions is evident in very practical ways. Carol Adams describes the interconnections between the violence against women and the violence against animals.[44] Various theorists describe the linguistic connection between the degradation of women and elements of nature, including animals. 'Mother Nature' is 'raped' and 'pilloried', while women are referred to as dogs, cats, old hens, bitches, queen bees and many other pejorative terms. Adams describes how the environment and animals are culturally feminised, while women are simultaneously culturally animalised.[45] Susan Griffin provides a particularly powerful account of the history of the western patriarchal domination of women and nature and how the traits typically characterised as male are systematically privileged over the traits typically associated with women.[46]

41 See Val Plumwood, 'The Ecopolitics Debate and the Politics of Nature', in Karen J. Warren (ed.), *Ecological Feminism* (Routledge, 1994) 64.

42 Warren and Wells-Howe, *Ecological Feminism*, 1.

43 Marti Kheel, 'The Liberation of Nature: A Circular Affair' (1985) 7(2) *Environmental Ethics* 135, 136.

44 Carol J. Adams, *The Sexual Politics of Meat: A Feminist–Vegetarian Critical Theory* (Continuum, 1990).

45 Adams, *Sexual Politics of Meat*.

46 Susan Griffin, *Woman and Nature: The Roaring Inside Her* (Harper & Row, 1978).

Recent research continues to show that women are largely absent from the field of conservation.[47]

2.3.2 *Oppression As a Conceptual Framework*

Because of the shared nature of the domination of women and the environment by a patriarchal worldview, it is argued that any movement to end either oppression includes a movement to end the other.[48] Thus, ecology is a feminist issue and feminism is an environmental issue. To understand the relationship of domination from a human–wildlife perspective, it is first necessary to understand the nature and source of the shared oppressions of women and nature.

The factors that contribute to oppression are theorised by Warren. She suggests there are a series of dominations that create an 'oppressive conceptual framework'. The framework is a socially created mindset that reinforces domination and oppression, and it is reflected in western patriarchal societies.[49] This framework is particularly useful for analysing the social and institutional factors surrounding human–wildlife conflict. Warren calls her first characteristic 'value-hierarchical thinking'.[50] This is the perception that greater value is always attributable to that which is higher in a metaphorical spatial hierarchy. This characteristic is demonstrative of the ineffectiveness of other theoretical frameworks discussed in Section 2.2, particularly in a conflict scenario. Followers of Leopold's land ethic place the good of the ecological community at the pinnacle of the hierarchy, and so it is given greater value than say an individual animal or the interests of a farmer struggling to protect his crop against a species that provides services to the surrounding natural ecosystem.[51] Animal liberationists, such as Regan and Singer, place value on either suffering or cognition of an individual over the environment as a whole, so that a member of a species considered to be damaging the environment is given more value than the environment it is damaging.[52] These hierarchies

[47] Robyn James et al., 'Conservation and Natural Resource Management: Where Are All the Women?' (2021) 55(6) *Oryx* 860–67.

[48] See Rosemary Ruether, 'Toward an Ecological–Feminist Theology of Nature', in Judith Plant (ed.), *Healing the Wounds: The Promise of Ecofeminism* (Green Print, 1989) 145.

[49] Karen J. Warren, 'Feminism and Ecology' (1987) 9(1) *Environmental Ethics* 3, 6.

[50] Warren, 'Feminism and Ecology', 6.

[51] Leopold's land ethic is centred on a sense of morality that protects the ecological whole, such that 'a thing is right when it tends to preserve the integrity, stability, and beauty of the biotic community'. See Leopold, *Sand County Almanac*, 262.

[52] Singer, *Animal Liberation*; Regan, *Case for Animal Rights*.

are not capable of being complementary or supporting compromise where it may be required in such circumstances, and instead create thinking that is reflective of 'normative dualisms', Warren's next oppressive characteristic.

Normative dualisms support oppositions that exclude conciliatory thinking. For example, consider the lifeboat scenario, a hypothetical not unlike the trolley problem, discussed by animal liberationist theorists that rely on rationalisations.[53] The scenario asks one to consider the following; if a lifeboat can hold only four sentient beings, but there are five, with one being an animal, which sentient being ought to be left behind? Regan and Singer debate the morality of throwing either the dog or one of the people overboard and the real-world ethical implications for their theoretical answer. This either–or analogy is consistent with the type of dualisms propounded by hierarchical forms of philosophy, when feminist theory argues that in reality there need not be a choice of a dualistic nature, and any such discussion ignores the intricacies of the circumstances of the conflict.[54]

Not only are these abstract, speculative, thought experiments divorced from practical reality but they are also divorced from the intricacies of social philosophy. That is to say, the social theories and building blocks that lead to the eventuation of a particular situation are ignored. For example, Deborah Slicer applies the hypothetical to the very real choice of using animals for research and the ethical argument commonly deployed that such research is necessary to save lives.[55] In effect, the dog is being sacrificed for the humans. She suggests that, when put in this context, the decision is not either/or, but instead the evidence increasingly shows that animal research is not a reliable model for human beings and so is largely worthless. Therefore, at least in cases where animal research is not reliable, the choice is not between animals and human welfare: both can be saved. An analysis of the complete context would result in altering institutional structures so that the lifeboat scenario would not eventuate in the first place. A critical social perspective would question the structures that put the animal in the testing facility in the first place. Josephine Donovan supports Slicer and argues that Slicer's contextual reasoning does not evade the basic moral dilemma posed by the lifeboat scenario (a common criticism of feminist theory in this area), but reframes it so that the political,

53 See the discussion in Tom Regan, reply by Peter Singer, 'The Dog in the Lifeboat: An Exchange', *The New York Review of Books* (New York), 25 April 1985. Available from www.nybooks.com/articles/1985/04/25/the-dog-in-the-lifeboat-an-exchange/ (last accessed 3 December 2021).

54 See, for example, Josephine Donovan, 'Animal Rights and Feminist Theory' (1990) 15(2) *Signs* 350.

55 Deborah Slicer, 'Your Daughter or Your Dog' (1991) 6(1) *Hypatia* 108.

social and legal contexts become relevant as part of the moral assessment.[56] In essence, discussion of moral dilemmas out of context is not helpful. Similarly, Warren suggests that normative dualisms such as this either/or debate separate aspects of reality that are not separable or that should be taken in tandem. In the wildlife conflict scenario, this is demonstrated by the separation of human interests from the ecosystem when human interests are actually consistent with ecosystem welfare.

Warren then argues that such value-hierarchical thinking gives rise to a 'logic of domination', the third characteristic in her oppressive conceptual framework.[57] The logic of domination relies on value-hierarchical thinking to justify the subordination of those lower in the hierarchy by those at the top. Such thinking justifies the extermination of entire groups of wildlife in the interests of human economic profit; the human interest is given hierarchical power that allows domination of wildlife to their detriment.

Warren attempts to clarify her conceptual framework by discussing a potential ecofeminist peace politic and, in doing so, adds two further characteristics that she argues are used to justify the logic of domination.[58] The first is 'power-over conceptions of power', wherein those in power maintain other people's conceptions of their power by coercive restriction of liberty, threat and use of force, sanctions and expressions of disapproval.[59] This power-over other's conceptions of power is evident in wildlife policy in two ways. First, there are policies that directly attempt to influence wildlife behaviour in such a manner, called aversive conditioning.[60] Second, those in power often seek to control conflict scenarios by establishing their power over the scenario and leaving out those who are directly affected. Often, this is demonstrated by policy and lawmakers asserting control in a manner that is not conducive to conflict resolution and contributes to the human–human side of the conflict. This is evident in situations where wildlife is given priority over human security, not because the wildlife is higher in the hierarchy, but because the wildlife interests are aligned with the power – over the conception of power.[61]

56 Josephine Donovan, 'Feminism and the Treatment of Animals: From Care to Dialogue' (2006) 31(2) *Signs* 305, 311.

57 Karen J. Warren, 'The Power and the Promise of Ecological Feminism' (1990) 12(2) *Environmental Ethics* 125.

58 Karen J. Warren, 'Toward an Ecofeminist Peace Politics', in Karen J. Warren (ed.), *Ecological Feminism* (Routledge, 1994) 179.

59 Warren, 'Toward an Ecofeminist Peace Politics', 182–84.

60 Conover, *Resolving Human–Wildlife Conflicts*, 53.

61 Jennifer Bond and Kennedy Mkutu, 'Exploring the Hidden Costs of Human–Wildlife Conflict in Northern Kenya' (2018) 61(1) *African Studies Review* 35; Daniel Brockington and James Igoe, 'Eviction for Conservation: A Global Overview' (2006) 4(3) *Conservation and Society* 424, 425.

A common example is the displacement of local people for neo-liberal conservation purposes, where displacement leads to loss of history, cultural identity and power, but the neo-liberal conservation has economic benefits for those with power.[62]

Warren's final characteristic is 'conceptions of privilege' which systematically benefit the already privileged.[63] Similar to the power conception, this is the notion that the privileged have qualities that should be attained by the non-privileged, such as wealth and power. Such conceptions are detrimental to wildlife when it means that attainment of said privilege leads to their destruction, and privileges values that are inconsistent with coexistence.

The social construction of conceptual frameworks that support dichotomisation and domination is a theoretical view shared by many ecofeminists, including Val Plumwood.[64] In demonstrating the social nature of the construction of the framework (as opposed to a biological nature), Plumwood states that such a framework provides a coherent theory of oppression wherein all dominations in society are interconnected: colonialism and capitalism are connected with racism, sexism, classism and environmental segregation and degradation. Plumwood asserts that all struggles are a link in a web, all related but sometimes separate, where the main oppression is the control of reason over nature.[65] It is certainly the case that the domination of wildlife is interlinked with other dominations in society and various dominations contribute to the imperfect institutionalisation of wildlife in law, which in turn affects individual relationships with wildlife, contributing to conflict.

2.3.3 *Interconnections, Holism and Avoiding the Descent into Relativism*

The existence of interconnections between various oppressions means that any theoretical position seeking to address the domination of wildlife must account for the shared oppressions of people and wildlife. Thus, when ecofeminists identify their theory as holistic, they are often referring to the need to view the conflict from differing oppressed positions. This differs from ecological holistic theory because ecological holists consider the whole of an

62 Bond and Mkutu, 'Exploring the Hidden Costs'. See also Atieno Mboya, 'Human Vulnerability and Environmental Rights: The Endorois Welfare Council v. Kenya Case', in Michael Faure (ed.), *Elgar Encyclopedia of Environmental Law*, Vol. VII.43 (Edward Elgar Publishing Limited, 2019) 543.

63 Warren, 'Toward an Ecofeminist Peace Politics', 184.

64 See Val Plumwood, 'Nature, Self and Gender: Feminism, Environmental Philosophy, and the Critique of Rationalism' (1991) 6(1) *Hypatia* 3; Plumwood, 'Ecopolitics Debate'.

65 Plumwood, 'Ecopolitics Debate', 74.

ecosystem to be the paramount concern, not any given individual or individual part.[66] This is particularly the case with theories of 'deep ecology' where the concept of 'human self' is one that is identified within and by nature. That is to say, humans are indistinguishable from their surrounding environment or the environment is inherently part of our identity.[67] Where deep ecology features 'sameness', or human equivalence with the surrounding environment, the feminist version of holism places humans in the overall biotic community whilst recognising the validity of different voices and experiences of individual components within that community. In recognising differences they ensure a type of equality that celebrates strength in difference and does not require uniformity. In this way, feminist holistic thought conceptualises personhood as relational, rather than autonomous. Every member of the biotic community has a different role to play and our relationship with the other members enables us to be a present member of society. The relationships that we form with other people and that we have with other aspects of the biotic community (whether we know they are there or not) contribute to our ability to be present in and participate in the community. This version of holism, including principles of difference and relational personhood, seeks to celebrate those differences by removing all versions of hierarchy, rather than flip the hierarchy and instil ecosystems or individual animals/people at the top.

This version of holism has been the subject of many critiques.[68] The difference principle, in particular, leads many rational and liberal theorists to criticise ecofeminist theory on the basis that it has no one utilisable ethic.[69] They argue it does not attempt to provide an objective moral point of view but lends itself to many voices of oppressed communities and has the potential to descend into moral relativism. Essentially, everyone has their own version of what is morally acceptable and we will never be able to agree on a solution to a problem if we accept every difference and individual voice on a given topic. In the age of 'alternative facts', relativism is not desirable, at least where those

[66] See, for example, J. Baird Callicott, *In Defense of the Land Ethic: Essays in Environmental Philosophy* (State University of New York Press, 1989) 21.

[67] For a thorough discussion on the concept of 'deep ecology' see Warwick Fox, 'The Intuition of Deep Ecology' (1984) 14(56) *Ecologist* 144; and George Sessions, *Deep Ecology for the Twenty-First Century* (Random House, 1995).

[68] See, for example, Janet Biehl, *Rethinking Ecofeminist Politics* (South End Press, 1991); Christine J. Cuomo, 'Unravelling the Problems in Ecofeminism' (1992) 14(4) *Environmental Ethics* 351; Lucy Sargisson, 'What's Wrong with Ecofeminism' (2001) 10(1) *Environmental Politics* 52.

[69] See, for example, Biehl, *Rethinking Ecofeminist Politics*, and the response of Douglas J. Buege, 'Rethinking Again: A Defence of Ecofeminist Philosophy', in Karen J. Warren (ed.), *Ecological Feminism* (Routledge, 1994) 42.

alternate versions of reality come from people or groups that are identified as the oppressors in Warren's conceptual framework. From a wildlife perspective, a relativist solution would simply not work when the goal is to address differences in values and attitudes, not hold stubbornly onto them.

Lori Gruen attempts to meet this criticism by suggesting that ecofeminist theory can assist in sorting 'true beliefs' and false ones and can justify coherent moral claims while at the same time adhering to a pluralist epistemological strategy that recognises differences.[70] She does this by relying not on value-free science and dispassionate reason as the basis for knowledge but instead relies on values determined by community, experience, and 'situatedness'.[71] However, in doing so, Gruen imposes her opinion on what constitutes 'true beliefs' and how to attain them. This is certainly an epistemological conundrum of much of ecofeminist theory. Various theorists criticise science for being overtly patriarchal and not emotive but do not deny it has a role to play.[72] Certainly, one thing we can take from such a discussion of the potential for difference to descend into relativism is the epistemological view that we need to change how we ascertain and respond to facts about the human–wildlife relationship. It is consistently demonstrated that it is human values, not objective data that drives the conflict.[73] The diversity in values that is being demonstrated by social sciences research cannot be reconciled with objective assessments of the value of nature and/or wildlife and the imposition of value onto a hierarchical structure of morality. Ecofeminism requires us to alter a hierarchical liberal framework into something horizontal and holistic and accounts for different values and voices, whilst maintaining some form of overall shared ethic. Vulnerability theory lays a foundation for that universality prerequisite.

2.4 VULNERABILITY: A THEORETICAL ANALYSIS

Theories on vulnerability are premised on the contention that to be human is to be vulnerable. Vulnerability and the dependency it creates is not limited to the groups of people we typically ascribe the term to, such as women, refugees, people of colour, LGBTIA+ individuals, people with low socioeconomic status and other minorities. Instead, we are all fundamentally vulnerable no

70 Lori Gruen, 'Toward an Ecofeminist Moral Epistemology', in Karen J. Warren (ed,), *Ecological Feminism* (Routledge, 1994) 120, 124.

71 Gruen, 'Toward an Ecofeminist Moral Epistemology', 126–33.

72 See, for example, Vandana Shiva, 'Reductionism and Regeneration: A Crisis in Science', in Maria Mies and Vandana Shiva (eds.), *Ecofeminism* (Spinifex Press, 1993) 22–35.

73 See Chapter 3 for a discussion of this evidence.

matter what wealth, power or privilege one may have – although those things increase our *resilience* to vulnerability. We are vulnerable as children, and as we grow older, to illness and death, natural disasters, societal changes and structures, individual torment and unforgiving and damaging relationships. Vulnerability theorists suggest that this vulnerability has been systemically eliminated from western liberal philosophy and politics and recognition in our day-to-day lives. Alisa Carse argues that much of philosophical history, especially that of western post-enlightenment thought, has embraced a notion of the self that has underplayed vulnerability and promotes a version of human flourishing that highlights 'self-sufficiency, independence, a capacity for deliberation, and rational transcendence of emotion'.[74] Vulnerability theory is an attempt to counter this suppression and to place the autonomous self into a larger relational framework of human existence.

In their edited collection on vulnerability, Mackenzie, Rogers and Dodds suggest that any vulnerability ethic ought to address four questions:[75]

1. What is vulnerability?
2. Why does vulnerability give rise to moral obligations and duties of justice?
3. Who bears primary responsibility for responding to vulnerability?
4. How are our obligations to the vulnerable best fulfilled?

I will now outline various theoretical responses to these questions, with an emphasis on Martha Fineman's politico-legal vulnerability analysis. Fineman's analysis is distinguished because of her emphasis on the role of institutions (and in particular the law) in producing and alleviating vulnerability.

2.4.1 *What Is Vulnerability?*

The concept of vulnerability is something that is commonly discussed in ecological theory, risk analysis, natural disaster management, medical ethics and psychology. In each of those areas, references to vulnerability are fragmented so that vulnerability is limited to particular situations. For example,

[74] Alisa L. Carse, 'Vulnerability, Agency, and Human Flourishing', in Carol R. Taylor and Roberto Dell'Oro (eds.), *Health and Human Flourishing* (Georgetown University Press, 2006) 33, 35.

[75] Catriona Mackenzie, Wendy Rogers and Susan Dodds (eds.), *Vulnerability: New Essays in Ethics and Feminist Philosophy* (Oxford University Press, 2014), 3–4.

individuals facing various forms of insecurity,[76] people in low lying areas susceptible to flooding[77] or someone that cannot give medical consent are referred to as vulnerable.[78] Each of these areas uses the concept of vulnerability to discuss particularised problems or groups. However, the significance of vulnerability in contemporary philosophy and legal systems is much deeper and broader than fragmented applications. Vulnerability is inherent to the human condition and various theorists consider that a full account and acknowledgement of vulnerability in daily life is required for human flourishing.[79] Essentially, being vulnerable is constitutive of what it means to be human.[80]

Mackenzie and others suggest there are two primary ways vulnerability is viewed in the literature.[81] The first is the universal application of vulnerability: the notion that because we are embodied, we are all inherently and equally vulnerable to threats to our body, such as sickness, death and ageing. The second is a relational view of vulnerability: vulnerability is not ontological but is particular to certain people in specific circumstances. Whilst every human has the potential to be in circumstances that make them vulnerable, some people or groups are especially vulnerable because of their particular position and an inability to protect themselves.

Most theorists, however, acknowledge the relevance of both kinds of vulnerability – the universal embodied version and the specific relational version.[82] Martha Nussbaum, for example, recognises universal embodied vulnerability as being interwoven with our 'human animality', based on her acceptance that humans are essentially animals.[83] Alasdair MacIntyre also

[76] For example, children or the elderly. See Amy Mullin, 'Children, Vulnerability, and Emotional Harm', in Catriona Mackenzie, Wendy Rogers and Susan Dodds (eds.), *Vulnerability: New Essays in Ethics and Feminist Philosophy* (Oxford University Press, 2014) 266.

[77] S. M. Tapsell et al., 'Vulnerability to Flooding: Health and Social Dimensions' (2002) 360 (1796) *Philosophical Transactions of the Royal Society of London. Series A: Mathematical, Physical and Engineering Sciences* 1511.

[78] Phil Bielby, *Competence and Vulnerability in Biomedical Research* (Springer, 2008).

[79] See for example Carse, 'Vulnerability, Agency, and Human Flourishing', 34; John Barry, *The Politics of Actually Existing Unsustainability: Human Flourishing in a Climate-Changed, Carbon Constrained World* (Oxford University Press, 2012) 33.

[80] This phrase is borrowed from Barry, Politics of Actually Existing Unsustainability, 36.

[81] Mackenzie, Rogers and Dodds, *Vulnerability*, 4.

[82] Fineman terms the latter 'embedded vulnerability'. See Martha Albertson Fineman, 'Vulnerability and Inevitable Inequality' (2017) 4(3) *Oslo Law Review* 133, 134.

[83] See Martha C. Nussbaum, *Frontiers of Justice: Disability, Nationality, Species Membership* (Harvard University Press, 2006); Martha C. Nussbaum, 'Human Capabilities, Female Human Beings', in Martha C. Nussbaum and Jonathon Glover (eds.), *Women, Culture and Development* (Calrendon Press, 1995) 61.

considers humans to be 'dependent rational animals'.[84] He states that humans are not just like animals but *are* animals. However, they both also note the existence of relational vulnerability, suggesting that our nature is dependent on social relations with others and those relations may give rise to specific instances of vulnerability, such as the need for care. Martha Fineman also discusses vulnerability as both a universal and particular concept[85] and notes that both types of vulnerability can be embodied (within our physical bodies, such as our characteristics, health, etc.) and embedded vulnerability (designated to us through repressive societal structures). However, she also notes embodied and embedded vulnerability are in themselves not autonomous concepts but are interlinked. Fineman says the particularity of bodies serves as a basis for legal claims and political positions, power and privilege, all of which contribute to and define embedded vulnerability, as has been demonstrated.[86] Our embodied experience marks and shapes our embedded experience and the opposite can also be true.

Fineman posits human and humanity's universal vulnerability as a conceptual ideology worthy of replacing autonomy as the dominant force in liberal political systems. She views autonomy as the current foundational myth of western liberal society. Further, the myth that individuals and families are capable of achieving complete autonomy limits the way society views equality and contributes to inequality by sheltering individuals from it. Fineman's theory is a worthy extension of the radical, postmodern and ecological feminist critique of western liberalism as it breaks down the discourse to a much more tangible and identifiable factor that is common to various oppressions (autonomy in liberal systems) while offering a potential solution.

Fineman begins by noting that in the United States (and other western liberal systems by extension), the notion of autonomy defines politics, governmental policy, law and the creation and maintenance of social structures and institutions.[87] She defines autonomy as independence or freedom, acting for oneself, not dependant on something else and an ability to supply one's own

84 Alisdair MacIntyre, *Dependent Rational Animals: Why Human Beings Need the Virtues* (Open Court, 1999).

85 Martha Albertson Fineman, 'The Vulnerable Subject and the Responsive State' (2010) 60(2) *Emory Law Journal* 251, 268.

86 Martha Albertson Fineman, 'Reasoning from the Body: Universal Vulnerability and Social Justice', in Chris Dietz, Mitchell Travis and Michael Thomson (eds.), *A Jurisprudence of the Body* (Springer International Publishing, 2020) 17.

87 Fineman traces the history of autonomy in the United States to the Declaration of Independence and the US Constitution. See Martha Fineman, *The Autonomy Myth: A Theory of Dependency* (New Press, 2004); Fineman, 'Vulnerable Subject and the Responsive State', 18–19.

needs.[88] Those without autonomy are stigmatised as dependent on government intervention. She states: 'Autonomy thus connotes on an ideological level that an individual who conforms to the dominant notions of independence and self-sufficiency is both freed *from* the prospect of regulatory governmental action and freed *through* governmental structures from interference by other private actors.'[89] Other authors are also critical of autonomy as the basis for political decision-making, particularly libertarian notions of autonomy.[90] Carse suggests that autonomy has 'held us captive' and that vulnerability ought to be more fundamental as a foundational concept in social and political structures.[91] Barry agrees and states that while vulnerability is a universal feature of the human condition, autonomy has to be socially and institutionally created and supported.[92] Anderson and Honneth argue that traditional autonomy is seen as being individualistic and so not conducive to the relationality that is required for human flourishing.[93]

Within her theory, Fineman raises specific concerns with autonomy as the primary basis for freedom and political decision-making. The first and most significant, as the title to her foundational text suggests, is that autonomy is, in fact, a myth. Realistically there is no such thing as an autonomous liberal being, despite any one person's belief that they are autonomously 'free' and despite the autonomous liberal subject being the informing aspect of our economic, legal and political principles. Anna Grear describes this as the 'decontextualisation of law's person'.[94] Indeed, it is the nature of interrelationships with others, along with bodily fragility, which makes all humans vulnerable. Every human is dependent on others. The sources of human vulnerability are inherent in our bodies but are also institutional and structural. An employee who earns their own income is dependent on their employer, the infrastructure that allows them to have an office, allows them

88 Fineman, *Autonomy Myth*, 7.

89 Fineman, *Autonomy Myth*, 9 (emphasis added).

90 See for example Catriona Mackenzie's critique of libertarian autonomy, although note that Mackenzie is critical of autonomy and vulnerability as 'oppositional'; Catriona Mackenzie, 'The Importance of Relational Autonomy and Capabilities for an Ethics of Vulnerability', in Catriona Mackenzie, Wendy Rogers and Susan Dodds (eds.), *Vulnerability: New Essays in Ethics and Feminist Philosophy* (Oxford University Press, 2014) 33, 41.

91 Carse, 'Vulnerability, Agency, and Human Flourishing', 36.

92 Barry, Politics of Actually Existing Unsustainability, 37.

93 Joel Anderson and Axel Honneth, 'Autonomy, Vulnerability, Recognition, and Justice', in John Chrisman and Joel Anderson (eds.), *Autonomy and the Challenges to Liberalism: New Essays* (Cambridge University Press, 2005) 127, 128.

94 Anna Grear, 'The Vulnerable Living Order: Human Rights and the Environment in a Critical and Philosophical Perspective' (2011) 2(1) *Journal of Human Rights and the Environment* 23, 32.

to commute to their place of employment and their customers/shareholders/ clients. A person earning that income is dependent on the partner and on the army of support that may consolidate and care for their family life. Existence is *relational*, not autonomous. The 'autonomy' promoted in these examples is socially and institutionally created and supported. Vulnerability can arise because of our dependency on this support and in situations where it is lacking.

This demonstration of dependency highlights human vulnerability and these examples demonstrate that vulnerability is not confined to groups of people who are typically considered 'vulnerable' – the poor, disabled, marginalised, etc. Instead, vulnerability is inherent in the human condition and so is inherent in the free liberal subject. Further, the fragile nature of human bodies makes the vulnerable condition more visible and demonstrates that vulnerability is the rule, not the exception.

Autonomy as the basis for human–wildlife conflict decision-making is equally problematic, and this is demonstrated in Section 2.4.5.

2.4.2 *Vulnerability As a Basis for Morality*

Many vulnerability theorists suggest that vulnerability itself is the source of moral obligations.[95] Robert Goodin argues just this, stating that vulnerability creates dependency and it is this fact of dependency that creates moral obligations.[96] Similarly, the feminist ethic of care is based on the contention that care and trust are dynamic aspects of interpersonal relationships so that if an individual has trust in someone to care for them, they are dependent on that person and so vulnerable in the relationship.[97]

Fineman also suggests that vulnerability is the basis for moral concern and argues that a vulnerability approach would lead to improved conceptual equality. Indeed, her second concern with the notion of autonomy is that it

95 Although note that others disagree that vulnerability creates moral obligations and instead argue that vulnerability is a signal that alerts us to the possibility of harms that lead to moral obligations. That is, the harm is the basis for the obligation, not the vulnerability to the harm. See Mackenzie, Rogers and Dodds, *Vulnerability*, 10.

96 Robert E. Goodin, *Protecting the Vulnerable: A Reanalysis of our Social Responsibilities* (University of Chicago Press, 1985) 132–33.

97 See, for example, Selma Sevenhuijsen, 'The Place of Care: The Relevance of the Feminist Ethic of Care for Social Policy' (2003) 4(2) *Feminist Theory* 179. See also the discussion of the relationship between care, dependency and vulnerability in Daniel Engster, 'Care Ethics, Dependency, and Vulnerability' (2019) 13(2) *Ethics and Social Welfare* 100.

limits the way we view and seek to achieve equality.[98] First, the conception of autonomy filters our view of equality so that it is defined as sameness of treatment. Fineman argues such equality is comparative between groups, not amenable to individual differences and circumstances. It does not allow for the State to readjust damaging relationships that result in inequality and simultaneously ignores existing inequalities of circumstance and assumes a standard baseline.[99] This is particularly so when the comparative methodology employed by sameness of treatment equality distorts our understanding of a variety of social problems that are not based on identity characteristics and where it is assumed that people should be able to take care of themselves and their family. It is this notion of equality and the use of vulnerability to create a 'better' equality that forms Fineman's basis of morality.

2.4.3 *Responsibility for Vulnerability?*

The myth of autonomy and its impact on equality is described by Fineman through analysis of the family as an autonomous structure.[100] In western liberal systems, the family is viewed as a private sphere that is separated from the public sphere. A parent can voluntarily care for their child or sick or elderly relatives inside the bubble of the private sphere but, once they leave for paid employment, they enter the public sphere and are then seen to be contributing to society at large. The family, as it lies in the private realm, is supposed to lay outside of political and governmental interference. But such a view fails to acknowledge the relationship between the private and public spheres. In many cases, having a partner at home to care for children within the private sphere allows the other to be present in the public sphere. Those children will grow and become part of the public sphere in their own right, contributing to society. Single-parent families, on the other hand, are expected to do both so as not to become welfare-dependent (a stigmatised state), so that they must pay for care and contribute to the public sphere. Whilst a simple analogy,[101] it is this type of difference and discrimination that

98 Martha Albertson Fineman, 'Equality, Autonomy, and the Vulnerable Subject in Law and Politics', in Martha Albertson Fineman and Anna Grear (eds.), *Vulnerability: Reflections on a New Ethical Foundation for Law and Politics* (Ashgate Publishing Company, 2013) 13, 14–16.

99 Martha Fineman and Anna Grear, *Vulnerability: Reflections on a New Ethical Foundation for Law and Politics* (Ashgate, 2013) 14; Fineman, 'Vulnerable Subject and the Responsive State', 251.

100 See, for example, Fineman, Autonomy Myth, chapter 3.

101 Care is often used as an example to demonstrate the unjust allocation of dependency and vulnerability; however, vulnerability is in no way limited to the family structure. For care see

arises from the family as a private unit, as well as the acknowledgment that we are all dependent on something at some time, that leads Fineman to the position that there ought to be *collective responsibility* for dependency. She asserts that collective responsibility would lead to greater equality. Fineman's concept of collective responsibility is primarily applied by her to the debt owed to caretakers. However, I will demonstrate in Sections 2.4.4 and 2.4.5 that collective responsibility is equally applicable to environmental concerns and human–wildlife conflict, under an ecofeminist lens.

Others view responsibility as much more individualised. Goodin suggests that the duty to protect the vulnerable falls on anyone who can assist and those who hold power over someone vulnerable.[102] However, such individual notions of responsibility can be dismissive of the very social structures that contribute to and cause vulnerability in the first instance and inevitably cause responsibility to fall on members of society who traditionally bear the burden of such work. Fineman's concept of collective responsibility is more attuned to the dependency created and channelled by society, as well as the individual responsibility it creates.

2.4.4 *Obligations to the Vulnerable – Fineman's 'Responsive State'*

Within the vulnerability literature, there is some theoretical argument concerning the question of how obligations to the vulnerable ought to be fulfilled.[103] The focus of the argument is whether the policy should seek to minimise vulnerability or promote autonomy.

Fineman's theory lies in the former arena. In advocating for collective responsibility, she argues that the notion of vulnerability as an inherent human condition ought to replace autonomy as the *dominant* driver of political and sociological direction. To do this, she makes an argument for a 'responsive' state, noting that the state is the only entity that can act for all.[104] The goal of addressing vulnerability is not necessarily increasing autonomy,

Eva Feder Kittay, *Love's Labor: Essays on Women, Equality, and Dependency* (Routledge, 1999).

[102] Goodin, Protecting the Vulnerable, 194.

[103] See for example the different conceptions of resilience between John Barry and Martha Fineman: Barry, *Politics of Actually Existing Unsustainability*, chapter 3; Fineman, *Autonomy Myth*, chapter 10. See also the varying approaches of the authors in Mackenzie, Rogers and Dodds, *Vulnerability*.

[104] Fineman, 'Vulnerable Subject and the Responsive State', 264.

but instead increasing resilience.[105] It is the responsive state that ought to link resilience with societal institutions.

In mapping out the requirements for the 'responsive state', Fineman focuses mostly (although not exclusively) on the societal debt owed to caretakers.[106] She states that 'the existence of this debt must be recognised, and payment accomplished, through policies and laws that provide both some economic compensation and structural accommodation to caretakers'.[107] However, the role of the state in implementing collective responsibility for shared vulnerabilities and oppressions is not limited to caring nor any broader human role or quality. Fineman also acknowledges this when she states that the 'obligation to caretakers can be perceived as one component of a *more general state obligation* to promote and ensure the conditions of equality, wherein all individuals have an opportunity to achieve security and exercise agency'.[108]

The concept of a responsive state entails a move away from the privatisation of resources and structures and the mantra of individual responsibility that is currently prevalent in law and politics. Instead, the state should be providing resources to societal institutions whose 'very content and meaning is defined through state processes'.[109] Further, the state should be monitoring, evaluating, updating and reforming societal institutions that impact equality of access and opportunity.[110]

2.4.5 *Critique of Fineman's Vulnerability*

One of the primary critiques of Fineman's theory on vulnerability is that she undervalues the human desire for and necessity of autonomy for a flourishing life in contemporary society.[111] Mackenzie is particularly vocal on Fineman's conception of the autonomous subject and the vulnerable subject as opposing

[105] Fineman, 'Vulnerable Subject and the Responsive State', 269. For a thorough description of the meaning of 'resilience', see Ellen Gordon-Bouvier, 'Theorising Resilience', in Ellen Gordon-Bouvier (ed.), *Relational Vulnerability: Theory, Law and the Private Family* (Springer International Publishing, 2020) 135.

[106] See, for example, the theory applied to employment law in Martha Albertson Fineman and Jonathon W. Fineman (eds.), *Vulnerability and the Legal Organization of Work* (Routledge, 2018); and bioethics in Henk ten Have, *Vulnerability: Challenging Bioethics* (Routledge, 2016).

[107] Fineman, *Autonomy Myth*, 263.

[108] Fineman, *Autonomy Myth*, 263 (emphasis added).

[109] Fineman, 'Vulnerable Subject and the Responsive State', 272.

[110] Fineman, 'Vulnerable Subject and the Responsive State', 273.

[111] See, for example, Morgan Cloud, 'More than Utopia', in Martha Fineman and Anna Grear (eds.), *Vulnerability: Reflections on a New Ethical Foundation for Law and Politics* (Ashgate, 2013) 77; Nina A. Kohn, 'Vulnerability Theory and the Role of Government' (2014) 26(1) *Yale Journal of Law and Feminism* 1; Mackenzie, 'Importance of Relational Autonomy'.

states, a dichotomy which she asserts is a mistake.[112] Mackenzie's criticisms take on two primary arguments. The first is that suppression of autonomy could be and historically has been associated with 'coercive or objectionably paternalistic social relations, policies, and institutions, which often function to compound rather than ameliorate the vulnerability of the persons or groups they are designed to assist'.[113] This is a point supported by Sean Coyle, who suggests that there are reasons to be concerned about the potential for Fineman's responsive state to become authoritarian.[114]

Mackenzie's second criticism is of Fineman's 'conflation' of autonomy with the libertarian conception of autonomy, and the subsequent failure to consider theories of relational autonomy as being useful in the conception of the autonomous self.[115] She argues that libertarian and individualistic autonomy is indeed harmful and ought to be rejected, but that autonomy itself is crucial as it is necessary to counter the feeling of powerlessness that is often associated with vulnerability, so as not to descend into 'objectionable paternalism'. As a result, any attempt to address vulnerability should be an attempt to increase relational autonomous agency.

In her attempts to demonstrate autonomy's synthesis with vulnerability, Mackenzie draws on theories of relational autonomy. She offers the following context:

> Autonomy involves the exercise of an array of skills and capacities: cognitive capacities, such as reasoning skills and the ability to understand and process information; capacities to question and reflect critically on social norms and values; introspective skills necessary for self-reflection and self-knowledge, emotional and affective capacities required for sustaining intimate personal relationships and for social cooperation: and imaginative capacities necessary for envisaging alternative courses of action. Relational theorists claim that these autonomy competencies emerge developmentally and are sustained and exercised in the context of significant social relationships and, hence, that such relationships are necessary background enabling conditions for autonomy.[116]

[112] Mackenzie, 'Importance of Relational Autonomy', 34.
[113] Mackenzie, 'Importance of Relational Autonomy', 34.
[114] Sean Coyle, 'Vulnerability and the Liberal Order', in Martha Fineman and Anna Grear (eds.), *Vulnerability: Reflections on a New Ethical Foundation for Law and Politics* (Ashgate, 2013) 61.
[115] Mackenzie, 'Importance of Relational Autonomy', 41. But note that this is a critique offered by various vulnerability theorists, including Kohn, 'Vulnerability Theory'; Cloud, 'More than Utopia'; Coyle, 'Vulnerability and the Liberal Order'.
[116] Mackenzie, 'Importance of Relational Autonomy', 43.

In contrast, libertarian conceptions of autonomy focus on minimally constrained freedom of choice and ignore the background social conditions that inform preferences. They focus on individualism and the removal of the state's ability to impact that individualism.

Mackenzie's critique of Fineman's description and use of autonomy is essentially a matter of semantics. Mackenzie's view is that autonomy, if viewed in a relational way, is necessary for human development and that Fineman does not consider that form of relational autonomy. However, Fineman's theory can and should be viewed as a case for relational autonomy, notwithstanding the absence of the phrase in her work. Fineman does not argue for the elimination of autonomy for the sake of addressing vulnerability nor does she say that vulnerability is the antithesis of autonomy. Instead, she argues against privileging the individualistic autonomy that has recently been demonstrated in politics in the United States over the notion of true equality: 'This would not mean casting aside autonomy, but rather that we realize that as desirable as autonomy is as an aspiration, it cannot be attained without an underlying provision of substantial assistance, subsidy, and support from society and its institutions, which give individuals the resources they need to create options and make choices.'[117]

Whilst Mackenzie acknowledges this point, she discounts it on the basis that Fineman does not further develop the argument or acknowledge the need for autonomy.[118] Again, such an argument is a matter of language. Mackenzie states that there is no inherent tension between an 'adequately theorised' conception of autonomy and acknowledgement of universal vulnerability. The fact that Fineman does not extend her argument or draw on theories of relational autonomy does not mean she is not advocating against the concept of autonomy per se, but the language of it. This is precisely her point; there is tension because autonomy is not viewed as relational nor does its current liberal conception acknowledge or make room for universal vulnerability.[119] Further, it is noteworthy that Fineman's theory analyses the dominant politico-legal atmosphere of autonomy and argues that vulnerability should be given priority at the institutional level. Fineman's theory addresses the institutional perspective. At the individual level, she is markedly less distant from the concept of autonomy.

[117] Fineman, 'Vulnerable Subject and the Responsive State', 260.

[118] Mackenzie, 'Importance of Relational Autonomy', 41.

[119] Note Fineman's vulnerability is particularly 'Americanised' and her examples relate specifically to the American context.

Nina Kohn offers a different critique in her attempt to refine Fineman's vulnerability theory.[120] Kohn suggests Fineman's analysis of vulnerability and her applications to caretaking and the elderly fail to be prescriptive at the level required to allocate resources between vulnerable groups. Kohn argues:

> . . . when Fineman moves beyond a relatively abstract discussion of vulnerability theory to recommend specific laws, she adopts the very type of targeted group approach to addressing vulnerability that she has vigorously opposed. Specifically, when Fineman attempts to use vulnerability theory to argue for particular policies to protect older adults, she embraces an approach that singles out older adults for special 'protections' on the basis of the perceived vulnerability of the group . . . By doing so, she moves away from the post-identity and substantive equality approaches that she espouses, and toward the formalistic equality and identity-based approaches that she criticizes.[121]

Again, such a critique is misguided. Instead of acknowledging the universality of old age, Kohn chooses to single out those who would currently benefit from changes to laws protecting the elderly, rather than the benefit experienced by all from our shared vulnerability to growing older. Further, the requirement for some with more resilience to contribute to the caretaking based on the collective responsibility outlined by Fineman. There are undoubtedly situations where an application of vulnerability theory will prioritise some vulnerable subjects over others, but that prioritisation must be done with the full acknowledgement that we are all inherently vulnerable and potentially in need of said protection. This prioritisation of protection based on our shared inherent vulnerability can inform the basis of a framework for addressing human–wildlife conflict.

2.5 AN ECOFEMINIST APPROACH TO VULNERABILITY THEORY: ECOLOGICAL VULNERABILITY

It is now time to turn to an ecofeminist approach to vulnerability theory. This is necessary to move the theory beyond a critique of institutional reliance on autonomy concerning care and the public/private divide, to a holistic earth ethic that accounts for the shared vulnerabilities of humans, wildlife and nature and theorises the social relationships and institutions surrounding those vulnerabilities. Critically, expanding vulnerability theory can help inform a response to current human–wildlife conflicts. An ecofeminist expansion is

120 Kohn, 'Vulnerability Theory'.
121 Kohn, 'Vulnerability Theory'.

necessary for three reasons. First, it places autonomy in a web of interrelated concepts that together are responsible for the continued oppression of particular groups and people in society and the domination of wildlife and nature as a whole. Second, it shows the fallacy of the argument that the autonomy/vulnerability dichotomy can only be resolved by inverting the hierarchy and focusing on vulnerability. Finally, it will move the theory beyond its current anthropocentric focus. This section will discuss those benefits of giving vulnerability theory an ecofeminist perspective, whilst explaining how they inform the human–wildlife conflict conundrum. An ecofeminist approach to vulnerability theory would also have the most potential to inform a legal and political model of human–wildlife coexistence, as is demonstrated over the remainder of this chapter.

2.5.1 *Autonomy in the Web of Domination*

Vulnerability theory is one that seeks to address inconsistent notions of equality in the law. Fineman states: 'Vulnerability theory provides a template with which to refocus critical attention, raising new questions and challenging established assumptions about individual and state responsibility and the role of law, as well as allowing us to address social relationships of inevitable inequality.'[122] This makes the theory adaptable to all sorts of social interactions. Social relationships involving the environment and wildlife clearly fall within this framework, with instances of environmental degradation and human–wildlife conflict proven to increase inequality and most affect those who are least resilient. But environmental destruction goes beyond responsibility for inequality and Fineman's theory fits within a larger 'web of domination', as outlined by Plumwood and discussed in Section 2.3.1. That is to say, the domination of wildlife is caused by a web of social and culturally constructed phenomena, including, but not limited to, the quest for individual autonomy. To start we must assess that web from an ecofeminist perspective. For example, Anna Grear shows how the 'liberal legal person emerges as an ideological construct intimately related to capitalism'.[123] Indeed, capitalism, technology, industrialisation, reductionist scientific practices, colonisation and privatisation, all critiqued by ecofeminist and vulnerability theorists, contribute to the damaging hierarchical attitudes toward wildlife and the willingness to minimise their value and moral worth in management

[122] Fineman, 'Vulnerability and Inevitable Inequality', 134.
[123] Grear, 'Vulnerable Living Order', 30.

practices. Many of these can be linked to the promotion of autonomy or may be viewed as 'symptoms' of the quest for autonomy but, in reality, neo-liberal autonomy is the result of a power structure created and maintained by societal institutions. This is why Fineman focuses on both individual and institutional autonomy (that is the promotion of individual autonomy by institutions). Autonomy is only one link in a related web because there are many instances when those within the power structure do not seek to promote the autonomy of those outside of it. In wildlife governance, this manifests in various ways, such as forced removal from protected areas to protect the 'resource' for those with power and the dominance of groups who are consumptive users of wildlife within the political sphere.

An ecofeminist critique of these patriarchal societal structures has previously been applied to other aspects of the biosphere. Plumwood and Shiva both discuss forestry as demonstrative of the patriarchal exploitation of nature. Shiva explains the reductionism associated with patriarchal commercial capitalism:

> Commercial capitalism is based on specialized commodity production and therefore demands uniformity in production, and the uni-functional use of natural resources. Reductionism thus reduces complex ecosystems to a single component, and a single component to a single function. Further, it allows for the manipulation of the ecosystem in a way that maximizes the single-function, single-component exploitation. In this reductionist paradigm, a forest is reduced to commercial wood, and wood is reduced to cellulose fibre for the pulp and paper industry. Forests, land and genetic resources are then manipulated to increase the production of pulpwood. This distortion is legitimized scientifically as overall productivity increase, regardless of whether it might decrease the output of water from the forest, or destroy the diversity of life forms that constitute a forest community.[124]

Plumwood discusses the resulting and connected oppressions:

> High technology agriculture and forestry in the third world which is ecologically destructive also strengthens the control of elites and social inequality, increasing for example men's control over the economy at the expense of women, and it does these things in a way which reflects structure, not coincidence ... The losers will be (and in many places already are) those, human and nonhuman, without market power, and issues of human justice and issues of the destruction of nature must increasingly converge.[125]

[124] Shiva, 'Reductionism and Regeneration', 24–25.
[125] Plumwood, 'Ecopolitics Debate', 64.

This reductionism and the oppressions it creates are equally evident in wildlife governance. Policies are often based on the instrumental or aesthetic value of the subject wildlife. There are entire books and monographs dedicated to methods of valuation in human terms.[126] The contention in neoliberal conservation is that, by giving wildlife 'value' and making them 'profitable', the incentive for conservation is stronger than the economic motivation behind destruction.[127] However, where the value is not found in adequate, immediate terms, wildlife will be sacrificed for the advancement of commercialism or human development. They will be removed to clear the way for a mine or property development, culled to avoid damage to crops and livestock or killed and sold for their parts (known ominously as 'extraction'). These actions, including many apparent 'conservation' actions, such as trophy hunting, also benefit the oppressors or, as Plumwood suggests, those with market power.

The monetary income associated with neoliberal conservation is rarely distributed to those who bear the cost of conflict but is diverted by those with power or status and, as a result, there is an increasing disconnect between those methods of conservation and human security as well as conservation of biodiversity.[128] Those who bear the cost of conservation, and work hard for it, are not receiving the benefit of increased autonomy, as institutional structures do not allow for it. This is because the liberal legal subject is a tool used to maintain the power-over conceptions of power, as outlined by Warren.[129] In maintaining conceptions of power, institutions focus on the attainment of autonomy by very particular methods and by very particular people. Thus, those with power in a community-run conservation project are those with the funds necessary to achieve the conservation goals. Although they may not be doing the groundwork or bearing the costs of the project, such as physical labour, increased negative interaction with species that are the focus of the project, loss of access to land, etc., they can use their power to maintain it to the detriment of others. Institutionally this is seen as acceptable and even necessary. Contract laws, for example, do not generally allow for unequal bargaining positions. Financial institutions that might lend to conservation groups with noble purposes but no assets will require a financial backer or guarantor. Once the power is obtained, the privileged can maintain the concept of privilege by suggesting that those at the ground level can only be

[126] See, for example, Daniel J. Decker and Gary R. Goff, *Valuing Wildlife: Economic and Social Perspectives* (Westview Press, 1987).
[127] See the discussion of neo-liberal conservation in Section 3.3.
[128] Bond and Mkutu, 'Exploring the Hidden Costs'.
[129] Warren, 'Toward an Ecofeminist Peace Politics'.

privileged if they fit a particular mould. Power is obtained in a very particular way and bearing the cost of someone else's conservation investment is not it. Instead, one must work at becoming 'autonomous' from others so one exerts one's own control. The autonomous liberal subject is free from State intervention and so is free to maintain the web of domination.

2.5.2 *Breaking Down Dichotomies*

Ecofeminists suggest that we need to remove oppressive dichotomies to overcome the web of domination.[130] Fineman's theory is premised on such a divide: the autonomy/vulnerability dichotomy. In the ecofeminist web of domination, dichotomies are used to maintain the power over conceptions of power discussed by Warren.[131] The dichotomy described by Fineman is just that. The need to achieve a particular type of autonomy that is defined by those with greater levels of inherent resilience leads to power over the concept of autonomy itself and a feeling that those with less resilience need to catch up.

The autonomy/vulnerability divide is also linked to Plumwood's contention that the main oppression linking feminism and environmental domination is reason over nature.[132] The vulnerability dichotomy *is* one of reason/nature. Autonomy is premised as something that can only be achieved via means of reason, through intelligence and perseverance, whilst vulnerability is human nature and something that needs to be overcome. Although not explicit in Fineman's version of the theory, the implication is that vulnerability instead needs to become the reasoned focus. However, ecofeminism warns against this flipping of the hierarchical dichotomy. Instead, it advocates for an equal balance between the two sides. Any dichotomy can lead to 'value-hierarchical thinking', as explained by Warren and discussed above in Section 2.3.2. As such, vulnerability theory needs to embrace the breakdown of that dichotomy so that emotion and nature are equally balanced with reason. Certainly, a reasoned approach to vulnerability is necessary and one of the strengths of Fineman's theory. However, an ecofeminist approach needs to go beyond that and argue for a balanced perspective that includes compassion and care in addition to the logical fallacy of autonomy. An ecofeminist approach to

[130] See, for example, Karen Morrow, 'Ecofeminism and the Environment: International Law and Climate Change', in Margaret Davies and Vanessa E. Munro (eds.), *The Ashgate Research Companion to Feminist Legal Theory* (Routledge, 2013) 377–93, 378; Griffin, Woman and Nature; Kheel, 'Liberation of Nature', 138–39; Plumwood, 'Ecopolitics Debate', 74.

[131] Warren, 'Toward an Ecofeminist Peace Politics'.

[132] Plumwood, 'Ecopolitics Debate', 74.

vulnerability theory would result in an argument that the State needs to promote both autonomy and address vulnerability, rather than replace autonomy with responses to vulnerability, as suggested by Fineman. This will have a very practical effect for methods of responding to human–wildlife conflict, as will be discussed in Chapters 5 and 6.

The reason/emotion divide in western dualistic thinking is also evident in the conflict literature and is informative of the human reluctance to be emotionally invested in the interests of wildlife which we come into conflict with. Emotional connections with wildlife and particularly problem wildlife are often discouraged in western societies. Whilst we love and care for domesticated household animals such as dogs and cats, and care about their experiences, pain and pleasure, we do not consider wildlife in the same manner, particularly those that are not 'cute' and 'lovable'. Wildlife species that conflict with human interests, even native species, are often called 'pests', a term that invokes a negative emotional response.[133] Leopold was aware of such emotional disconnection and the realisation that he felt something for a dying wolf he had just shot is thought to have informed his ecological theory.[134] Even in circumstances where we do feel an emotional connection with wildlife, such connection is often dominated by competing arguments of logic. Reason is prioritised over emotion. Zoos are an apt example. One of the conservation premises of voyeuristic zoos is that people will become emotionally engaged with the animal species and so be more willing to support their conservation. Yet, they care little about the interests of the wild animal confined to an enclosure and the evidence that the experience of a zoo actually leads to an increased conservation ethic is lacking.[135]

Notwithstanding the attempted use of emotion as a tool in certain conservation arenas, it continues to be subjected to intense scrutiny from theorists in the animal and environmental sphere. For example, Singer and Regan reject emotion as being a point of relevance.[136] Feminist theorists argue that emotion should not be excluded but should be as useful as reason in

[133] For example, kangaroos have a long history of being considered 'pests' by landholders in Australia; D. Ben-Ami et al, 'The Welfare Ethics of the Commercial Killing of Free-Ranging Kangaroos: An Evaluation of the Benefits and Costs of the Industry' (2014) 23(1) *Animal Welfare* 1, 3.

[134] Leopold, *Sand County Almanac*, 138. Note though that Leopold did not abandon hunting, even after his wolf epiphany.

[135] Joanne Vining, 'The Connection to Other Animals and Caring for Nature' (2003) 10(2) *Research in Human Ecology* 87, 88.

[136] See Marti Kheel's discussion of the absence of emotion in the theories of Singer and Regan; Kheel, 'Liberation of Nature', 23–26.

issues of social justice. This is particularly demonstrated in the use of care, empathy and compassion and is evident in Carol Gilligan's care and sympathy theory, supplemented by Josephine Donovan.[137] Indeed, care theory can be inherently linked with vulnerability theory.[138] The relationality of vulnerability and the care required for those at certain stages of vulnerability, such as infancy, is the basis of a compassionate view of the relationship between the carer and cared for and the institutional reflection of that relationship. Care theory adds to the logical arguments of inherent vulnerability posited by Fineman and allows for those emotions to be utilised in a vulnerability framework. An effective coexistence model would harness the compassionate emotional pull of certain species of wildlife and use it in conjunction with logic to overcome conflict.

2.5.3 *Highlighting the Vulnerable 'Other' and Extending the Vulnerability Voice*

From a vulnerability perspective, the autonomy myth not only precludes a full understanding of equality but also the way we think about the environment in general and wildlife specifically. An ecofeminist account of vulnerability theory would expand vulnerability from a universal human condition to a universal condition of all living beings and the Earth itself. In so doing we not only begin to recognise the inherent vulnerability of wildlife but how their vulnerability is connected to ours. It is vital to note that the vulnerability of wildlife affects human resilience, whilst human vulnerability affects wildlife resilience. The relationality runs in both directions.

To elucidate, consider how our embodied and embedded vulnerability is linked with that of wildlife and how that link can create conflict. Human actions affect the embedded vulnerability of wildlife. Habitat can be destroyed, leaving wildlife homeless and hungry, increasing the chance of them

[137] See Carol Gilligan, *In a Different Voice: Psychological Theory and Women's Development* (Harvard University Press, 1982); Donovan, 'Animal Rights and Feminist Theory'. There are three central principles to care theory. First, care theory does not rely on autonomous individual rights. Instead, it is predicated on the existence of unequal relationships, where there is a carer and the cared for. Second, care theory values emotions and considers sympathy, empathy and love as paramount. Third, care theory is more focused on the particulars of a given situation, such that there is no single solution to the global human–wildlife conflict phenomena. Applying this, there is an acknowledgement that every conflict situation results in a different set of interests, rights and values and, as a result, no one rule or set of rules can be established.

[138] Engster, 'Care Ethics, Dependency, and Vulnerability'.

expanding their range and coming into contact with people. More fundamentally, our resilience depends on their resilience. We rely on the ecosystem services provided by wildlife and their contribution to the greater environment.

Similarly, our vulnerabilities can leave wildlife less resilient. By way of example, a conservation ethic is less likely to be held by those in poverty, who are more likely to be concerned about finding food and sources of income for themselves and their family.[139] Our economic situation, as a symptom of our embedded vulnerability, affects the steps that need to be taken and our ability to take them to stem biodiversity loss.

Conceptions of vulnerability are not familiarised within western political ideology. Instead, they are hidden away from public thought and consideration. Anthony Giddens defines the processes involved in the minimisation of vulnerability as 'sequestration': the institutional systemic exclusion and concealment from social life of anything that would undermine our ontological security and lead to an existential crisis, such as madness, sickness and nature – things often associated with vulnerability.[140] This sequestration of vulnerability arises because the powers in western liberal politic favour, prioritise and reward autonomy over-dependence, whilst western philosophical thought posits autonomy as the basis for a healthy human existence. The role of the biosphere in human flourishing is often 'sequestered' or overridden by concerns of the self. The plight of prairie dogs in the United States is an apt example. Species of prairie dogs come into conflict with humans for two primary reasons.[141] Many people consider them to spread zoonotic disease such as sylvatic plague, and so argue they pose a health risk. It has also been historically asserted that their herbivorous diet impacts livestock's ability to graze. More recently, both of these arguments have been found to be scientifically untrue.[142] Yet, the ecological role of the prairie dog is still minimised by

[139] Adrian Treves, R. B. Wallace and S. White, 'Participatory Planning of Interventions to Mitigate Human–Wildlife Conflicts' (2009) 23(6) *Conservation Biology* 1577, 1583.

[140] Anthony Giddens, *Modernity and Self-Identity: Self and Society in the Late Modern Age* (Polity, 1991) 156.

[141] Christopher Pepper et al., 'Threatened or Endangered-Keystone Species or Public Health Threat – The Black-Tailed Prairie Dog, the Endangered Species Act, and the Imminent Threat of Bubonic Plague' (2004) 24(3) *Journal of Land, Resources, & Environmental Law* 355, 363.

[142] See Pepper et al., 'Threatened or Endangered-Keystone Species'; Ron J. Johnson, Ronald M. Case and Mary M. Beck, 'Biodeterioration of the Biosphere: Where does Wildlife Damage Management Stand?' (1995) 36(1) *International Biodeterioration & Biodegradation* 7.

relevant stakeholders and, in some instances, public perceptions remain so dire that the actual ecological facts do not matter to policy decision-makers.[143]

The sequestration of the role of wildlife suggests we are autonomous from the environment and our need for wildlife does not go beyond their instrumental value. Yet our vulnerabilities are inherently connected with theirs. Evidence suggests that eliminating prairie dogs from a locality actually increases the risk of plague to humans.[144] Further, they have more recently been identified as a keystone species – they are integral to the functioning of the surrounding grasslands ecosystem and so increase grazeability for livestock over the long-term.[145]

Application of vulnerability theory to the conundrum of human–wildlife conflict would necessarily involve several key features. The first and most important is to encourage the removal of the sequestration of the role of wildlife and recognise our shared vulnerability. Inherent in this step is an understanding that the concept of vulnerability needs to be viewed holistically. Vulnerability is not only a human condition. Wildlife is vulnerable, as individuals and species. This means that we must make evident how our vulnerability is connected to wildlife and the greater environment and how their vulnerability is largely caused by human action and continues to be related to it. This is the universal aspect of ecological vulnerability. However, we cannot consider the vulnerability of wildlife only so far as it impacts our own vulnerability, but we also must consider their vulnerability to us, outside of their instrumentality. In essence, wildlife needs to be given their own vulnerability voice, as does the ecological community that they inhabit. Extending moral consideration to the vulnerability of wildlife is a necessary part of care and vulnerability theories and ensures emotional investment in their wellbeing. It is also necessary to truly remove hierarchy and facilitate a relationship of coexistence. Listening to different voices allows for a particular vulnerability to be considered. Further, an analysis of those differences leads to questions as to how they are treated. As Fineman herself notes, 'the process of analyzing differences that arise from individual experience within social structures does not begin with the particular characteristics of the individual but with the nature of social arrangements'.[146]

[143] Richard P. Reading et al., 'Understanding and Resolving the Black-Tailed Prairie Dog Conservation Challenge', in Rosie Woodroffe, Simon Thirgood and Alan Rabinowitz (eds.), *People and Wildlife: Conflict or Coexistence?* (Cambridge University Press, 2005) 209, 222–23.

[144] Pepper et al., 'Threatened or Endangered-Keystone Species'.

[145] Pepper et al., 'Threatened or Endangered-Keystone Species'.

[146] Martha Albertson Fineman, 'The Limits of Equality: Vulnerability and Inevitable Inequality', in Robin West and Cynthia G. Bowman (eds.), *Research Handbook on Feminist Jurisprudence* (Edward Elgar Publishing, 2019) 84.

Recognition of our shared vulnerability would lead to redefining the relationship as relational instead of one defined by one-sided use and instrumental value. Also, the need for collective responsibility for reducing wildlife loss becomes evident. There is an 'environmental social debt' that is like Fineman's caretaker debt, and that debt is one specifically owed to wildlife, given what humans have taken at their expense.

Given the need for collective responsibility, the state or in this instance the laws and policies created by the state need to go beyond concern for embodied vulnerability and also consider ecological vulnerability. The state needs to be responsive to and act responsible for our interconnected vulnerabilities. Fineman herself briefly acknowledges the importance of state responsibility for ecological vulnerability as she discusses the types of resources that can be provided by societal institutions to increase resilience, albeit she does so in a way that is superficial and human-centric:

> We live in an environment and are dependent on things like clean air and water. We experience the environment in immediate and cosmic sense. The state of our neighbourhood park is important, but so too are Arctic ice flows or floods in Pakistan. A variety of external factors and physical actions can alter the environments in which we live and have profound influence over our needs and well-being.[147]

Because of this, she argues that ecological resources must be provided to societal institutions by the State, as part of acknowledging the collective responsibility for environmental degradation. Angela Harris takes this argument further.[148] She argues that there is a need for recognition of an 'environmentally embedded subject', together with Fineman's 'vulnerable subject', and discusses in depth the connections between human flourishing, social justice and both macro- and micro-level ecologies:

> 'Ecological vulnerability' recognizes that human lives are part of complex ecosystems that operate on various levels of scale, from the local to the global. Particularly in the age of the Anthropocene, when human activity is rapidly causing large-scale, not fully predictable, and potentially irreversible changes to our inner and outer environments, the fully responsive state should recognize that soil degradation, water scarcity, warming oceans, and depleted fishing stocks structure our options and create opportunities just as market and family relations do. In the age of the Anthropocene, it can no longer be

[147] Fineman, 'Vulnerable Subject and the Responsive State', 271.
[148] Angela P. Harris, 'Vulnerability and Power in the Age of the Anthropocene' (2014) 6(1) *Washington and Lee Journal of Energy, Climate, and the Environment* 98.

> argued that these environmental processes and events are outside the circle of justice. 'Human behavior' and 'the natural world' are now locked in an ever-tightening feedback loop. To care for its citizens, the responsive state must care for the systems that make its citizens' flourishing possible.[149]

Harris' analysis is a positive contribution to the vulnerability literature but is also posited from a human-centric view, not an ecological one. As a result, it is not holistic and not considerate of ecofeminist philosophy. Whilst she touches on the state's responsibility to 'nonhuman entities and processes', she does so for the sake of human flourishing, not to give such 'entities' a valid voice as vulnerable subjects themselves.[150]

Whilst our laws and policies must be collective and acknowledge the debt owed to wildlife, to be feminist they must be open to an individual voice. As Kohn suggests, sometimes individuals are best placed to decide what makes them safe and secure and such a premise must extend to both individual humans bearing the cost of human–wildlife conflict and individual animals.[151] For this reason, ecological vulnerability must have an element of care and be implemented based on shared and lived experience.

2.6 CONCLUSION

To commence an exploration of the potential for law and policy to assist the resolution of human–wildlife conflict, it is first necessary to reach an understanding of the theoretical framework that underpins our motivations. Current philosophical approaches to the human–wildlife relationship are not appropriate for instances of conflict, because they are not prescriptive, there is no ability to tailor a solution to the specific needs of any given situation and they do not consider the diverse array of voices that are impacted by said conflict and which are influenced by personal feeling and experience. This chapter sought to fill the gap by formulating a theoretical framework, referred to as 'ecological vulnerability' that explains the deficiencies in the human–wildlife relationship and how it may be improved.

Vulnerability theory is useful for explaining the institutional aspects of our social relationships and their impact on wildlife. However, as a holistic Earth ethic, vulnerability theory needs development. If we were to make it an Earth ethic to address conservation conflicts such as human–wildlife conflicts, it would eventually become a theory that fits within the ecofeminist blanket due

149 Harris, 'Vulnerability and Power', 127.
150 Harris, 'Vulnerability and Power', 127.
151 Kohn, 'Vulnerability Theory', 14.

to the theoretical similarities in the first place. Therefore, using ecofeminism to expand it outward is logical. It becomes not only a theory that questions the role of institutions (including law) in creating a social discourse that results in inequality but adds environmental vulnerability and compassion for non-human 'others' to that social discourse.

An ecofeminist application of vulnerability theory leads to a theoretical framework that is based on the connection and inter-dependency of our shared vulnerabilities, both human and environmental. In having 'vulnerability' as the basis for social and environmental justice, such theory can overcome the relativism criticism encountered by ecofeminism, whilst still maintaining a sense of shared identity with the environment.

The framework has the potential to do what other theories cannot and turn seemingly either/or situations into contextual moral responses. Thus, ecological vulnerability is based on the premise that humans and wildlife are inherently vulnerable and the circumstances that increase or prolong that vulnerability are connected. As a result, we must engage with the state, via its role in law and policy development, to respond to our shared vulnerabilities, decrease conflict and contribute to a healthy and flourishing environment for both humans and wildlife.

In Chapter 3, I will move ecological vulnerability from a philosophical argument and take the concept into the real world of human–wildlife conflict. I will explain the use of ecological vulnerability in a model of human–wildlife coexistence and how the concepts embodied in ecological vulnerability should be embodied in law and other governance institutions. The theoretical framework developed in this chapter will be further explored through the remaining chapters of this book.

3

Friends in the Wild?

The Problem of Human–Wildlife Conflict and Its Governance

3.1 INTRODUCTION

In Australia, more shark attacks occurred in 2020 than in the preceding 86 years.[1] This fact hit news around the world, raising questions as to the safety of beach-going in Australia and the necessity of further protective measures.[2] In Queensland, shark nets were reinstated after a local Member of Parliament questioned the 'non-lethal' shark management policies that the Queensland government had adopted, suggesting that recent attacks had 'knocked our tourism industry around'.[3] In Western Australia, managers were permitted to shoot the sharks deemed responsible for the attacks.[4] The public discourse around the governance of this type of conflict still lies heavily within the realm of 'to kill or not to kill'. Yet, experts suggest that several other human-related

1 Elias Visontay, 'High Number of Fatal Australian Shark Attacks Prompts Concern Hunting Grounds Are Shifting', *the Guardian* (Online), 13 October 2020. Available at: www.theguardian.com/environment/2020/oct/14/high-number-of-fatal-australian-shark-attacks-prompts-concern-hunting-grounds-are-shifting (last accessed 31 January 2022).

2 Livia Albeck-Ripka, 'Death by Shark Is at a High in Australia. What's Going On?', *The New York Times* (Online), 25 November 2020. Available at: www.nytimes.com/2020/11/24/world/australia/shark-attack.html (last accessed 31 January 2022); 'Is Australia Really Seeing More Shark Attacks?', *BBC News* (Online), 14 October 2020. Available at: www.bbc.com/news/world-australia-54112992 (last accessed 31 January 2022).

3 Stephanie Zillman, 'Smart Drum Lines, Nets and Drones Part of New Shark Control Measures', *ABC News* (Online), 4 February 2020. Available at: www.abc.net.au/news/2020-02-04/smart-drum-lines-nets-drones-new-shark-control-measures/11927260 (last accessed 31 January 2022). As a side note, it was 2020; a pandemic was more likely to blame for the fall in tourism numbers.

4 Lauren Pilat and Michael Genovese, 'Police Shot up to 25 Bullets at Shark That Killed Broome Local Charles Cernobori', *WAtoday* (Online), 23 November 2020. Available at: www.watoday.com.au/national/western-australia/police-shot-up-to-25-bullets-at-shark-that-killed-broome-local-charles-cernobori-20201123-p56h60.html (last accessed 31 January 2022).

environmental changes may be at play, such as climate change.[5] This dissonance is indicative of how we define, contextualise and manage the larger problem of human–wildlife conflict and the continued promotion of autonomy from the environment that we inhabit and our effect on it (and, in turn, the flow-on effects to us).

This chapter is an analysis of this dissonance around the problem of human–wildlife conflict. It provides context for the legal response to the problem by outlining the scientific, sociological, cultural and historical aspects of the conflict, the way it is defined, the way it is managed and the way it is studied. I will show that the individual liberal notion of autonomy discussed in Chapter 2 has been integrated into wildlife governance and will demonstrate the dire effect that has on conflict and the human relationship with wildlife. I will also consider the usefulness of the terms 'coexistence' and 'resilience' as the antonym to conflict.

Finally, the chapter will end on a more positive note with a summary of some of the developments in wildlife governance currently being undertaken by wildlife managers and researchers, including exciting innovations around the inclusion of emotional connections with wildlife and expansion to include traditional forms of knowledge, education and collaboration. These are several new and innovative techniques and policies that take on more of a eco-vulnerability approach to conflict and that can be used to focus on the role of institutions and assist the responsive state.

3.2 CURRENT APPROACHES TO HUMAN–WILDLIFE CONFLICT

In 2020, the International Union for the Conservation of Nature (IUCN) amended its definition of human–wildlife conflict at the World Conservation Congress in Marseilles.[6] The amended definition suggests that human–wildlife conflict involves 'negative interactions between people and wild animals, with consequences for both people and their resources and wildlife and their habitats'.[7] Previously, the definition was that human–wildlife conflict involves any interaction between humans and wildlife when

5 Yuri Niella et al., 'Predicting Changes in Distribution of a Large Coastal Shark in the Face of the Strengthening East Australian Current' (2020) 642 *Marine Ecology Progress Series* 163; 'Is Australia Really Seeing More Shark Attacks?'.

6 IUCN World Congress, *Motion 117 – Addressing Human–Wildlife Conflict: Fostering a Safe and Beneficial Coexistence of People and Wildlife*, 1 September 2020, https://iucncongress2020.org/motion/117 (last accessed 31 January 2022).

7 IUCN World Congress, preambular recital.

they harm or threaten one another in the course of pursuing their goals.[8] This definition was most commonly accepted by academics, the international community and local wildlife managers[9] and suggests that the conflict flows both ways; that is, humans and wildlife negatively impact each other. As defined, both before and after 2020, it is apparent our vulnerabilities are intertwined. These definitions would include interactions whereby humans remove, pollute or otherwise destroy wildlife habitat, remove species for monitoring or conservation purposes and alternatively when wildlife impact human health and safety and the financial viability of tourism or development projects, as just a few examples.

However, this wide range of possible negative interactions is not how the conflict has been historically viewed in practice. The IUCN definitions in this sense are somewhat of a fallacy. Instead, it was often only the impact that wildlife had on human autonomy and well-being that was addressed in the traditional governance of the issue: the conflict (or at least its management) generally ran one way only. For example, wildlife are 'managed' when they eat livestock and crops, damage property and pose a direct risk to our safety via death, injury or disease.[10] The governance techniques involved in this type of expression of the problem commonly include translocation of problem animals, lethal control or 'culling' of single animals or populations, fertility control, scare tactics (also known as 'fear-provoking stimuli'), exclusion by creating wildlife zones and habitat manipulation.[11] Where wildlife infringes upon the perceived autonomy or rights of people, their own freedom is disrupted or removed. As a result, the 'human' side of human–wildlife conflict was ignored for some time, both within the research and by wildlife managers.

However, a shift in public attitudes towards animal welfare and environmentalism has seen a shift in governance strategies in recent decades. Endangered species protection has become paramount and certain species are protected legally. However, different groups of people still have different ideas as to how wildlife should be managed and what the focus of conservation

8 IUCN, *Benefits Beyond Boundaries. Proceedings of the Vth IUCN World Parks Congress* (IUCN, 2005), 185.

9 See, for example, Terry A. Messmer, 'The Emergence of Human–Wildlife Conflict Management: Turning Challenges into Opportunities' (2000) 45(3) *International Biodeterioration & Biodegradation* 97–102, 97; Francine M. Madden, 'The Growing Conflict between Humans and Wildlife: Law and Policy As Contributing and Mitigating Factors' (2008) 11(2) *Journal of International Wildlife Law & Policy* 189–206, 189.

10 For a thorough discussion of the risks posed by wildlife to people, see Conover, *Resolving Human–Wildlife Conflicts*, chapters 3–6.

11 Conover, *Resolving Human–Wildlife Conflicts*, introduction.

strategies should be more generally. These differences in values started to take on a greater role when considering responses to human–wildlife conflict.

The more that individual and group values clashed over appropriate wildlife governance and responses to human–wildlife conflict, the more evident it became that human–wildlife conflict was not solely about negative interactions between people and wildlife, but instead was a social conflict. As a result, the phrase 'human–wildlife conflict' has been related to 'conservation conflicts' or 'human–human conflicts', acknowledgements in the ecological and socio-environmental literature that the scope of the problem has expanded.[12] These phrases signal recognition of the diverse set of environmental values and factors that can create conflict between people over wildlife.

In the last two decades, an increase in these types of conflicts has seen the field of wildlife research shift from strategies to deal with 'problem wildlife' and remove or mitigate human–wildlife conflicts, to researching the 'human' side of the equation.[13] Research on the 'human dimensions' of wildlife involves multidisciplinary studies of the human attitudes, behaviours and values that contribute to or exacerbate human–wildlife conflict and biodiversity decline. Often the research is dedicated to analysing human values to find governance solutions that are amenable to a very diverse range of people, so as to appease all and minimise stakeholder conflicts.[14]

This shift has also seen increased discussion around the definition and phrasing of 'human–wildlife conflict' itself. The phrasing of the problem as 'conflict' is seen to have negative connotations that can have unfavourable consequences.[15] Some commentators have acknowledged it does not encompass the full scope of relationships, actions and values that foreground

[12] See the use of the terms in F. Nsonsi et al., 'Attitudes Towards Forest Elephant Conservation Around a Protected Area in Northern Congo' (2017) 15(1) *Conservation & Society* 59–73; Catherine M. Hill, 'Perspectives of "Conflict" at the Wildlife–Agriculture Boundary: 10 Years On' (2015) 20(4) *Human Dimensions of Wildlife* 296.

[13] See, for example, the advent of journals such as *Human Dimensions of Wildlife* published by Taylor & Francis Online, and *People and Nature*, published by the British Ecological Society.

[14] See, for example, Heidi Bencin, John Kioko and Christian Kiffner, 'Local People's Perceptions of Wildlife Species in Two Distinct Landscapes of Northern Tanzania' (2016) 34 *Journal for Nature Conservation* 82; Nathan J. Bennett et al., 'Conservation Social Science: Understanding and Integrating Human Dimensions to Improve Conservation' (2017) 205 *Biological Conservation* 93; Simi Talukdar and Abhik Gupta, 'Attitudes Towards Forest and Wildlife, and Conservation Oriented Traditions, around Chakrashila Wildlife Sanctuary, Assam, India' (2017) 1–11 *Oryx* 508.

[15] Saloni Bhatia et al., 'Beyond Conflict: Exploring the Spectrum of Human–Wildlife Interactions and Their Underlying Mechanisms' (2020) 54(5) *Oryx* 621, 621.

conflicts.[16] The term has also been criticised for portraying wildlife as combative.[17] Like me, some authors have argued that the concept reinforces the human–nature dichotomy and others suggest it should be refocussed towards the concept of coexistence.[18]

Whilst this development in research and management is certainly an improvement over unfettered elimination of animals and entire species, based on perceived human wants and needs, it is still based on the human over wildlife hierarchy and plays to the maintenance of human autonomy over greater vulnerabilities. The focus in this research is managing wildlife whilst maintaining economic development or the individual autonomy that allows for such development, at the expense of wildlife and their habitat. In this sense, autonomy in wildlife governance is defined with a neo-liberal capitalist backdrop. Here, our deeper relationship with wildlife is not addressed, but rather our current ideological viewpoints assessed to ascertain what we will accept and what we will not. Returning to our shark examples, the underlying causes of the increase in shark attacks do not enter into public debate but, rather, managers seek a public expression of values based on an either/or scenario: would you prefer that the sharks are killed or would you rather let them be? The answer becomes dichotomised based on the public response to this narrow question and creates social conflicts between the two camps. This type of practice is also often done by assessing the monetary value we associate with a species or specific wildlife interactions or by assessing our social values towards wildlife.[19] For example, would you spend $10 to ensure that bears are not killed so that your national park hike is safe, or $100? That information is then used to justify wildlife governance decisions. The vulnerability of wildlife is not considered, except where our own values, attitudes and cost-benefit analysis allows for it.

In addition to this issue, broader gaps remain in the literature in this area. As a social and ecological conflict, the problem of human–wildlife conflict becomes one much broader than simple 'wildlife management'. We need to assess the relationships, views, attitudes, structures, rules and processes that lead to instances of individual conflict as symptoms of a greater social and ecological issue. There remains an 'institutional gap' in the human–wildlife conflict

16 Jeremy T. Bruskotter et al., 'Assessing Tolerance for Wildlife: Clarifying Relations between Concepts and Measures' (2015) 20(3) *Human Dimensions of Wildlife* 255.

17 S. Pooley et al., 'An Interdisciplinary Review of Current and Future Approaches to Improving Human–Predator Relations' (2017) 31(3) *Conservation Biology* 513.

18 Pooley, 'Improving Human–Predator Relations'.

19 Pooley, 'Improving Human–Predator Relations'.

literature and governance processes.[20] The gap is occasionally acknowledged in the literature. For example, Yurco and others state that the human–wildlife conflict scholarship is missing a 'nuanced understanding of the conditions that arise to produce conflict in the first place, including appreciation for how conflict varies over time and space, even among the same individuals, households, communities or wildlife species'.[21] Lute and others suggest that a greater understanding of influences on wildlife conservation is needed.[22]

There has been some movement toward institutional analysis in very recent years, although such research is in its fledgling stages and requires further development. For example, DeMotts and Hoon use a political ecology framework to focus on a construction of human–wildlife conflict that situates it as a conflict of institutions rather than over wildlife.[23] Bhatia has discussed the institutional influences of religion and its role in shaping values towards large carnivores in Northern India.[24] There has also been research undertaken on early childhood education and the role it has in shaping values towards wildlife into adulthood.[25]

So, what should be the purpose of governance in this arena? If responses to individual conflicts are not sufficient in isolation, what can an institutional approach offer? In Section 3.3, I will answer this question with an eco-vulnerability analysis of the institutional and individual factors associated with human–wildlife conflict.

3.3 THE ROLE OF AUTONOMY AND INTERRELATED DOMINATIONS IN WILDLIFE GOVERNANCE STRATEGIES

The human relationship with wildlife is one of dominance, which sits within the web of domination espoused by Plumwood.[26] The attitude of human

[20] Katie Woolaston et al., 'A Review of the Role of Law and Policy in Human–Wildlife Conflict' (2021) 19(3) *Conservation and Society* 172–83.

[21] Kayla Yurco et al., 'Human–Wildlife Interactions and Environmental Dynamics in the Okavango Delta, Botswana' (2017) 30(9) *Society & Natural Resources* 1112, 1113.

[22] Michelle L. Lute et al., 'Conservation Professionals Agree on Challenges to Coexisting with Large Carnivores but not on Solutions' (2018) 218 *Biological Conservation* 223, 231.

[23] Rachel DeMotts and Parakh Hoon, 'Whose Elephants? Conserving, Compensating, and Competing in Northern Botswana' (2012) 25(9) *Society & Natural Resources* 837.

[24] Saloni Bhatia et al., 'The Relationship between Religion and Attitudes Toward Large Carnivores in Northern India?' (2017) 22(1) *Human Dimensions of Wildlife* 30.

[25] See, for example, the research described by Halimah Ilavarasi, 'Researching out of Cultural Depth: Positioning within the Insider–Outsider Continuum' (2017) 22(2) *Waikato Journal of Education* 17.

[26] See Section 2.3.2.

dominance within wildlife governance has a long history, dating back to the first instances of domestication of farm animals and earlier. Conover suggests that 'management' of wildlife has existed since prehistoric times, when humans learned to use tools and collectively hunt, suppressing populations of their prey.[27] People have sought to reduce wildlife numbers for reasons of safety, prosperity or simple convenience throughout history.[28] Present methods of traditional governance continue to attempt resolution of conflict by managing the wildlife, for example relocating animals that do not fit within the human described mode of behaviour or creating barriers that do not allow natural roaming and migration.[29] This dominance within the conflict and how it is dealt with is also seen in the deeper level causes of conflict between humans and wildlife. For example, loss of habitat as a result of urban sprawl and climate change are both a result of human understanding that the environment is a resource to be used for human ends.

However, methods of traditional governance that seek to dominate and control can be unreliable in their outcome.[30] Methods such as lethal management (also known as culling), population control via sterilisation and segregation via fencing and other means have questionable strike rates and, in some instances, are not scientifically sound methods of achieving the desired outcome (that is, a reduction in conflict between humans and wildlife). For example, lethal management of problem animals or species (culls) is of limited value in eliminating conflict. Evidence suggests they do not work in reducing population levels unless the species is reduced to dangerously low levels.[31] As a specific example, evidence suggests that shark drum-line programmes do not increase beach-goer safety.[32] There are similar issues with

[27] Conover, *Resolving Human–Wildlife Conflicts*, 18.

[28] Frank and Conover, 'Thank Goodness They Got All the Dragons', 156.

[29] Philip J. Nyhus, 'Human–Wildlife Conflict and Coexistence' (2016) 41(1) *Annual Review of Environment and Resources* 143, 154–56.

[30] Long-term conflict resolution is rare, even where such traditional management strategies have been implemented. See A. J. Dickman, 'Complexities of Conflict: The Importance of Considering Social Factors for Effectively Resolving Human–Wildlife Conflict' (2010) 13(5) *Animal Conservation* 458, 459.

[31] Species have a biological carrying capacity and reducing their numbers can mean they breed at a faster rate, die naturally at a slower rate and other animals from nearby locations may fill the gap. See Conover, *Resolving Human–Wildlife Conflicts*, 153–57.

[32] Woolaston and Hamman, 'Operation of the Precautionary Principle in Australian Environmental Law', 337–38.

translocation of animals involved in conflicts,[33] fencing and habitat fragmentation.[34]

Neo-liberal conservation is another commonly used method of traditional governance. This involves compensating people directly involved in the conflict, in the hope that their tolerance of wildlife will increase, or alternatively paying them to carry out conservation or conflict mitigation techniques (with payments usually made by the state or a non-government organisation).[35] Researchers thus use the term 'neo-liberal' to describe the approach, as it expands the market by using a cost-benefit analysis to regulate people's interactions with the environment and essentially commodifies wildlife and nature. The use of these types of schemes is controversial. The evidence suggests that sometimes they are successful in increasing tolerance and/or conservation,[36] whilst at other times the schemes can antagonise those involved and increase conflict.[37] Some research has found that economic considerations are not as influential as expected.[38] Bureaucratic inadequacies and barriers in the payment system, together with inadequate and late payments, can lead to a backlash from participants, many of whom retaliate against the wildlife.[39] Whilst economic factors *may* influence the decision-making and behaviour of the people involved in the conflict,[40] the consensus

[33] Conover, *Resolving Human–Wildlife Conflicts*, chapter 9.

[34] Andrew Gonzalez, Nicolas Mouquet and Michel Loreau, 'Biodiversity As Spatial Insurance: The Effects of Habitat Fragmentation and Dispersal on Ecosystem Functioning', in Shahid Naeem et al. (eds.), *Biodiversity, Ecosystem Functioning, and Human Wellbeing: An Ecological and Economic Perspective* (Oxford University Press, 2009) 134.

[35] Philip J. Nyhus et al., 'Bearing the Costs of Human–Wildlife Conflict: The Challenge of Compensation Schemes', in Rosie Woodroffe, Simon Thirgood and Alan Rabinowitz (eds.), *People and Wildlife: Conflict or Coexistence* (Cambridge University Press, 2005) 110.

[36] See, for example, the results of the Namibian HWCSRS Insurance Scheme Model, discussed in M. Karidozo, M. La Grange and F. V. Osborn, *Assessment of the Human Wildlife Conflict Mitigation Measures being Implemented by the Kavango-Zambezi Transfrontier Conservation Area (KAZA TFCA) Partner Countries. Report to the KAZA TFCA Secretariat (BMZ No.: 2009 66 788 and BMZ No.: 2006 65 646)* (2016) 50.

[37] Nyhus et al., 'Bearing the Costs of Human–Wildlife Conflict', 117.

[38] A. Koziarski, B. Kissui and C. Kiffner, 'Patterns and Correlates of Perceived Conflict between Humans and Large Carnivores in Northern Tanzania' (2016) 199 *Biological Conservation* 41.

[39] Maan Barua, Shonil A. Bhagwat and Sushrut Jadhav, 'The Hidden Dimensions of Human–Wildlife Conflict: Health Impacts, Opportunity and Transaction Costs' (2013) 157 *Biological Conservation* 309, 310.

[40] Anja Kollmuss and Julian Agyeman, 'Mind the Gap: Why do People Act Environmentally and What Are the Barriers to Pro-Environmental Behavior?' (2002) 8(3) *Environmental Education Research* 239, 249.

in the literature is that such schemes are usually structurally ineffective in administration.[41]

In addition to their potential ineffectiveness and ability to court public controversy, methods of traditional governance perpetuate the human over wildlife hierarchy and promote the fallacy that people are not vulnerable to the loss of wildlife and species. Because people often consider that they do not need wildlife, especially when the wildlife is interfering with a human interest in some way and so are viewed as a 'problem', we justify domination to the detriment of the well-being of the animal and species. Sometimes we even justify the extermination of a species.

The promotion of autonomy plays an integral role in our relationship with wildlife and an ingrained sense of the right of autonomy is most often detrimental to the human–wildlife relationship. The negative effects of immovable individual rights manifest in many ways. First, conflicts can be created or exacerbated when that autonomy is infringed upon or when it is perceived that rights are being removed or not prioritised. This is particularly the case when governance or management steps are put in place with no or little regard to the individual affected and when the individual views those steps as being less effective than their own or an infringement of other personal interests. Catherine Hill discusses this phenomenon in the context of farmer's attitudes and responses to crop-raiding by wildlife.[42] She suggests that animosity towards the wildlife is rooted in frustration over the lack of autonomy they have in situations of conflict and with outsiders and government officials who they consider threatening to the security of the community.

The notion of autonomy can also create an immovable belief that one's actions are right or justifiable, regardless of the consequences on the 'other', whether that be another person or group, an animal or species or the greater environment. Studies conducted on the illegal taking of wildlife demonstrate such a link. In 2004 Stephen Eliason conducted interviews with American 'wildlife law violators' and conservation officers to determine their motivations.[43] Amongst the rationale for illegal fishing and hunting was a sense of

[41] See, for example, Jeremy Ravenelle and Philip J. Nyhus, 'Global Patterns and Trends in Human–Wildlife Conflict Compensation' (2017) 31(6) *Conservation Biology* 1247; J. Linnell, J. Thomassen and K. Jones, *Wildlife–Human Interactions: From Conflict to Coexistence in Sustainable Landscapes* (Norwegian Institute for Nature Research, 2011) 45.

[42] See Catherine M. Hill, 'Farmers' Perspectives of Conflict at the Wildlife–Agriculture Boundary: Some Lessons Learned from African Subsistence Farmers' (2004) 9(4) *Human Dimensions of Wildlife* 279; Hill, 'Perspectives of "Conflict"'.

[43] Stephen L. Eliason, 'Accounts of Wildlife Law Violators: Motivations and Rationalizations' (2004) 9(2) *Human Dimensions of Wildlife* 119.

entitlement and a view that they held a traditional right of use, despite the prohibitive laws.[44]

A further issue with the notions of autonomy and personal rights in these types of conflicts is that situations are approached with pre-conceived ideas of 'what works best for me', instead of 'what works best for my community, the animals and species involved, and the environment'. Stakeholders start from a position of conflict and individual interests and rights detract from the relational links between environmental, societal and individual well-being. Economic answers are found to address individualised economic interests. The scope for compassion, care and compromise is automatically reduced,[45] as is a concern for the ecosystem and greater environment.

Along with these explicit examples where the participants openly acknowledge their 'rebellion' or belief in their personal right, there lies a greater level of autonomy in conflict. This can be characterised as the people who have negative feelings towards being told what to do generally, with no consultation or acknowledgement. A sense of powerlessness can arise from having autonomy stripped in certain circumstances when that autonomy has been institutionalised and there is a belief that it is all-encompassing.

Individual notions of 'right of use' and autonomy are institutionalised in many legal traditions. For example, the North American Model of Wildlife Conservation (NAMWC) includes such ideals in its formative tenets, wherein the purpose is to emphasise that all citizens have a legally protected right to use wildlife.[46] Similarly, institutions such as the law are often responsible for stripping that autonomy. This 'institutional conflict' trickles down to communities, groups and individuals and adds to (or can create) situations of human–wildlife conflict. People can take on that conflict and hold onto one side over the other. Importantly, if institutions are promoting different things, it is very difficult for individuals to agree and work collaboratively to solve instances of human–wildlife conflict.

Neo-liberal conservation techniques are another example of the institutionalisation of concepts of hierarchy and individual autonomy. Notwithstanding, neo-liberal conservation schemes continue to be prevalent and are, thus, an institutional focus in building resilience and creating coexistence. In reality, these schemes, like other traditional governance techniques, are focused on

44 Eliason, 'Accounts of Wildlife Law Violators', 120, 126.

45 Jonathan Herring, 'Compassion, Ethics of Care and Legal Rights' (2017) 13(2) *International Journal of Law in Context* 158, 162.

46 J. F. Organ et al., *The North American Model of Wildlife Conservation; The Wildlife Society Technical Review* (The Wildlife Society, 2012) 12-04, Tenet 3.

building resilience through fostering liberal autonomy. That is to say, the choice to conserve is in the hands of individuals, with payments made to encourage certain types of behaviours. Those payments in themselves add to the perceived autonomy of those individuals within a neo-liberal system. Similarly, conservation payments such as this can also create institutional conflicts. For example, Zabel and Engel discuss the differing policy goals inherent in many performance payment schemes.[47] They suggest that such schemes commonly have a primary goal of environmental conservation with secondary goals such as poverty alleviation or provision of income support to farmers.[48] The presence of these secondary goals creates constraints and limits the attainability of the primary goal. Further, secondary goals can predominate schemes and be self-defeating, where they compromise the provision of the primary goal, that of conservation.

The inherent benefit of the 'human dimensions of wildlife' research is that it prima facie shifts the focus to the human side of the conflict and so may be viewed as an attempt to remove the hierarchy. However, even this interdisciplinary body of scientific literature tends to focus on using findings on values and attitudes to assess the viability and acceptance rates of different types of wildlife governance options, rather than addressing or seeking to understand and amend the values and attitudes themselves. That is to say, the research does not lead to a decrease in human domination, but often seeks to perpetuate it by discovering the most 'acceptable' method of wildlife governance. There are of course many exceptions, with research that seeks to shift attitudes towards a less dominant approach.[49] These examples are in the minority though and overall the research itself is an exercise in autonomy. That is to say, how can we conserve wildlife or remove the problem without encroaching on an individual's sense of autonomy? Related vulnerabilities are not the focus and many of the interrelated dominations are not considered as relevant. For example, there is very little gender analysis within the human–wildlife conflict literature. However, the little research that does exist shows that women are identified as bearing the greater brunt of the 'hidden costs' of human–wildlife conflict.[50] They experience decreased food security and well-being (both physical and emotional) and increased workload as a result of

47 Astrid Zabel and Stefanie Engel, 'Performance Payments: A New Strategy to Conserve Large Carnivores in the Tropics?' (2010) 70 *Ecological Economics* 405.

48 Zabel and Engel, 'Performance Payments', 406.

49 For example, see Rocky D. Spencer, Richard A. Beausoleil and Donald A. Martorello, 'How Agencies Respond to Human–Black Bear Conflicts: A Survey of Wildlife Agencies in North America' (2007) 18(2) *Ursus* 217.

50 Nyhus, 'Human–Wildlife Conflict and Coexistence', 154.

many typical instances of conflict.[51] It has been found that crop-raiding resulted in the women of the family eating less,[52] while injury or death to male members of the family usually transferred the income responsibility to women, who were also still required to fulfil child-raising and household duties.[53] In addition, the economic and social benefits of neo-liberal models of conservation (where there are benefits) are unevenly distributed, such that women are often allocated a disproportionately smaller amount compared to their contribution, reducing their resilience and simultaneously reducing their perceived autonomy.[54] Nyhus suggests a resolution of the conflict is thus more difficult in areas where there is a larger equality gap.[55]

Although they are often more affected by conflict, evidence suggests that women on average have higher rates of pro-environmental behaviour than men.[56] There is evidence of a positive relationship between the engagement of women and environmental outcomes.[57] Women often interact differently with the environment than men so, if they are excluded, their knowledge and perspectives may not be included.[58] Women are more likely to change and to accept compassionate means of conflict resolution, even when they have higher levels of concern or fear concerning the animal or species involved.[59]

The dominance exerted in these hierarchies is not limited to that of human over wildlife and, in true eco-feminist style, is also not limited to the man/woman dichotomy. Research suggests that hierarchies amongst stakeholders also exist, so that some people are granted a higher level of 'autonomy' than others, with the result that the resilience of the others is reduced. This is consistent with Warren's Oppressive Conceptual Framework and, in particular, the power held over other's conceptions of power and conceptions of

51 Monica V. Ogra, 'Human–Wildlife Conflict and Gender in Protected Area Borderlands: A Case Study of Costs, Perceptions, and Vulnerabilities from Uttarakhand (Uttaranchal), India' (2008) 39(3) *GEOFORUM* 1408, 1419.

52 Ogra, 'Human–Wildlife Conflict and Gender'.

53 Barua, Bhagwat and Jadhav, 'Hidden Dimensions of Human–Wildlife Conflict', 311.

54 Kathryn Elizabeth Khumalo and Laurie Ann Yung, 'Women, Human–Wildlife Conflict, and CBNRM: Hidden Impacts and Vulnerabilities in Kwandu Conservancy, Namibia' (2015) 13(3) *Conservation & Society* 232, 233.

55 Nyhus, 'Human–Wildlife Conflict and Coexistence', 156.

56 D. H. Ting and C. F. C. Cheng, 'Measuring the Marginal Effect of Pro-Environmental Behaviour: Guided Learning and Behavioural Enhancement' (2017) 20 *Journal of Hospitality Leisure Sport & Tourism Education* 16, 18.

57 James et al., 'Conservation and Natural Resource Management', 1.

58 James et al., 'Conservation and Natural Resource Management', 1.

59 Harry C. Zinn and Cynthia L. Pierce, 'Values, Gender, and Concern about Potentially Dangerous Wildlife' (2002) 34(2) *Environment and Behavior* 239, 250; Kollmuss and Agyeman, 'Mind the Gap', 248.

privilege.[60] These stakeholder hierarchies can have dire consequences for human security. For example, Bond describes reports that there are often times when individuals in Kenya feel that wildlife is placed above humans on the hierarchy when wildlife is of economic benefit to prioritised stakeholders.[61] Mboya also provides evidence that humans can be displaced when it suits the conservation needs of people higher in the hierarchy.[62] Indeed, conservation may be economically beneficial to some in positions of power, which can lead to exploitation and displacement of locals in some instances, say for example where they live in an area that has been declared a protected one.[63] Conservation displacement is growing in recognition and has two appearances: the forced removal of people from their homes to create protected areas and the exclusion of people from particular areas that they are dependent on for their livelihoods.[64] This kind of displacement often causes conflict between human security groups and conservation scientists. It has even been reported that people have been killed to maintain this hierarchy.[65]

These stakeholder hierarchies also have negative consequences for wildlife. A study by Nsonsi and others of stakeholder attitudes in the Congo made evident the perceived distinction between Indigenous villagers and the typically white people in positions of power. Local villagers perceived elephants to be 'owned' by white people, expressing anger because elephant conservation was prioritised over their security. One respondent stated that 'white people do not compensate us when their elephants destroy our fields, but when we kill an elephant they arrest us'.[66] Another suggested retaliation, stating that 'if the white people don't help [... in reducing crop raiding ...] we will kill their elephants'.[67]

But the exclusion of certain people over others is not limited to race. The NAMWC has institutionalised some of these hierarchies that relate to different types of users of wildlife. Feldpausch-Parker and others have argued that the NAMWC exhibits an exclusionary discourse that prioritises consumptive use of wildlife over non-consumptive use and so 'places hunters on a conservation pedestal over other conservation practitioners and reinforces

60 As described in Section 2.3.2.
61 Bond and Mkutu, 'Exploring the Hidden Costs'.
62 Mboya, 'Human Vulnerability and Environmental Rights'.
63 See, for example, Brockington and Igoe, 'Eviction for Conservation', 424.
64 Brockington and Igoe, 'Eviction for Conservation', 425.
65 Bond and Mkutu, 'Exploring the Hidden Costs', 3.
66 Nsonsi et al., 'Attitudes Towards Forest Elephant Conservation'.
67 Nsonsi et al., 'Attitudes Towards Forest Elephant Conservation', 5.

hunting as an important conservation practice'.[68] Zuardo suggests that state law in the United States actually requires the state wildlife agency commissions to be stacked with 'consumptive wildlife users' and that these agencies depend heavily on revenues directly connected to consumptive use, making the opinions of other interest groups largely irrelevant.[69] This contributes to a culture of hierarchy in the United States system. Similarly, in Australia, economic arguments that favour industry interests tend to dominate policy decisions concerning kangaroos, while animal protection advocates, who have no economic mechanism to voice their interests, are placed lower in the stakeholder hierarchy.[70]

As discussed in Chapter 2, such hierarchy emanates from the oppressive framework that supports western dualistic thinking and promotes a form of neo-liberal capitalism that is detrimental to a substantive, holistic and positive relationship between humans and their surrounding environment and between humans themselves. In order to promote a transformation of the human–wildlife relationship, this type of permanent and institutionalised hierarchy needs to be disassembled.

However, one might ask what is the purpose of disassembling the dominant hierarchy?, what is it that we are working towards?, or what is the favoured outcome in addressing human–wildlife conflict? In Section 3.4 I will analyse the current research around conflict resolution and the language used. I will show that current governance goals might be furthered with the help of eco-vulnerability theory.

3.4 CONFLICT RESOLUTION: ACHIEVING COEXISTENCE OR BUILDING RESILIENCE?

Human–wildlife coexistence is often considered the antonym of human–wildlife conflict. Many have conceptualised coexistence differently and some consider the meaning to be so evident it does not require an explicit definition. An exploration of those different approaches to coexistence is useful to first determine what we are trying to achieve by addressing human–wildlife

68 A. M. Feldpausch-Parker, I. D. Parker and E. S. Vidon, 'Privileging Consumptive Use: A Critique of Ideology, Power, and Discourse in the North American Model of Wildlife Conservation' (2017) 15(1) *Conservation & Society* 33, 37.

69 Tara Zuardo, 'How the United States was Able to Dodge International Reforms Designed to Make Wildlife Trapping Less Cruel' (2017) 20(1) *Journal of International Wildlife Law & Policy* 73, 85–86.

70 See Peter Simmons, 'Transparency and Communication Can Improve Wildlife Welfare Outcomes: A Case of Kangaroos' (2017) 33 *SHS Web of Conferences* 73.

conflict. What is the goal of wildlife and conflict governance policies? What should be the objective of laws addressing human–wildlife conflict? More specifically, is 'coexistence' capable of a definition that would assist responses to conflict and can that definition be of any use to a vulnerability framework that seeks to address human–wildlife conflict?

'Coexistence' is largely undefined or under-defined in the wildlife governance literature and, instead, the meaning is considered to be self-evident. For example, prominent statements surrounding coexistence include: 'Resolving such conflicts will be crucial to the success of conservation development plans that require coexistence of people with wildlife.'[71] 'Coexistence, the theme of this volume, is the only possible solution'.[72]

More recent studies on the term take the same approach.[73] Instead of clarifying the nature of coexistence, statements like these lead to more questions. Why is coexistence required? Is it the only way to achieve resolution of the conflict, and if so why? What would coexistence look like? How do we get there? The seemingly stable use of the word in the literature is countered by the unstable nature of the way in which conflict is addressed. The conflict has various descriptions, it is addressed in countless different ways and it is theoretically construed by differing approaches where there is often no common theme. In such circumstances, it cannot be said that all researchers and managers are working towards a common, well-defined goal, despite many stating that goal is in fact 'coexistence'.

Notwithstanding the lack of precise meaning, the literature *is* useful in eliminating concepts and terms that are *not* considered to be coexistence. For example, in discussing the challenges to a peaceful coexistence, Fascione, Delach and Smith remark that the key questions facing society are 'whether we will make room for predators, and whether we will tolerate them'.[74] That is to say, tolerance of negative interactions is being equated with coexistence. However, various writers have suggested that coexistence is something more than tolerance and have discussed the importance of experiencing positive interactions to facilitate an improved human–wildlife relationship, in addition

[71] Woodroffe, Thirgood and Rabinowitz, *People and Wildlife*, 2.

[72] Nina Fascione, Aimee Delach and Martin E. Smith (eds.), *People and Predators: From Conflict to Coexistence* (Island Press, 2004) xii.

[73] See, for example, Amit and Jacobson, 'Understanding Rancher Coexistence', 1353; Varun R. Goswami et al., 'Mechanistic Understanding of Human–Wildlife Conflict through a Novel Application of Dynamic Occupancy Models: Dynamics of Human–Wildlife Conflict' (2015) 29(4) *Conservation Biology* 1100.

[74] Fascione, Delach and Smith, People and Predators, 6.

to tolerating the negative ones. Frank is one such author.[75] In describing one of the more developed coexistence frameworks, she posits a 'conflict-to-coexistence continuum' with extreme negative reactions to wildlife placed at one end and a positive, all-encompassing relationship at the other.[76] Frank identifies tolerance as being somewhat 'less positive' than coexistence or, at the least, a form of 'passive coexistence' when tolerance is defined as an acceptance of behaviour that one disagrees with or dislikes.[77]

In consideration of this, the questions asked by Fascione, Delach and Smith concerning tolerance might be conceptually incorrect from a coexistence perspective. Tolerance and coexistence do not appear as equal notions when considering human–wildlife interactions. Tolerance not only results from a reduction in negative interactions or a reason to tolerate them (such as financial incentives) but can *itself* be classified as a negative interaction, as it tends to assume the negativity of the interaction but refuses to react to it. Coexistence, on the other hand, results from both a reduction of negative interactions and an increase in *positive* ones, thus forming a more cohesive and rounded *relationship* between humans and wildlife. Inevitably tolerance must be one part of a coexistence framework, but it must also be paired with the promotion of positive interactions and increase in constructive attitudes and values towards wildlife. Taking this further, it is arguably easier to 'tolerate' behaviour when such tolerance is derived from a positive understanding of shared vulnerabilities.

Another concept that is often confused with coexistence is 'co-occurrence'. This particular misperception has caused some academic disagreement between authors. In 2012, Neil H. Carter and others published a paper titled 'Coexistence between wildlife and humans at fine spatial scales'.[78] They argued that their empirical studies undertaken in Nepal's Chitwan National Park demonstrated tiger–human coexistence, as they recorded high tiger densities and human presence within a defined area. In response, a letter was penned by Abishek Harihar and others, suggesting that the authors had made a fundamental error of logic 'by conflating 'co-occurrence' with

75 Beatrice Frank, 'Human–Wildlife Conflicts and the Need to Include Tolerance and Coexistence: An Introductory Comment' (2016) 29(6) *Society & Natural Resources* 738.

76 Frank, 'Human–Wildlife Conflicts'.

77 Cambridge Dictionary. Available at: http://dictionary.cambridge.org/dictionary/english/tolerance (last accessed 31 January 2022).

78 Neil H. Carter et al., 'Coexistence between Wildlife and Humans at Fine Spatial Scales' (2012) 109(38) *Proceedings of the National Academy of Sciences (USA)* 15360.

'coexistence'.[79] Simply put they argued that the two terms did not equate to the same thing. Theoretically, co-occurrence is more akin to Frank's passive coexistence and so suffers the same failings. If humans and wildlife are simply co-occurring, there is no framework for dealing with negative interactions when they occur. Conversely, a coexistence framework should set a foundation for returning positive relationships after negative interactions.

Another key feature of the wildlife governance literature is the insistence that attaining coexistence will not result in the elimination of all negative human–wildlife interactions. Coexistence is not a perfect-shared experience. Of course, we cannot control all actions of wildlife and some instances of negative interactions are inevitable, despite the use of our best governance strategies. Experience in the Kavango-Zambezi National Park highlights this misperception. A 2016 report to the Kavango-Zambezi Transfrontier Conservation Area stressed the goal of reducing the intensity of conflict, rather than eliminating it.[80] Wildlife by its nature is uncontrollable and unpredictable and so full resolution is an unrealistic goal. Instead, the report authors stated that 'management of people's attitudes and values is critical'.[81] This might suggest that coexistence should be portrayed publicly as any normal significant relationship, with 'ups and downs', although hopefully with more positive experiences than negative ones. As a result, coexistence is not an end game, as it does not equate to the resolution of conflict. It is a continually evolving set of circumstances and an interactive relationship between wildlife and people that requires frequent attention.

Just as coexistence is not an end game, it is also not a short-term resolution. Various scholars acknowledge that long-term planning and management is necessary for sustained coexistence.[82] The Kavango-Zambezi report states that coexistence requires a 'holistic approach that addresses root causes over the long term as well as short-term mitigation'.[83] Dubois and others suggest that coexistence is a culture.[84] They also suggest that a resolution of the

79 Abishek Harihar et al., 'Conflating "Co-occurrence" with "Coexistence"' (2013) 110(2) *Proceedings of the National Academy of Sciences (USA)* E109.

80 Karidozo, La Grange and Osborn, *Assessment of the Human Wildlife Conflict Mitigation Measures*.

81 Karidozo, La Grange and Osborn, *Assessment of the Human Wildlife Conflict Mitigation Measures*, 3.

82 See Amit and Jacobson, 'Understanding Rancher Coexistence'; Bencin, Kioko and Kiffner, 'Local People's Perceptions', 82–92.

83 Karidozo, La Grange and Osborn, *Assessment of the Human Wildlife Conflict Mitigation Measures*, 3.

84 Sara Dubois et al., 'International Consensus Principles for Ethical Wildlife Control' (2017) 31 (4) *Conservation Biology* 753.

'problematic outcome' is not helpful and that alteration of the 'root causes' of conflict is necessary; one of those being the culture that leads to human behaviour affecting the ecosystem.[85] As such, to promote a culture of coexistence, a cultural shift away from domination is necessary. If we consider the longstanding nature of cultural human domination over wildlife, we can begin to understand the kind of long-term commitment required to facilitate a change in values and attitudes necessary for a cultural shift.

This is where an eco-feminist approach to vulnerability theory can provide the greatest assistance. It can give the human–wildlife conflict literature a macro focus by developing the concepts of conflict and coexistence beyond the individualised constructions inherent in governance so far. Conflict and coexistence do require a holistic response, one that accounts for individual manifestations, cultural values and attitudes and institutional responses. It also requires an analysis of the link between all these things. Eco-vulnerability theory gives us the relationality framework and the critical perspective of institutions required for such analysis. It highlights the connections between our individual and institutional vulnerabilities, ecological and human vulnerabilities and the different oppressive factors that influence all those things. In doing this, eco-vulnerability highlights the autonomy fallacy or the prevailing notion that conflict can be overcome through autonomy of human *action*, rather than through the acknowledgement of the interdependence or shared nature of the vulnerability of *being*.

Given the difficulty with the concept of 'coexistence', it is useful to consider the alternative goals of addressing human–wildlife conflict. Here, again, vulnerability theory is particularly useful. The range of concepts in the literature that can be linked to coexistence seems to correlate with a broad term contained within the vulnerability literature: resilience. It is discussed as an essential response to vulnerability, just as coexistence is positioned as the resolution of conflict. Fineman writes: 'Resilience is the essential, but incomplete antidote to our vulnerability. Resilience is what provides an individual with the means and ability to recover from harm or setbacks . . . Resilience is not something we are born with; it is accumulated over the course of our lifetimes within social structures or institutions over which individuals may have little control.'[86] Within Fineman's vulnerability theory, resilience to vulnerability is posited as the alternative to the institutional promotion of liberal autonomy. The building of resilience is achieved through 'subsidy

[85] Dubois et al., 'International Consensus Principles', 755.
[86] Martha Albertson Fineman, 'Vulnerability, Resilience, and LGBT Youth' (2013) 23 *Temple Political & Civil Rights Law Review* 307, 320.

and support' and promoting the 'webs of economic and social relationships that sustain us'.[87] Acknowledgement of the whole of the interrelated web is a first step in building resilience, including recognition of the groups that safeguard human security. For example, when discussing disaster relief, Kuo and Means suggest that an effective response to disaster is 'the aggregation of individually vulnerable people into a resilient group'.[88]

Fineman argues for State responsiveness to achieve peak resilience.[89] That is to say, people cannot maintain a high level of resilience to vulnerability unless States or a responsible institution or governance regime work to promote that resilience. Moreover, the State response needs to be aligned with promoting holism and group connections to achieve resilience to vulnerability, instead of promoting individual autonomy.

With respect to human–wildlife conflict, the meaning of resilience could have two dimensions. First, individual resilience could be, as Fineman suggests it should, the goal of State responsiveness to the shared vulnerabilities of people and wildlife. Second, resilience could refer to relationship resilience, both as a matter of improving conservation or human–human conflicts, and the more direct human–wildlife conflict. A resilient relationship is one that survives. Institutions need to promote both individual and relationship resilience. When considered this way, the answer to conflict is still coexistence, but with that coexistence supported by resilience. The question then evolves into what factors are required to build resilience and how can institutions support and/or promote those factors? I will now consider the drivers of resilience in situations of human–wildlife conflict.

3.5 VULNERABILITY APPROACHES TO CONFLICT GOVERNANCE

The literature on human–wildlife conflict demonstrates a number of common themes that are necessary to increase the resilience of people and wildlife to conflict. In fact, much of the literature leads to the same conclusion: that a holistic, relational approach is required when seeking to address human–wildlife conflict. This research is vital when formulating an appropriate State or institutional response to human–wildlife conflict, yet there remains a gap between the research and the responses to date. As a result,

[87] Fineman, *Autonomy Myth*, 28.

[88] Susan S. Kuo and Benjamin Means, 'After the Storm: The Vulnerability and Resilience of Locally Owned Business', in Martha Albertson Fineman and Anna Grear (eds.), *Vulnerability: Reflections on a New Ethical Foundation for Law and Politics* (Routledge, 2013) 95, 98.

[89] Martha Albertson Fineman, 'Equality and Difference – The Restrained State' (2015) 66(3) *Alabama Law Review* 609, 625.

this section will detail the common themes that come from the research and how they support an eco-vulnerability approach to wildlife governance, before discussing how each theme might be implemented into a legal framework in the following chapters.

3.5.1 *Contextual Relevance*

Vitally, the literature is largely united in describing the contextual relevance of each conflict. There are few, if any, universal variables that predict conservation behaviour or an improved human–wildlife relationship.[90] Every conflict is different, from both the human side and the wildlife side. Conflict is dependent on locality, individual relationships, notions of morality and held values, culture, relevant stakeholders, governance models and historical context. Even in specific conflict situations, researchers are finding that coexistence programmes need to be more targeted. For example, Amit and Jacobson found there were at least four types of 'ranchers' coming into conflict with jaguars and puma in Costa Rica, and each type required something different to build resilience to conflict.[91] They suggest constructing 'typologies' for stakeholder groups in situations of conflict to understand the different motivations, factors and attitudes that contribute to negative interactions. Specifically, they found that the presence of wildlife managers to 'provide technical assistance on a case-by-case basis' to be successful.

This contextual relevance is something that is accepted and reinforced by eco-vulnerability theory. As noted in Chapter 2, the existence of interconnections between dominations and oppression means that any solution must account for all of those shared oppressions and dominations. The differences between ecologies, habitats, people and wildlife should be celebrated, not minimised. As a result, flexibility in governance is required even where there is a set goal, but always driven by the need to be sensitive to context. For example, if conservation is a goal, the vulnerability of human inhabitants of a relevant area may need to be considered above conservation in specific situations. Bond discusses examples of the human vulnerability being ignored for the sake of neoliberal conservation, to the extent that interviewees suggest people are often killed in the name of conservation when there is a large neo-colonial aspect in the said conservation plan.[92] While human life should never be sacrificed, the goal of human security may need to sometimes make

90 Goodale, Parsons and Sherren, 'The Nature of the Nuisance', 320.
91 Amit and Jacobson, 'Understanding Rancher Coexistence'.
92 Bond and Mkutu, 'Exploring the Hidden Costs'.

way for conservation or animal/species welfare, particularly when that security is premised on economic development that is detrimental to species.

The need to allow for context and difference in specific conflict situations may seem at odds with a legal or another institutional framework that requires generalisations and underlying principles. Indeed, this need for relativism is an inherent critique of eco-feminism, as described in Chapter 2.[93] However, this critique can be met in practicality if the law or a governance framework were to be driven first and foremost by the prioritisation of building resilience to vulnerability. Vulnerability is the universal principle on which to build an institutional response to conflict, even when it is acknowledged that each conflict is different and each stakeholder (be it person or animal) in the conflict has different levels of resilience. An eco-vulnerability framework should allow for assessment of respective levels of resilience and the application of rules depending on those different contexts. That is to say, flexibility in governance is mandated by generalised law that insists on vulnerability contextualisation before regulating specific conduct, as will be demonstrated in Chapters 5 and 6.

3.5.2 *The Role of History, Sociology and Political Ecology*

A second theme within the human dimensions of wildlife literature is the acknowledgement that conflicts are often centred on historical and sociological conflicts between different human stakeholders, rather than a direct result of damage or injury caused by wildlife. As noted in Chapter 2, all dominations are interrelated and this has a very real manifestation in certain situations of human–wildlife conflict.[94] For example, in India, the traditional custodian style of forest management and conservation was disintegrated with the coming of colonial rule and stringent government controls were put in place.[95] The traditional forest dwellers were deprived of many of their traditional rights and this history has contributed to increased antagonism toward forest officials today. Biru and others have found that locals in Ethiopia have attitudes towards wildlife that are affected by their relationship with park authorities.[96] The studies of Hill have also demonstrated the link between

93 See Section 2.3.3.

94 See Section 2.3.

95 Talukdar and Gupta, 'Attitudes Towards Forest and Wildlife', 1 and 7.

96 Yihew Biru, Zewdu K. Tessema and Mengistu Urge, 'Perception and Attitude of Pastoralists on Livestock–Wildlife Interactions around Awash National Park, Ethiopia: Implication for Biodiversity Conservation' (2017) 6 *Ecological Processes* 13, 13.

social conflicts concerning past conservation policy and current attitudes to wildlife.[97]

The historical oppression and ongoing societal inequities need to at least be acknowledged, if not reconciled, in order to build the most resilience to the direct human–wildlife conflict. This process would necessarily be part of an eco-vulnerability framework that seeks to understand the web of oppressions surrounding any given human–wildlife conflict.

3.5.3 *Positive Experience*

A further theme found in the human–wildlife conflict literature is the necessity of positive wildlife experiences to balance the negative interactions. Positive encounters and interactions are required to increase the social, cultural and emotional connection with wildlife and so transform the human–wildlife relationship. Mentioned in Section 3.2 was the suggestion that coexistence is not equivalent to tolerance and a primary difference between the two is the inclusion of positive experience with wildlife.[98] The literature is supportive of such a need for positive experience as one necessary factor in developing positive attitudes toward wildlife and so contributing to increased relationship resilience.[99] Kansky and others have found that attitudes can be more negative when there is less interaction with wildlife.[100] Likewise, a study undertaken by Ting and others found that positive experiences can create environmental awareness and, when combined with other factors, can lead to behavioural change.[101] There are also several studies which show that experiencing nature in a positive way, for example through outdoor recreation, is correlated with higher pro-environmental attitudes, environmental awareness and support for conservation.[102] Sharing of those experiences

97 Hill, 'Farmers' Perspectives of Conflict'; Hill, 'Perspectives of "Conflict"'.

98 See Section 3.4.

99 See, for example, Amit and Jacobson, 'Understanding Rancher Coexistence'; Susan Clayton et al., 'Transformation of Experience: Toward a New Relationship with Nature' (2017) 10(5) *Conservation Letters* 645; Ting and Cheng, 'Measuring the Marginal Effect'; Bencin, Kioko and Kiffner, 'Local People's Perceptions'.

100 Ruth Kansky, Martin Kidd and Andrew T. Knight, 'Meta-Analysis of Attitudes toward Damage-Causing Mammalian Wildlife: Attitudes to Damage-Causing Wildlife' (2014) 28(4) *Conservation Biology* 924.

101 Ting and Cheng, 'Measuring the Marginal Effect'.

102 Michael A. Tarrant and Gary T. Green, 'Outdoor Recreation and the Predictive Validity of Environmental Attitudes' (1999) 21(1) *Leisure Sciences* 17; Peter Kareiva, 'Ominous Trends in Nature Recreation' (2008) 105(8) *Proceedings of the National Academy of Sciences (USA)* 2757; Michael J. Manfredo, *Who Cares about Wildlife?: Social Science Concepts for Exploring Human–Wildlife Relationships and Conservation Issues* (Springer, 2008).

with friends and relatives can transmit positive attitudes and support to others and contribute to a greater social identity and concern toward nature.[103]

Unfortunately, there is a growing disconnect between humans and their natural environment, despite the need for a greater emotional connection with nature. The disconnect can lead to a progressive disaffection and displays of negative behaviour towards wildlife and their habitat.[104] Robert Pyle and others have called this 'extinction of experience' and it is associated with negative impacts on human security as a whole and specifically impacts people's individual emotional, attitudinal and behavioural relations to nature.[105] Market sceptics and 'new conservation' theorists are among the many who acknowledge that this separation is the greatest threat to our environment and suggest conservation strategies should focus on reducing this emotional and physical separation from nature.[106]

There are a number of ways that positive experience could be implemented into an eco-vulnerability framework. Siemer and others found links between people who spent more time recreating outdoors, local place attachment and pro-environmental behaviours.[107] However, encouraging outdoor activity is not enough. Societal institutions need to place a greater focus on allowing the formation of place meanings. A sense of place refers to the 'entire group of cognitions and affective sentiments people hold regarding a particular geographic locale, including the meanings one attributes to a place'.[108] Place meanings must include the non-human animals that inhabit a place. Siemer and others have found that an individual's satisfaction with various aspects of place may affect their bond with that environmental setting and, so it can be construed, their attachment with the wildlife of the place.

In addition, local councils and state-based organisations should ensure that a sense of place is linked with supporting and encouraging environmental education and wildlife encounters. McIntosh and Wright suggest that

[103] Louise Chawla, 'Significant Life Experiences Revisited: A Review of Research on Sources of Environmental Sensitivity' (1998) 4(4) *Environmental Education Research* 369.

[104] Masashi Soga and Kevin J. Gaston, 'Extinction of Experience: The Loss of Human–Nature Interactions' (2016) 14(2) *Frontiers in Ecology and the Environment* 94.

[105] See the description in Clayton et al., 'Transformation of Experience', 1.

[106] See George Holmes, Chris Sandbrook and Janet A. Fisher, 'Understanding Conservationists' Perspectives on the New-Conservation Debate' (2017) 31(2) *Conservation Biology* 353, 359–60. See also Manfredo, Who Cares about Wildlife?, 173; William F. Siemer et al., *Measuring Complex Connections between Conservation and Recreation: An Overview of Key Indicators*, Human Dimensions Research Unit Publication Series, 17-3, Deparment of Natural Resources, College of Agriculture and Life Sciences, Cornell University (2017).

[107] Siemer et al., *Measuring Complex Connections*, 5.

[108] Siemer et al., *Measuring Complex Connections*, 5.

meaningful positive experiences need to be developed through a variety of stages, including pre-encounter, actual encounter, post-encounter and long-term reflection.[109] As a result, she suggests that managers of parks and protected areas (this can be extended to local authorities such as councils) should pay greater attention to positive wildlife connections and use these relationships to facilitate more meaningful experiences.

3.5.4 *Emotional Connection*

Linked with the literature on positive experiences is a distinct but related theme – the role of emotion. The role of emotional connection, affect and attachment in the human–wildlife relationship is not something that has been extensively researched. As such, there is very little research on the topic directly, with most of the sociological tools used to discern attitudes towards wildlife being distinctly rational, to the exclusion of emotion.[110] Manfredo goes so far as to say that the use of emotion has been chastised in wildlife management[111] and this certainly fits within the eco-feminist paradigm where the prioritisation of reason over emotion is a source of critique. Many of the sociological tools used to discern attitudes toward wildlife are distinctly rational and do not include assessment of emotional responses.[112]

However, a relational holistic view of our relationship with wildlife demands attention be given to the role of emotion and there are suggestions that the utilisation of emotive states may be useful for dealing with other wildlife stakeholders in collaborative processes and for improving our relationship with wildlife overall. As Manfredo suggests, current views of emotions

[109] Danielle McIntosh and Pamela A. Wright, 'Emotional Processing As an Important Part of the Wildlife Viewing Experience' (2017) 18 *Journal of Outdoor Recreation and Tourism* 1, 5.

[110] See, for example, the Theory of Planned Behaviour in Icek Ajzen, 'From Intentions to Actions: A Theory of Planned Behavior', in Julius Kuhl and Jürgen Beckmann (eds.), *Action Control: From Cognition to Behavior* (Springer, 1985) 11; and the Wildlife Acceptance Model in Daniel J. Decker and Ken G. Purdy, 'Toward a Concept of Wildlife Acceptance Capacity in Wildlife Management' (1988) 16(1) *Wildlife Society Bulletin* 53.

[111] Manfredo, *Who Cares about Wildlife?*, 50.

[112] See, for example, the Theory of Planned Behaviour that suggests the intention to perform a behaviour is a decidedly rational decision, predicted by attitude, subjective norms and perceived behavioural control; Ajzen, 'From Intentions to Actions'. See also the model of Wildlife Acceptance Capacity, which includes such factors as perceived competition of a species with another of interest to people, the role of wildlife in disease transmission and the rational economic, aesthetic ecological and intrinsic values placed on wildlife; Decker and Purdy, 'Toward a Concept of Wildlife Acceptance'.

emphasise their importance in rational decision processes, whilst the emotional state of an individual has a significant effect on their judgement.[113]

Despite the lack of detailed consideration of affect in the human dimensions of wildlife literature, we can utilise other areas of research that have a stronger association with emotion. For example, there are theories that suggest necessary factors for a pro-environmental attitude incorporate affect[114] and these are backed by scientific studies to this effect.[115] Further, emotional determinants can be powerful predictors of wildlife-related behaviour. For example, Amit and Jacobson conducted research with ranchers in Costa Rica and found that human behaviour in big cat conflicts was influenced by pre-existing negative emotions towards big cats.[116] As a result, they suggest that emotions must necessarily be integrated into theoretical frameworks concerning human–wildlife conflicts because 'emotions are used for decision-making in a gradient of analytical versus experiential processes, and must be addressed if interventions are to be successful'.[117]

Positive wildlife-related emotions and emotional states are likely to assist in collaborative efforts to implement compassionate wildlife management programmes.[118] Positive affect facilitates constructive collaborative processes because it leads to more creative and innovative responses and solutions, results in people being more likely to evaluate a solution as positive and means that people are less likely to break agreements and use aggressive negotiating tactics.[119]

However, emotion will not have these impacts where judgements are already made going into decision-making processes[120] and that is more likely to be the case if they have experience only of negative wildlife interactions or overwhelmingly negative interactions in the past. As a result, emotions such as compassion are closely linked with the experience of positive wildlife interactions and the facilitation of a sense of place and sense of home, discussed in Section 3.5.3. In fact, emotional connection and the degree of connection felt

[113] Manfredo, *Who Cares about Wildlife?*, 59–60.

[114] For example, see the Theory of Nature Relatedness in Amanda Obery and Arthur Bangert, 'Exploring the Influence of Nature Relatedness and Perceived Science Knowledge on Proenvironmental Behavior' (2017) 7(1) *Education Sciences* 17, 19.

[115] Katrina Brown et al., 'Empathy, Place and Identity Interactions for Sustainability' (2019) 56 *Global Environmental Change* 11; Jaime Berenguer 'The Effect of Empathy in Environmental Moral Reasoning' (2010) 42 *Environment and Behavior* 110.

[116] Amit and Jacobson, 'Understanding Rancher Coexistence'.

[117] Amit and Jacobson, 'Understanding Rancher Coexistence', 1370.

[118] The role of community collaboration is further discussed in Section 3.6.

[119] Manfredo, *Who Cares about Wildlife?*, 60.

[120] Manfredo, *Who Cares about Wildlife?*, 60.

with the places in which we live is linked with community growth, development and pro-environmental behaviours.[121] This is because an emotional connection assists in the development of a sense of place, which is likely to increase community involvement, which increases both ecological and community resilience.[122] As a result, positive emotional connections can be linked with participation in community decisions regarding wildlife and ecosystems (to be discussed in Section 3.6), together with an increase in positive wildlife interactions.

3.5.5 *The Role of Education*

The literature suggests that educational tools should be utilised in order to maximise positive experience, emotional connection and a sense of place and home. In addition, specific types of education are associated with an increase in pro-environmental behaviour, and also serve to counter negative associations and stereotypes of specific wildlife and wildlife-related problems.[123]

Whilst level of education is correlated with a conservation ethic,[124] the necessity or efficacy of environmental education as a conservation tool, in general, is debated. There is disagreement with respect to whether environmental education is a driver of environmental attitudes and behaviours. Kollmuss suggests that 'most researchers agree that only a small fraction of pro-environmental behaviour can be directly linked to environmental knowledge and environmental awareness'.[125] Indeed, there is a low correlation between people that identify as environmentalists and factual knowledge of environmental issues.[126] However, there is a correlation between perceived knowledge and identification/non-identification as an environmentalist, suggesting that cultural models influence the interpretation of environmental information, as do emotional constructs.[127] It is this link that is worthy of further discussion.

[121] Siemer et al., *Measuring Complex Connections*, 1.
[122] Siemer et al., *Measuring Complex Connections*, 1.
[123] See, for example, Kiyo Kurisu, *Pro-Environmental Behaviors*, 1st ed. (Springer Japan, 2015), chapter 6.
[124] Kang Min Ngo, Tetsuro Hosaka and Shinya Numata, 'The Influence of Childhood Nature Experience on Attitudes and Tolerance towards Problem-Causing Animals in Singapore' (2019) 41 *Urban Forestry & Urban Greening* 150, 152.
[125] Kollmuss and Agyeman, 'Mind the Gap', 250.
[126] Beth Robelia and Tony Murphy, 'What do People Know about Key Environmental Issues? A Review of Environmental Knowledge Surveys' (2012) 18(3) *Environmental Education Research* 299.
[127] Obery and Bangert, 'Exploring the Influence of Nature Relatedness', 11.

The connection was demonstrated by Ting and others in 2016 when they found that environmental awareness was not a dominant factor in predicting pro-environmental behaviours.[128] However, they also found that respondents exposed to nature at a younger age would have higher levels of pro-environmental behaviours, leading them to the conclusion that 'educating people at an early age and the transferable values and knowledge which they developed to play a significant role in establishing PEB (pro-environmental behaviours)'.[129] These findings have been replicated more recently in a Singaporean study.[130] Further, specific active types of education, like experiential education conducted with coyote conflicts, have been found to have much greater effect on the dynamic of the relationship.[131]

On the whole, there is significant evidence to support the contention that education initiatives are necessary to increase positive attitudes towards wildlife.[132] Indeed, a number of international wildlife researchers and practitioners agree that a 'long-term education-based process, based on preventative action and increased tolerance, is also necessary to move toward a culture of greater coexistence with wildlife'.[133]

More specifically, many ecologists and wildlife managers consider conservation education to be a viable ongoing tool in the governance of human–wildlife conflict.[134] A number of studies have found that education in specific contexts can assist conflict situations and environmental awareness more broadly. For example, there is some evidence that providing basic biological facts about an animal increases acceptance of that species.[135] In 2017, Marley found that for each per cent of the population that was taught about waste management, there was a 5 per cent decrease in the probability that a bear will become involved in human–wildlife conflict.[136] Conover states

[128] Ting and Cheng, 'Measuring the Marginal Effect'.

[129] Ting and Cheng, 'Measuring the Marginal Effect'.

[130] Ngo, Hosaka and Numata, 'Influence of Childhood Nature Experience'.

[131] Carly C. Sponarski et al., 'Changing Attitudes and Emotions toward Coyotes with Experiential Education' (2016) 47(4) *The Journal of Environmental Education* 296; Carly C. Sponarski et al., 'Retaining Change in Attitudes and Emotions toward Coyotes Using Experiential Education' (2019) 46(2) *Wildlife Research* 97.

[132] In addition to the studies mentioned, see also Bencin, Kioko and Kiffner, 'Local People's Perceptions'.

[133] Dubois et al., 'International Consensus Principles', 755.

[134] Danson K. Mwangi et al., 'Socioeconomic and Health Implications of Human–Wildlife Interactions in Nthongoni, Eastern Kenya' (2016) 46(2) *African Journal of Wildlife Research* 87.

[135] Goodale, Parsons and Sherren, 'The Nature of the Nuisance', 323.

[136] Jessa Marley et al., 'Does Human Education Reduce Conflicts between Humans and Bears? An Agent-Based Modelling Approach' (2017) 343 *Ecological Modelling* 15.

that simple educational initiatives, such as teaching people not to get too close to bison, can significantly reduce conflicts.[137]

Although educational initiatives are of use to human–wildlife conflict responses and resilience, the manner of delivery will influence the outcome. For example, education will likely be ineffective if used as a tool in persuading the public of decisions already made. Crowley suggests such an approach can 'trigger and rapidly polarize management conflicts' and does not give consideration to differences in social values and risk perceptions.[138] Defending decisions through educational initiatives can result in the reinforcement of the conflict and cause stakeholders to declare either for or against the proposal and drive the conflict further.[139]

In order to promote conflict resilience, educational initiatives need to be specific as well as create general environmental awareness. There ought to be a focus on the vulnerabilities of the relevant groups and the wider environment, rather than further education on the rights of respective stakeholders and consideration of those. What is vital is that perceptions of vulnerability are challenged, so that it becomes more commonplace knowledge that our vulnerability is linked with that of wildlife.

The themes discussed in this section are supported by many studies with very diverse practical objectives, disciplinary tools and epistemological frames. Yet, taken together, they assist with providing a critique of the ideology of autonomy as it relates to human–wildlife conflict. While the themes may not assist in addressing every conflict, given the individual nature of each instance of human–wildlife conflict, they do provide a starting point for an eco-vulnerability framework. Section 3.6 will continue with exploration of that framework and commence construction of the themes into a generalisable governance framework that can be utilised by the State, the law and other institutions.

3.6 PUTTING IT ALL TOGETHER; COLLABORATIVE GOVERNANCE AND COMMUNITY PARTICIPATION

The nature of human–wildlife conflicts, the links between history, society and wildlife values and the need to create a sense of place with emotional connection all suggest that community involvement in conflict resolution is

[137] Conover, *Resolving Human–Wildlife Conflicts*, 53.
[138] Sarah L. Crowley, Steve Hinchliffe and Robbie A. McDonald, 'Conflict in Invasive Species Management' (2017) 15(3) *Frontiers in Ecology and the Environment* 133, 137.
[139] Crowley, Hinchliffe and McDonald, 'Conflict in Invasive Species Management', 137.

necessary. In this section I show that the themes of contextual relevance, the role of history, sociology and political ecology, emotional connection and education can all be incorporated into a collaborative governance framework.

Indeed, community participation is another theme that arises from the wildlife literature. There are various suggestions that often it is a lack of communication with the community that results in or exacerbates the conflict. For example, Biru, Tessema and Urge conducted a study of attitudes around Awash National Park, Ethiopia, and found that although 73 per cent of households would be 'ready to live in harmony' with the park, 85 per cent of park staff considered the community as a threat.[140] Involving the community in planning and implementation necessarily allows everyone a seat at the table and opens lines of communication. Whilst undertaking research on conflict in India and Norway, Linnell, Thomassen and Jones found that simply undertaking the research itself opened dialogue with the community and assisted in reducing conflict.[141] Nsonsi and others found a lack of communication on the role of the local conservation agency contributed to human–elephant conflict in northern Congo.[142] The findings of Zajac and others also support this notion. They suggest that interventions were more successful when they involved individual community members and increased their social trust and feelings of control.[143]

These studies provide an answer to the deeper ideological premise that liberal autonomy is not an appropriate starting principle for responses to human–wildlife conflict and that something else is required, something that includes collaboration and communication between all stakeholders. Fineman also argues that vulnerability, and the dependency it creates, requires a *collective* response. She states: '(T)he essential and society-preserving work inevitable dependency demands has been channelled by society in such a way as to make only *some* of its members bear the burdens of this work.' [144] This is arguably the case with the protection and conservation of wildlife. To start, there is most certainly a link between societal preservation and conservation of biodiversity.[145] Second, while our laws and societal 'group think' acknowledge the need for conservation and protection, our institutions, on the whole, actually work against it. Our capitalist economy demands

140 Biru, Tessema and Urge, 'Perception and Attitude of Pastoralists', 13.
141 Linnell, Thomassen and Jones, *Wildlife–Human Interactions*, 7.
142 Nsonsi et al., 'Attitudes Towards Forest Elephant Conservation', 6.
143 Ryan M. Zajac et al., 'Learning to Live with Black Bears: A Psychological Model of Acceptance' (2012) 76(7) *The Journal of Wildlife Management* 1331–40.
144 Fineman, Autonomy Myth, 263 (original emphasis).
145 Harris, 'Vulnerability and Power in the Age of the Anthropocene', 98.

collective ignorance of the plight of wildlife. As an institution, the economic system promotes development and capital as the only means of achieving utilitarian notions of human security. That development destroys ecosystems and wildlife habitat, allows consumption of species on the brink of collapse and fosters a belief that neoliberal conservation is working, both to protect wildlife and promote human security.

As a result of these societal barriers, the majority of wildlife conservation is performed by a few select individuals, groups and NGOs that bear the burden of the work (in keeping with Fineman's framework they will be referred to as 'caretakers'). The caretakers are working with less State and institutional assistance each year. State conservation funding is shrinking in many parts of the world.[146] Likewise, National Parks and Conservation areas are being reduced.[147]

Yet, the linkages between our vulnerability and that of wildlife create a societal debt that must be acknowledged and paid at a broader level. This does not just involve paying the caretakers more money or compensating for their time and emotional and physical energy, but necessarily involves reducing their burden significantly, so that they do not have to work against society, but with it. The state needs to be *responsive* to the vulnerabilities of people, wildlife and ecosystems. This responsiveness involves implementing institutional arrangements that are based on increasing resilience and supporting the vulnerabilities that cannot be eliminated, rather than focusing on autonomy and individual rights of a capitalist nature.

However, when utilising the concept of a responsive state to alter the human–wildlife relationship, we need to be aware that pure top-down approaches of governance create animosity and can fuel the conflicts and this is likely to be the case with any regulatory management, whether it be based on vulnerability or not.[148] Specifically, researchers have noted that the values of the wider public are often different from the government agencies responsible for wildlife decision-making and the views of large numbers of people are

[146] See, for example, Adam Morton, 'Environment Funding Slashed by Third since Coalition Took Office', *The Guardian* (Online), 13 December 2017. Available at: www.theguardian.com/australia-news/2017/dec/13/environment-funding-slashed-by-third-since-coalition-took-office (last accessed 31 January 2022); Joe Avary, 'Conservation Council Report Shows Shrinking Environmental Protection Fund', *Cayman* 27 (19 March 2018). Available at: cayman27.ky/2018/03/conservation-council-report-shows-shrinking-environmental-protection-fund (last accessed 28 August 2019).

[147] See Brittany Patterson, 'Trump Poised to Shrink Two National Monuments', *ClimateWire* (4 December 2017). Available at: www.scientificamerican.com/article/trump-poised-to-shrink-two-national-monuments/ (last accessed 31 January 2022).

[148] Treves, Wallace and White, 'Participatory Planning of Interventions', 1584.

ignored.[149] For these reasons, there is wide consensus in the wildlife management literature that a bottom-up system of governance with community participation and consultation is required.[150]

One such bottom-up mechanism that is already being used in many instances of natural resource management and beyond is community-based governance (also referred to as collaborative governance and multi-party governance).[151] Ansell and others suggest that collaborative governance is useful for collective decision-making that aims to implement public policy or manage public programmes and challenges old forms of adversarial and managerial modes of policy-making and implementation.[152] They define collaborative governance as '(a) governing arrangement where one or more public agencies directly engage non-state stakeholders in a collective decision-making process that is formal, consensus-oriented, and deliberative and that aims to make or implement public policy or manage public programs or assets'.[153] Wondolleck and Yaffee discuss collaborative governance in natural resource management.[154] They suggest such a style of governance has a number of identifying features, including that it is context-dependent, place-based, rooted in cooperation and multiparty involvement, encompasses high-quality information and essentially builds relationships between people who have been isolated or alienated from each other.[155]

Another important feature of this type of governance is the devolution of state power in some way. The state is giving up some of their decision-making power, in order for the community to either make their own decisions or have a real say in the decision itself.[156] This is separate from the notion of

[149] Simmons, 'Transparency and Communication', 2.

[150] See Crowley, Hinchliffe and McDonald, 'Conflict in Invasive Species Management'; Biru, Tessema and Urge, 'Perception and Attitude of Pastoralists'; Obery and Bangert, 'Exploring the Influence of Nature Relatedness'; Linnell, Thomassen and Jones, *Wildlife–Human Interactions*; Treves, Wallace and White, 'Participatory Planning of Interventions'.

[151] See Chris Ansell and Alison Gash, 'Collaborative Governance in Theory and Practice' (2008) 18(4) *Journal of Public Administration Research and Theory* 543; Julia M. Wondolleck and Steven L. Yaffee, *Making Collarboration Work: Lessons from Innovation in Natural Resource Management* (Island Press, 2000); Arun Agrawal and Maria Carmen Lemos, 'A Greener Revolution in the Making?: Environmental Governance in the 21st Century' (2007) 49(5) *Environment: Science and Policy for Sustainable Development* 36.

[152] Ansell and Gash, 'Collaborative Governance', 544.

[153] Ansell and Gash, 'Collaborative Governance', 544.

[154] Wondolleck and Yaffee, Making Collarboration Work.

[155] Wondolleck and Yaffee, Making Collarboration Work, 4.

[156] Holley and Lawson actually suggest that 'pure' collaborative governance would involve no State input at all and involve regulatory mechanisms such as shaming and other informal social control. See Cameron Holley and Andrew Lawson, 'Implementing Environmental Law and

'stakeholder engagement' or 'public participation', wherein the consultation process is only one step in a larger decision-making process. Stakeholders are usually afforded the opportunity to voice their concerns and ideas for governance, but that is where the collaboration ends. The state-based decision-makers will then choose whether to use that information or not, with little transparency on the factors that lead to the final decision. This form of stakeholder engagement does not have the desired effect of placating stakeholders but instead has been shown to antagonise them and contribute to the conflict.[157] They become frustrated that their concerns are not considered or that decisions are made despite their protests.[158] Crowley defines the processes that seek out concerns but do not act on them, as 'internal exclusion'.[159]

On the other hand, collaborative governance involves stakeholders and the larger community at all stages of information gathering and decision-making, leading to a more consultative and 'group-think' process and result. Decisions are usually (although not always) accepted when the parties have a direct say in that particular outcome. The process is also inclusive of a diverse range of voices within the community, not just those considered relevant or that operate within the same ideology. Internal exclusion can arguably be achieved via this alternative process; engaging only a certain set of stakeholders or collaborating with selective members of the community. For example, Feldpausch notes that the NAMWC has only included consumptive users such as hunters and wildlife managers and scientists in its tenets,[160] thereby promoting internal exclusion of conservationists and specific communities.

Community-based governance also has other related benefits. Involving the community in decision-making naturally ensures increased transparency.[161] The human–wildlife conflict literature also suggests that community-based governance may be useful in promoting cultural change.[162] That is, there is a

Collaborative Governance', in Paul Martin and Amanda Kennedy (eds.), *Implementing Environmental Law* (Edward Elgar, 2015) 238, 239.

157 Crowley, Hinchliffe and McDonald, 'Conflict in Invasive Species Management', 137. See also Amanda Kennedy, *Environmental Justice and Land Use Conflict: The Governance of Mineral and Gas Resource Development* (Routledge, 2017) 280.

158 For example, see the experience recorded in Bruce F. Mackenzie and Brendon M. H. Larson, 'Participation under Time Constraints: Landowner Perceptions of Rapid Response to the Emerald Ash Borer' (2010) 23(10) *Society & Natural Resources* 1013.

159 Crowley, Hinchliffe and McDonald, 'Conflict in Invasive Species Management', 5.

160 Feldpausch-Parker, Parker and Vidon, 'Privileging Consumptive Use', 34.

161 Simmons, 'Transparency and Communication', 6.

162 Chanda L. Meek, 'Forms of Collaboration and Social Fit in Wildlife Management: A Comparison of Policy Networks in Alaska' (2013) 23(1) *Global Environmental Change* 217, 218.

potential for it to be used to adjust attitudes and values away from individual autonomy and disputes over rights, to understanding and appreciation of shared vulnerabilities.

Prima facie, it is arguable that the mode of governance arising from a responsive state is incompatible with community-based governance. Indeed, community-based governance necessarily involves the state stepping away from its position of power in some way and so a responsive state may be argued to be diametrically opposed to community-based governance.

However, any such argument is misleading and not indicative of what it means for a state to be 'responsive'. On the contrary, in order to be truly responsive, a state *requires* a collaborative style of governance. Without consultation with the community, key stakeholders and local knowledge of community ecosystems and wildlife behaviour, a state simply cannot be responsive to the needs of those who are most vulnerable. For example, one of the ideas behind community governance is that it has a problem-solving orientation. If the state was to assist managers in solving a conflict problem, there would be less push back from stakeholders who view their autonomy to be at risk, allowing the state and the managers to focus on vulnerability. Meek argues just this when she states that collaboration promotes 'social fit', leading to a more democratic and responsive policy whilst respecting human rights.[163] She states collaborative policy can be 'effective in the short term, and perhaps even more responsive to change if it is (1) legitimate to those who are to be governed, and (2) incorporates local knowledge of the context in which policy is to be implemented'.[164]

Further, while community-based governance might be informal and temporal, a responsive state has a duty to institutionalise such arrangements to allow for easier access to funding and support and to assist in the collaboration.[165] Temporal, agency-based collaborative methods, for example, may still come into conflict with arrangements at the district or state level that are contrary to community involvement if those arrangements are not institutionalised at every level.

A potential critique of a community–state collaborative alliance for wildlife governance is the contention by Fineman that local rule cannot be effective

[163] Meek, 'Forms of Collaboration and Social Fit'.

[164] Meek, 'Forms of Collaboration and Social Fit'.

[165] Richardson and Razzaque argue that there is a need to shift the onus from the public to the State to better institutionalise the process and ensure equity; Benjamin J. Richardson and Jona Razzaque, 'Public Participation in Environmental Decision-Making', in Benjamin J. Richardson and Stepan Wood (eds.), *Environmental Law for Sustainability* (Hart Publishing, 2006) 193.

and instead sometimes leads to more discrimination and greater inequality as a result of 'concession to local passion and prejudice'.[166] This kind of critique is similar to those who critique eco-feminist theory for accommodating too many views that leads to moral relativism. However, Fineman's argument is centred on comparing top-down state governance to market regulation. She does not consider a collaborative approach to regulation as an alternative to the involvement of the market. She states,

> to abandon progressive aspirations for the state given this history of *failure of the market* to make progressive adjustments without coercion is to abandon all hope for progressive change. The national government is the only organisation with the potential to impose such measures. At a minimum, the state must strive to eliminate major disparities that result from unequal social relations.[167]

While market failures is one issue that a vulnerability focus seeks to rectify, a top-down state response is not the only way to do this, nor is it necessarily the best way.

Others have considered a collaborative alternative and consider public involvement to be a viable counter to market-based regulatory failures. For example, Maria Lee and Carolyn Abbot argue that a public participation approach allows us to see participation as not only a response to ineffective autonomous bureaucracy but also an alternative to the commonly implemented market-based alternatives of pricing and privatisation.[168] Further, market-based responses are not consistent with participatory models as they tend to exclude the public from governance processes.[169]

Moreover, all of the themes discussed in Section 3.5 are linked with community involvement and collaboration in some way. An individualised community response is required where each human–wildlife conflict scenario is different and depends on the surrounding social, natural and political context. Getting people in the same room can help to resolve deeply embedded social conflicts. Sharing positive wildlife experiences with others can add to a connection with place, increasing both individual and community resilience. Finally, community education is only effective if the community

[166] Fineman makes this comment when considering U.S. political history. See Fineman, *Autonomy Myth*, 269–71.

[167] Fineman, *Autonomy Myth*, 270 (emphasis added).

[168] Maria Lee and Carolyn Abbot, 'The Usual Suspects? Public Participation under the Aarhus Convention' (2003) 66(1) *The Modern Law Review* 80, 81.

[169] Lee and Abbot, 'The Usual Suspects?'.

is given real input into solutions, not where they are only educated about previously made decisions.

When it comes to human–wildlife conflict, the answer lies not in pure state regulation or pure participation. Instead, a prerequisite of effective community-based governance is a responsive, amenable state that creates clear guidelines for collaboration and assists with the shift of focus from individual rights and autonomy to collective responsibility and assessments of vulnerability. Without this initial involvement, community collaboration might, as Fineman suggests, pander to local biases and worsen instances of human–wildlife conflict. A vital difference between this theory and that of Fineman's though is a recognition of the limits of state power. Fineman states that '(t)here must be a change in the discourse of politics, with a new paradigm to guide state policy replacing that of the free market, in which there is no collective responsibility, but only an exaggerated sense of individual autonomy'.[170] The notion of collective responsibility, leading to collaborative governance, achieves the change that Fineman requires. Collective responsibility for community-state governance necessarily moves away from ineffective market fixes, whilst focusing on the vulnerable.

3.7 CONCLUSION

Overall, the human–wildlife conflict literature makes some important inroads into the sociological and emotional nature of the relationships that exist between people and wildlife and the conflicts therein. As a result, the human–wildlife governance literature as a whole now errs on being in favour of an interdisciplinary model that seeks to adjust both wildlife *and* human behaviour, a giant leap from the traditional methods of governance focusing on animal behaviour. Nsonsi and others capture this sentiment when they state that 'true understanding of conservation conflicts goes well beyond knowledge of the site-specific crop-raiding patterns, to assessing the ecological basis of wildlife impacts on people and perceptions'.[171] This type of understanding is indeed necessary to build resilience to conservation conflicts and would be a rational place to continue with addressing the conflicts surrounding shark attacks in Australia, for example. However, something is still missing from this body of literature. It does not connect the dots, from a holistic, ontological point of view. The ecological basis of impacts on people and their perceptions and vice versa is the basis of much of this literature, but the

170 Fineman, *Autonomy Myth*, 271.

171 Nsonsi et al., 'Attitudes Towards Forest Elephant Conservation', 2.

sociological and institutional impact on people and their perceptions and how that, in turn, influences the human–wildlife relationship, is lacking.[172] That is to say, the missing link is how societal structures and methods of governance influence and shape people's attitudes and values that are detrimental to coexistence.

The question remains: what are the larger relationships and structures that have led us to this particular point, or to a particular conflict? An ecofeminist ontology can shape and broaden the perspective and fill in the gaps provided by the narrowness of specific empirical data, whilst the theory of vulnerability adds depth to the proposed solutions. Together, the empirical evidence and an ecological vulnerability ontology can formulate a more holistic account of appropriate responses to human–wildlife conflict. They suggest that the state and institutions should respond to human–wildlife conflict by creating and formalising collaborative governance structures, that are guided by the themes of vulnerability, positive experience, emotional connection and education, and seek to address longstanding related conflicts. The remainder of this book will begin to place this method of response in context with discussion and analysis of case studies.

[172] There are limited examples of authors attempting this leap. See the critique of the North American Model of Wildlife Conservation's ideological foundations and exclusionary discourse, in Feldpausch-Parker, Parker and Vidon, 'Privileging Consumptive Use'.

4

Friends in Law?

The Critical Complexities of International Wildlife Law

4.1 INTRODUCTION

The international wildlife law regime itself does not afford protection to all wildlife, either within or outside of conflict with humans. Instead, specific protection is given to threatened species and populations,[1] other specifically named species[2] and certain areas and habitats that are especially rich in biodiversity.[3] The most commonly discussed multi-party international wildlife agreements include the *Convention on Biological Diversity* (CBD),[4] the *Convention on International Trade in Endangered Species* (CITES),[5] and the *Convention on Migratory Species* (CMS).[6] Habitat agreements such as the *Ramsar Convention*[7] and the *World Heritage Convention* (WHC)[8] are also commonly discussed.

1 See, for example, *United Nations Convention on Biological Diversity*, opened for signature 5 June 1992, 31 ILM 822 (entered into force 29 December 1993) Article 8(k); the listing provisions of *Convention on International Trade in Endangered Species of Wild Fauna and Flora*, opened for signature 3 March 1973, 993 UNTS 234 (entered into force 1 July 1975); and *Convention on the Conservation of Migratory Species of Wild Animals*, opened for signature 23 June 1979, 1651 UNTS 333 (entered into force 1 November 1983).

2 See, for example, *Agreement on Conservation of Polar Bears*, opened for signature 15 November 1973, 13 ILM 13 (entered into force 26 May 1976).

3 See *Convention on Wetlands of International Importance especially as Waterfowl Habitat ('Ramsar Convention')*, opened for signature 2 Feburary 1971, 11 ILM 963 (entered into force 21 December 1975); and *Convention Concerning the Protection of the World Cultural and Natural Heritage*, opened for signature 23 November 1972, 1037 UNTS 151 (entered into force 15 December 1975).

4 *United Nations Convention on Biological Diversity.*

5 *Convention on International Trade in Endangered Species of Wild Fauna and Flora.*

6 *Convention on the Conservation of Migratory Species of Wild Animals.*

7 *Convention on Wetlands of International Importance especially as Waterfowl Habitat.*

8 *Convention Concerning the Protection of the World Cultural and Natural Heritage.*

It is important to note that international wildlife law is a much more complicated network of agreements and decisions than those mentioned in the preceding paragraph. International wildlife law is not a discrete body of rules.[9] There are hundreds of multilateral agreements that have the potential to affect wildlife governance.[10] These include agreements specifically addressing biodiversity and particular species, broader environmental agreements that deal with habitat, pollution and climate change, trade treaties that affect the way we exploit wildlife and a State's ability to pursue environmental policies, treaties concerning food and agriculture, patent agreements addressing genetic resources and human rights treaties that prioritise certain inalienable rights over environmental and wildlife protection. This system of international agreements is also naturally supplemented by the other sources of international law, including customary international law, general principles and international case law.[11] Adding to the complexity of the regime, there are hundreds of soft law instruments,[12] such as the *World Charter for Nature*,[13] a multitude of Conference of the Parties decisions under a host of wildlife treaties, Memorandums of Understanding and Action Plans. Finally, there is an increasing number of international environmental institutions that influence the shaping and implementation of international wildlife law and particular organisations that are primarily tasked with the conservation of wildlife and/or their habitat.[14] Indeed, to find the relevant international law, one must start with a particular species or locale and work out from there.

9 Similar claims were made about International Environmental Law initially. See Patricia W. Birnie and Alan Boyle, *International Law and the Environment*, 2nd ed. (Oxford University Press, 2002), 1; D. M. Johnston, 'International Environmental Law: Recent Developments and Canadian Contributions', in R. St J. MacDonald et al. (eds.), *Canadian Perspectives on International Law and Organization* (University of Toronto Press, 1974) 555.

10 See, for example, Mark Austen and Tamara Richards, *Basic Legal Documents on International Animal Welfare and Wildlife Conservation* (Kluwer Law International, 2000), although note that the number of agreements has increased in the last 18 years, particularly soft law agreements such as Action Plans and Memoranda of Understanding arising out of the main treaties.

11 *Statute of the International Court of Justice*, opened for signature 26 June 1945, 3 Bevans 1179 (entered into force 24 October 1945), Article 38(1).

12 Soft law instruments can be persuasive but are not enforceable, such as hard law documents like treaties.

13 *World Charter for Nature*, 37th session, 48th plenary meeting, UN Doc A/RES/37/7 (28 October 1982).

14 See, for example, the International Union for the Conservation of Nature's Red List of Threatened Species. Available at: www.iucnredlist.org/ (last accessed 6 February 2022) and Species Survival Commission. Available at: www.iucn.org/species/about/species-survival-commission (last accessed 6 February 2022).

This chapter contains the first case study demonstrating the effects of *institutional* promotion of autonomy on instances of human–wildlife conflict. International wildlife law is a normative institution that reflects our relationship with wildlife and simultaneously shapes it.[15] It can, and should, promote a resilient relationship with wildlife. However, in this chapter, I will suggest that international wildlife law is premised on human autonomy and requires separation and domination of the environment, species and individual animals. As currently structured, the law is not conducive to a positive relationship between humans and non-humans but still situates the relationship in use-value and human benefit, factors which may instead increase the prevalence of the conflict.

4.2 INTERNATIONAL WILDLIFE LAW: LEGAL AND PRACTICAL CHALLENGES IN NEGOTIATING THROUGH CONFLICT

I begin this chapter by illuminating how and where the conflict is addressed within the institution of international wildlife law. In short, human–wildlife conflict is not mentioned explicitly in any of the main wildlife treaties, despite its contribution to biodiversity loss. There are several references to certain elements of the conflict, such as the 'taking' of wildlife, which is defined in the CMS.[16] Of course, there are also references to preventing the causes of biodiversity and wildlife loss, although, again, human–wildlife conflict is not specifically mentioned as one of the causes.[17] The *World Charter for Nature* does mention conflict,[18] somewhat contrary to the 'hard' law of CITES, CMS and the CBD, although the conflict mentioned is that of human–human warfare and armed conflict, not human–wildlife conflict and related conflicts that concern conservation values.[19]

[15] This is certainly not unique to wildlife, nor is it a revelation. See, for example, the discussion of the symbiotic relationship between law and culture in society in Naomi Mezey, 'Law as Culture' (2001) 13 *Yale Journal of Law and the Humanities* 35.

[16] *Convention on the Conservation of Migratory Species of Wild Animals*, preamble definition i, art 3(5), 4(5)(k).

[17] See, for example, the preamble to the CBD, *United Nations Convention on Biological Diversity*; 'Noting that it is vital to anticipate, prevent and attack the causes of significant reduction or loss of biological diversity at source'. See also article 7(c), which requires identification of the processes and categories of activities which have or are likely to have significant adverse impacts on the conservation and sustainable use of biological diversity and monitor their effects through sampling and other techniques.

[18] *World Charter for Nature*.

[19] Although many human–wildlife conflicts do involve arms and can lead to human–human armed conflict, this expression of the conflict is outside the scope of this book. However, it is worth noting that this type of conflict as it is related to the environment is subject to treaty law.

References to the conflict in CMS subsidiary action plans such as the Gorilla Agreement are perhaps the most comprehensive in international wildlife law.[20] The Agreement, signed by all 10 African gorilla range states, covers the four gorilla species and notes in the Preamble that the conservation of gorillas has 'unique implications in terms of interaction with human use of the land and its resources as well as in relation to human health'. The Agreement mandates that parties shall take coordinated measures to maintain or restore populations,[21] including specifically to 'take all efforts to prevent conflicts between humans and gorillas through appropriate land-use planning. Where human–gorilla conflict occurs, parties must take measures to reduce the conflict, with expert advice. These measures must be humane, consistent with the terms of this Agreement and to *the benefit of both humans and gorillas*'.[22] The method for achieving these mandates was to be included in the Agreement's Action Plans. Despite Action Plans being drafted for all four species, solid guidelines are yet to be produced[23] so, while the conflict is noted in this agreement, the inclusion is yet to translate into actionable and substantial policy points.

Notwithstanding the lack of comprehensive coverage in the main treaty instruments, the language and symptoms of human–wildlife conflict have infiltrated elsewhere in the international realm.[24] State reports, CoP decisions and other sources often explicitly note the widespread nature of the conflict

See for example, the *Environmental Modification Convention* (formerly known as the *Convention on the Prohibition of Military or Any Other Hostile Use of Environmental Modification Techniques*), opened for signature 18 May 1977 (entered into force 5 October 1978).

20 *Agreement on the Conservation of Gorillas and Their Habitats*, opened for signature 24 October 2007, UNEP/CMS/GOR-TC1/Inf.8.4 (entered into force 1 June 2008).

21 *Agreement on the Conservation of Gorillas and Their Habitats*, Art II.

22 *Agreement on the Conservation of Gorillas and Their Habitats*, Art II (emphasis added).

23 This is not to say that the Action Plans do not refer to conflict. For example, the 2015 Regional Action Plan for the Conservation of Western Lowland Gorillas and Central Chimpanzees allows limited funds to 'develop and sustain a human–gorilla conflict mitigation programme, including a disease-risk prevention strategy'; IUCN, *Regional Action Plan for the Conservation of Western Lowland Gorillas and Central Chimpanzees 2015–2025* (IUCN/SSC Primate Specialist Group, 2014). Similarly, the 2014 Revised Regional Action Plan for the Conservation of the Cross River Gorilla has a focus on methods to reduce illegal grazing and conflict with graziers; see Andrew Dunn et al., *Revised Regional Action Plan for the Conservation of the Cross River Gorilla (Gorilla gorilla diehli) 2014–2019* (IUCN/SSC Primate Specialist Group and Wildlife Conservation Society, 2014).

24 The following discussion is not a complete summary of the instances of human–wildlife conflict rhetoric in International Wildlife Law, but some of the more prominent examples. For example, there are also some documents on wildlife tourism conflicts with local people, other CoP decisions and agreements between CMS and CITES and brief mentions in some of the many documents concerning specific species.

and its impact on a State's ability to appropriately protect and conserve the environment. For example, the conflict is mentioned in directions to range states under CITES, concerning particular species, such as wild dogs, cheetahs and tigers.[25] The CITES Secretary-General has often remarked on the conflict as being a driver of species loss,[26] whilst the CITES programme 'Monitoring the Illegal Killing of Elephants' also mentions the importance of monitoring conflict.[27] Recent Ramsar Country Reports of Tanzania, Belize, Thailand, Zimbabwe, Namibia and Indonesia all mention the presence and difficulty of conflicts.[28]

There are also more implicit references to the conflict. For example, the CITES Conference of the Parties has acknowledged that in-situ conservation of species often conflicts with the livelihoods of locals and recommends that Parties 'adopt mitigation strategies for human–wildlife conflict with respect to CITES-listed species'.[29]

More urgently, States and international bodies have not been shy in calling for help in mitigating specific conflicts. CITES parties have requested States be provided with assistance in mitigating conflict with apes[30] and tigers.[31] The CBD Conference of the Parties have requested conflict management and reduction programmes concerning mountain biodiversity and recommends this be done via appropriate land-use planning.[32]

[25] CITES (2015), *CITES to discuss initiatives to dismantle criminal networks involved in tiger and rhino poaching* (Press Release, 20 October 2015). Available at: www.cites.org/eng/news/pr/2010/20100315_tiger-rhino.shtml (last accessed 14 February 2022); CITES (2015) *CITES Secretary-General's welcoming remarks at the Workshop on illegal trade in cheetahs* (Press Release, 3 November 2015). Available at: www.cites.org/eng/news/sg/cites_sg_welcoming_remarks_at_the_workshop_on_illegal_trade_in_cheetahs_03112015 (last accessed 14 February 2022).

[26] CITES-CMS (2016) *Joint statement by John E. Scanlon, Secretary-General of CITES and Badnee Chambers, Executive Secretary of CMS* (Press Release 30 May 2016). Available at: www.cites.org/eng/news/sg/Lion_Range_State_Meeting_Joint_statement_by_CITES_CMS_300516 (last accessed 14 February 2022).

[27] See CITES Program 'Monitoring the Illegal Killing of Elephants (MIKE)'. Available at: www.cites.org/eng/prog/mike/index.php (last accessed 14 February 2022).

[28] COP13 National Reports. Available at: www.ramsar.org (last accessed 14 February 2022).

[29] CITES, *CITES and Livelihoods*, Resolution Conf. 16.6, (Rev. CoP17). Available at: https://cites.org/sites/default/files/document/E-Res-16-06-R18.pdf (last accessed 16 February 2022).

[30] CITES, *Conservation of and Trade in Great Apes*, Resolution Conf 13.4 (Rev. CoP16). Available at: https://cites.org/sites/default/files/document/E-Res-13-04-R18.pdf (last accessed 16 February 2022).

[31] CITES, 'CITES seeks meeting with Prime Minister Singh to discuss India's tiger crisis' (Press Release, 12 April 2005). Available at: www.cites.org/eng/news/pr/2005/050412_tiger.shtml (last accessed 14 February 2022).

[32] See SBSTTA 9 Recommendation IX/12 Mountain biological diversity, and COP 7 Decision VII/12 Sustainable Use (Article 10); SBSTTA 14 Recommendation XIV/1 XIV/1. In-depth review

Despite the increasing recognition of the issue in the international realm, there has not been substantial international guidance in managing and preventing human–wildlife conflicts to date, although the tide may be starting to shift on this as well. The IUCN has released a limited number of species-specific best practice management guidelines.[33] There are also certain areas of promising development relevant to international governance of the issue. For example, in 2016 the IUCN's Species Survival Commission (SSC) set up a human–wildlife conflict taskforce.[34] The mission statement of the task force suggests the 'main aim is to support the IUCN SSC network in addressing human–wildlife conflict by providing interdisciplinary guidance and expert support, through the integration of ecological and social sciences'.[35] They are not tasked with bringing the problem further to the fore in international law, nor do they address specific or non-specific instances of conflict from an international legal perspective. The task force suggests that one of its objectives is to 'build capacity to support the SSC network by developing technical or framework guidance materials, resources, tools and training as needed by those working on human–wildlife conflict issues'.[36] Unfortunately, at this early stage in the development of the task force, there are no framework guidance materials and the resources referred to are a bibliography of outside scholarly articles. That said, the task force is working toward developing these guidelines and they will be a welcome development. The task force has been successful in gaining IUCN support for a 'position statement on the Management of Human–Wildlife Conflict', that sets out many of the parameters of conflict governance addressed in Chapter 3.[37]

In 2018, the CITES sponsored London Conference on Illegal Wildlife Trade resulted in the 'London Declaration' which recognised 'the importance of engaging communities living with wildlife as active partners in

of the implementation of the programme of work on mountain biological diversity, and COP 10 Decision X/30 X/30. Mountain biological diversity.

33 See, for example, Kimberley Hockings and Tatyana Humle, *Best Practice Guidelines for the Prevention and Mitigation of Conflict Between Humans and Great Apes* (IUCN, Conservation International, Center for Applied Biodiversity Science (CABS), IUCN Species Survival Commission (SSC) Primate Specialist Group, 2009). Available at: https://portals.iucn.org/library/efiles/documents/ssc-op-037.pdf (last accessed 16 February 2022).

34 IUCN-SSC, 'Human–Wildlife Conflict Task Force'. Available at: www.hwctf.org/ (last accessed 14 February 2022).

35 IUCN-SSC, 'Human–Wildlife Conflict Task Force – What We Do'. Available at: www.hwctf.org/about/what-we-do (last accessed 14 February 2022).

36 IUCN-SSC, 'Human–Wildlife Conflict Task Force – What We Do'..

37 IUCN, *Position Statement on the Management of Human–Wildlife Conflict* (IUCN, 2020). Available at: www.iucn.org/sites/dev/files/ssc_human_wildlife_conflict_position_statement.pdf (last accessed 14 February 2022).

conservation, by reducing human–wildlife conflict and supporting community efforts to advance their rights and capacity to manage and benefit from wildlife and their habitats'.[38] Of great promise, the UN Development Programme, together with the IUCN and the International Institute on Environment and Development (IIED), released a report in February 2018 proposing improved community-based wildlife management in situations of conflict and beyond.[39] The report includes a review of mechanisms for community engagement at the international level and this will be further discussed in Section 4.5.

It seems things are starting to happen around the issue of conflict in the international sphere. However, examples of that direct kind of language remain few, with the paradigms of welfare, consumption and biodiversity conservation favoured instead.[40] The framework as a whole speaks in terms of human values, without giving any guidance to addressing the individual conflicts of values that surround human–wildlife conflict. So why hasn't conflict been included more substantially? Pragmatically the understanding of conflict as both an environmental and social issue post-dates the real push in drafting the international wildlife law framework. Yet, the way that the main documents were drafted has still left us with a specific problem when it comes to human–wildlife conflict and that makes it difficult to now include specific principles that may assist in the resolution of conflict. The social nature of the problem has become increasingly accepted and the imposition of values and the ideology of autonomy from the top-down has been acknowledged as prohibitive to effectively addressing conflict. Yet, this is precisely what international wildlife law does. With perhaps the exception of the CMS Gorilla Action Plans and the IUCN Task Force position statement, the documents that do acknowledge conflict also prioritise autonomy, separation and domination over shared vulnerability and resilience. Section 4.3 will demonstrate the presence of values that result in the persistence of the autonomy ideology within the institution of international wildlife law.

[38] CITES (2014), 'London Conference on The Illegal Wildlife Trade – Declaration'. Available at: https://cites.org/sites/default/files/eng/news/sundry/2014/london-wildlife-conference-declaration-140213.pdf (last accessed 14 February 2022).

[39] UNEP (2018), *Wildlife, Wild Livelihoods: Involving Communities in Sustainable Wildlife Management and Combatting the Illegal Wildlife Trade*. Available at: http://wedocs.unep.org/bitstream/handle/20.500.11822/22864/WLWL_Report_web.pdf (last accessed 14 February 2022).

[40] Benjamin Cretois et al., 'What Form of Human–Wildlife Coexistence Is Mandated by Legislation? A Comparative Analysis of International and National Instruments' (2019) 28(7) *Biodiversity and Conservation* 1729.

4.3 THE PRESENCE OF VALUES: HUMAN–WILDLIFE CONFLICT AND ENVIRONMENTAL JURISPRUDENCE

It is necessary to look to the theoretical foundations and broad objectives of international wildlife law, given it does not explicitly provide a framework for mitigating and addressing human–wildlife conflict. Various commentators discuss paradigms and principles based on philosophies of protectionism, preservation, conservation and sustainable use.[41] However, a close analysis of these and other dominant theories of environmental justice shows that there are conflicts in international jurisprudence that bear striking resemblance to the different sets of values held by people in situations of human–wildlife conflict and described as the 'philosophical dilemma of conflict' in Chapter 2. Values around use to humans, ecosystems and individual animal welfare are all evident within the jurisprudence and the laws themselves. This demonstrates that the theoretical conflict is present at all levels and the lack of substantive acknowledgement of the conflict in international wildlife law means that resolution at the ground level is impractical at best and impossible at worst.

4.3.1 *Representation of Value in the Development of International Wildlife Law*

The philosophical conflict has not always been an underlying theme in the development of international environmental law. The earliest agreements were strictly anthropocentric and were concluded to prolong the viability of wildlife as an economic resource for human use into the future.[42] For example, the *Treaty for the Preservation and Protection of Fur Seals* and the first *Convention on the Regulation of Whaling* were signed in 1911 and 1931, respectively. Those agreements implicitly acknowledged the loss of use and human attributed value that would come with the loss of the species protected under the treaty banners and so put 'take' limits on species to preserve their long-term utilisation.

[41] For an outline see Rosemary Rayfuse, 'Biological Resources', in Daniel Bodansky, Jutta Brunnée and Ellen Hey (eds.), *The Oxford Handbook of International Environmental Law* (Oxford University Press, 2007) 362, 370–74.

[42] See, for example, *International Convention on the Regulation of Whaling*, opened for signature 24 September 1931, 155 LNTS 349 (entered into force 16 January 1935); *Fisheries Convention*, opened for signature 9 March 1964, UNTS No. 35 (1966) (entered into force 16 March 1966).

A human-centred philosophy continues to dominate international wildlife law. For example, the anthropocentric nature of CITES is evidenced by the description of the value of 'wild fauna and flora', which is limited to value from 'aesthetic, scientific, cultural, recreational and economic points of view'.[43] All these values are held by people and judged by people and result in species being categorised based on the value placed on them. Similarly, the CMS notes that wild animals must be conserved for the 'good of mankind' and lists a similar set of values,[44] whilst the *World Heritage Convention* relies on the anthropocentric value of the areas it seeks to protect.[45] The use of particular concepts within international wildlife law is also supportive of this premise. For example, Otomo argues that the conceptualisation of 'common heritage' in the CBD and CITES places wildlife in the realm of human commerce, making the concept entirely anthropocentric.[46]

The human focus in international wildlife law was particularly evident around the 'seminal' UN Conference on the Human Environment (the Stockholm Conference).[47] The *Stockholm Declaration* in itself was focused on the protection of the environment as a means of meeting the needs and rights of humankind. This construction and safeguarding of the universalising values attached to 'humanity' and 'mankind' were viewed as necessary to garner widespread support for propositions and laws that were not necessarily meant to be entirely anthropocentric.

This focus has meant that most commentators agree on the anthropocentric nature of the framework. Bowman, Davies and Redgwell, in their leading text on international wildlife law, suggest that the *Stockholm Declaration* is 'marked by its heavy anthropocentric bias towards developmental issues' and 'nature itself does not receive prominent mention'.[48] The preamble establishes the 'environmental goal' that informs the Declaration: 'To defend and

43 *Convention on International Trade in Endangered Species of Wild Fauna and Flora*, second preambular recital.

44 Albeit the preamble also includes environmental, ecological, genetic, educational and social value. See Preambular recital 1 and 3.

45 The sixth preambular recital suggests 'preservation as part of the world heritage of mankind as a whole'; *Convention Concerning the Protection of the World Cultural and Natural Heritage*.

46 Yoriko Otomo, 'Species, Scarcity and the Secular State', in Yoriko Otomo and Edward Mussawir (eds.), *Law and the Question of the Animal: A Critical Jurisprudence* (Routledge, 2013) 166, 170.

47 This conference has been described as the 'beginnings of an organised system of international environmental policy and law', although several key environmental instruments were concluded beforehand, such as the 1971 *Ramsar Convention on the Conservation of Wetlands of International Importance*; Michael Bowman, Peter Davies and Catherine Redgwell, *Lyster's International Wildlife Law* (Cambridge University Press, 2010), 12–13.

48 Bowman, Davies and Redgewell, Lyster's International Wildlife Law, 17.

improve the human environment for present and future generations has become an imperative goal for mankind – a goal to be pursued together with, and in harmony with, the established and fundamental goals of peace and of worldwide economic and social development.'[49] This 'goal' is further established in Principle 1, which reaffirms 'man's fundamental right to freedom, equality, adequate conditions of life, in an environment of a quality that permits a life of dignity and well-being'. In essence, the advent of solid commitments to the environment in international law is tempered by the need to comply with already existing human rights obligations, alleviate worldwide poverty, and increase human security globally. Highlighting these goals was necessary to universalise support for the agreement.

Recent developments in international environmental law have been made based on poverty and conservation being inextricably linked. This concept was the focus of the Brundtland Report:

> There has been a growing realization in national governments and multilateral institutions that it is impossible to separate economic development issues from environment issues; many forms of development erode the environmental resources upon which they must be based, and environmental degradation can undermine economic development. Poverty is a major cause and effect of global environmental problems. It is therefore futile to attempt to deal with environmental problems without a broader perspective that encompasses the factors underlying world poverty and international inequality.[50]

People in poverty are less concerned with issues that do not immediately affect their security and ability to provide for their family.[51] In this light, an anthropocentric focus, especially in low-income countries, is not only understandable but *prima facie* necessary. Human vulnerability is a vital consideration in environmental actions and poverty is an interrelated oppression that must be addressed in conjunction with human–wildlife conflict. However, the argument as made in the Brundtland report suggests that an anthropocentric focus in international wildlife law is the only way of achieving a reduction in global poverty and conservation together and equates economic development with

49 *Declaration of the United Nations Conference on the Human Environment ('Stockholm Declaration')*, U.N. Doc. A/Conf.48/14/Rev. 1(1973), Stockholm, UN (1972), preambular recital 6.

50 World Commission on Environment and Development, *Our Common Future ('the Brundtland Report')*, (1987), paragraph 8.

51 Susan Shearing, 'Biodiversity', in David Leary and Balakrishna Pisupati (eds.), *The Future of International Environmental Law* (United Nations University Press, 2010) 42, 51.

social development. This assumption is interrogated by a vulnerability analysis and I will discuss it further in Section 4.4.

4.3.2 *Anthropocentricity versus Ecological Holism*

To conclude that international wildlife law is clearly anthropocentric though is overly simplistic. International wildlife agreements have included notions of the intrinsic value of nature as a whole, implying that nature is worth saving because of the value it holds in and of itself. This is especially true of many of the soft agreements such as the *World Charter for Nature*.[52]

Ecological holism as a philosophy has been transformed into a principled 'ecosystem approach' in international wildlife law. This approach was developed by the CBD Conference of the Parties (CoP) and is said to be the 'fundamental paradigm' of the CBD.[53] The CoP specifically developed 12 principles at its fifth meeting, known as the 'Malawi Principles', and also set the context for the approach:

> The ecosystem approach is a strategy for the integrated management of land, water and living resources that promotes conservation and sustainable use in an equitable way ... An ecosystem approach is based on the application of appropriate scientific methodologies focused on levels of biological organization, which encompass the essential structure, processes, functions and interactions among organisms and their environment. It recognizes that humans, with their cultural diversity, are an integral component of many ecosystems.[54]

The approach is meant to be environmentally holistic and one would think that environmental decision-making should therefore consider the vulnerability of the whole of the ecosystem at the first instance. This is certainly evident in the Malawi Principles, where, for example, Principle 3 states: 'Ecosystem managers should consider the effects (actual or potential) of their activities on adjacent and other ecosystems'. Such an approach would be a welcome departure from a system that has traditionally prioritised liberal autonomy.

[52] The Preamble states that '(e)very form of life is unique, warranting respect regardless of its worth to man'; *World Charter for Nature*.

[53] Bowman, Davies and Redgwell, *Lyster's International Wildlife Law*, 603.

[54] Conference of the Parties, *United Nations Convention on Biological Diversity, Decisions Adopted by the Conference of the Parties to the Convention on Biological Diversity at its Fifth Meeting*, held in Nairobi from 15 to 26 May 2000, UN Doc UNEP/CBD/COP/5/23, Decision V/6, Annex III Principles 1 and 2, 104–5.

However, the Principles include other considerations that appear to overshadow a pure ecosystem approach that would allow focus on the shared vulnerability of people, ecosystems and wildlife. These principles concern things such as economics[55] and human use.[56] As a result of these and other social inclusions, the Malawi Principles are not limited to an ecosystem approach but, in fact, encompass a socioecological approach. Whilst a socioecological approach is vital for resolving social conflict, in this context it means that the intended ecosystem approach ends up falling into the dominant hierarchical paradigm.

This is because ecological holism (and socioecological holism) can essentially be viewed in two ways. The first is arguably how Leopold intended it, a philosophy that breaks down the traditional hierarchy of human dominance and places humans as an element of an ecosystem, such that the ecosystem takes priority when it comes to decision-making. The sociological aspect of this approach would see a de-assembling of the structures that do not support the precedence of the ecosystem. The alternate viewpoint is arguably how ecological holism has been implemented and interpreted in international wildlife law via the Malawi Principles; as a means to an end, with that end being liberal autonomy. In this interpretation, ecological holism is just another anthropocentric perspective. Although the whole of the ecosystem is considered, it is another way of ensuring the same outcome; the continued human utilisation of the environment to maintain autonomy into the future. The ecosystem approach is not the dominant paradigm itself in the CBD, it is instead a theory of environmental governance, with the purpose being to sustain the world's human population and ultimately provide resources to the individual. Rayfuse argues just this and suggests that the approach is actually posed as a method of implementation of 'sustainable use'.[57] Therefore, it is a governance technique used to implement an ostensibly anthropocentric paradigm based on human 'use' (albeit in a way that sustains the resource for use by future generations). The objectives outlined in the Convention itself are dominantly human-centred and the later adoption of the Malawi Principles was then required to fit that dominant paradigm.[58] Further, as a CoP decision, the Malawi Principles do not carry the same weight as the

55 Principle 4, 105.
56 Principle 10, 107.
57 Rayfuse, 'Biological Resources'.
58 Noting that the 'intrinsic value' of biological diversity outlined in the first preambular recital is not reflected in the substantive provisions of the Convention.

Convention itself and so must bow to the dominant philosophy in that respect.[59]

Indeed, the Malawi Principles have been interpreted as providing for specific governance theories, rather than an overall narrative or paradigm.[60] To be clear, these theories on their own are not necessarily anthropocentric, but when placed into an existing anthropocentric paradigm they become tools for that paradigm. Implementation of ecological holism into international wildlife law has thus far not been successful in building environmental resilience.

4.3.3 *Ecological Holism versus Welfare Individualism*

Ecological holism, in the Leopoldian sense, has not yet successfully been integrated into international wildlife law and its potential for overthrowing the dominant paradigm is currently tempered by its interpretation as a governance practice that supports ongoing human utilisation. Another hurdle is that ecological holism is meeting resistance from another value point, welfare individualism or the push to have animal rights and welfare considered in international wildlife law.

The welfare of wildlife and the intrinsic value of nature as a whole have become more prominent in internationals agreements that concern wildlife since the Stockholm Conference.[61] Intrinsic value is noted in the preamble of several wildlife agreements, including the *Bern Convention*,[62] the *World*

59 See, for example, Donald R. Rothwell et al., *International Law: Cases and Materials with Australian Perspectives*, 3rd ed. (Cambridge University Press, 2018) 107. Although note that the status of CoP decisions is somewhat contested. See, for example, Annecoos Wiersema, 'The New International Law-Makers? Conferences of the Parties to Multilateral Environmental Agreements' (2009) 31(1) *Michigan Journal of International Law* 231.

60 For example, it has been argued that the ecosystem approach furthers three specific management theories; Ecosystem Services Approach, Ecosystem Management and Community-Based Natural Resource Management. See K. A. Waylen et al., 'The Need to Disentangle Key Concepts from Ecosystem-Approach Jargon' (2014) 28(5) *Conservation Biology* 1215.

61 It is arguable that intrinsic value was evident in Principle 4 of the Stockholm Declaration; 'Man has a special responsibility to safeguard and wisely manage the heritage of wildlife and its habitat, which are now gravely imperilled by a combination of adverse factors. Nature conservation, including wildlife, must therefore receive importance in planning for economic development'. However, overall the Declaration is focused on the rights of 'Man' and the necessity of the environment in furthering those rights now and into the future; see the *Stockholm Declaration*.

62 *Convention on the Conservation of European Wildlife and Natural Habitats ('Bern Convention')*, opened for signature 19 September 1979, 1284 UNTS 209 (entered into force 1 June 1982).

Charter for Nature[63] and the CBD (although note that Article 8 of the CBD requires eradication of invasive species, so the semantics here are not equal to the substantive obligations).[64] It is also evident in a limited number of substantive treaty provisions, such as in the *Environmental Protocol to the Antarctic Treaty*[65] and the *African Nature Conservation Convention.*[66] Some ancillary agreements promote intrinsic value to a higher extent, such as the CMS ancillary agreement concerning gorillas, which affords gorillas' almost absolute protection against killing or taking and requires conflicts to be mitigated to the benefit of both gorillas and humans.[67] The Addis Ababa Guidelines on Sustainable Use, an ancillary agreement of the CBD Conference of the Parties, also somewhat paradoxically confirms the intrinsic value of biological diversity.[68]

Welfare principles are also somewhat present and reflect the intrinsic value of the wildlife they concern. For example, CITES has limited welfare provisions concerning the transport of live animals (called 'specimen' in the text itself), so that export minimises the 'risk of injury, damage to health or cruel treatment'.[69] The Schedule to the *International Convention on the Regulation of Whaling* initially limited how whales could be killed.[70] Overall though, a global welfare approach is missing and international law is yet to catch up to the prominence of welfare laws in domestic spheres.[71] However, the push for

63 *World Charter for Nature.*

64 *United Nations Convention on Biological Diversity*, preamble, first recital.

65 Although the use of the term is somewhat inconsistent with its definition, as it states that the intrinsic value of Antarctica *includes* its wilderness and aesthetic values and its value as an area for scientific research, all of which are instrumental and inherent values; *Protocol on Environmental Protection to the Antarctic Treaty*, opened for signature 4 October 1991, 30 ILM 1455 (entered into force 14 January 1998), Article 3(1).

66 The Convention lists 'environmental protection' as an objective (noting that a protection regime is usually discussed as being synonymous with intrinsic value) and also refers to 'ethical values'; *African Convention on the Conservation of Nature and Natural Resources*, opened for signature 15 September 1968, 1001 UNTS 4 (entered into force 16 June 1969), Article 4.

67 *Agreement on the Conservation of Gorillas and their Habitats.* This is one of the only agreements that discusses human–wildlife conflict and will be considered in more detail in Chapter 5.

68 Conference of the Parties, *Convention on Biological Diversity, Decision Adopted by the Conference of the Parties to the Convention on Biological Diversity at its Seventh Meeting VII/12, Sustainable Use (Article* 10), UNEP/CBD/COP/DEC/VII/12, 13 April 2004, practical principle 10.

69 See, for example, Article 3(2)(c).

70 See *International Convention on the Regulation of Whaling*, schedule paragraph 6.

71 For a thorough discussion of welfare in international law, see Sabine Brels, 'A Global Approach to Animal Protection' (2017) 20(1) *Journal of International Wildlife Law & Policy* 105; Werner Scholtz (ed.), *Animal Welfare and International Environmental Law* (Edward Elgar, 2019).

global animal welfare principles has resulted in intergovernmental adoption of several animal welfare standards, drafted by the World Organisation for Animal Health.[72]

International wildlife law is also plagued with prima facie ideological differences when it comes to individual animal welfare that limit the ability to promote resilience to vulnerability. There is a current line of argument in scholarship concerning welfare and international law that positions international wildlife law as being concerned with the conservation of species as a whole; this is inconsistent with a welfare approach.[73] Indeed, the ecosystem approach written into international wildlife law is inconsistent with welfare, but not solely because of the differences in those philosophical positions (being the difference between principles arising out of ecological holism versus individual welfare). They argue that, ostensibly, a form of 'land ethic' is imposed and the welfare of individual animals is placed at the bottom of the decision-making hierarchy.[74] As a result, both philosophies are fighting to wrestle dominance away from anthropocentrism.

As a result, the theoretical battle does not have only two sides but is a triangular struggle between human use, ecological holism and animal welfare positions. As suggested in Section 4.3.2, the ecological holism model currently being favoured by international wildlife law is, in fact, a means of achieving anthropocentric goals. Therefore, the real philosophical discrepancy is not between ecological holism and welfare individualism, but between anthropocentrism and intrinsic value.

The fact that multiple forms of value are found in international wildlife law is not, in itself, problematic. Each aspect of the natural world can exhibit multiple forms of value and each is a necessary consideration in a holistic, relational framework. Indeed, it is a premise of the arguments in this book that recognition of different types of value is necessary to overcome human–wildlife conflicts based on alternate values. However, the methods of considering value in international wildlife law are neither holistic nor relational. Instead, the framework creates a hierarchy of value with anthropocentric values placed at the pinnacle, so that wildlife and other elements of nature are categorised based on their value to humans. Any detailed study of the framework will show representations of ecological holism and welfare

[72] OIE World Organisation for Animal Health, *OIE Global Animal Welfare Strategy* (2017). Available at: www.oie.int/animalwelfare.

[73] See, for example, Werner Scholtz, 'Injecting Compassion into International Wildlife Law: From Conservation to Protection?' (2017) 6(3) *Transnational Environmental Law* 463.

[74] See, for example, Arie Trouwborst et al., 'International Wildlife Law: Understanding and Enhancing Its Role in Conservation' (2017) 37(9) *BioScience* 784.

individualism as well, but this is the problem of the framework and the conflict it creates. The framework is based on an anthropocentric perspective that fosters individual autonomy and that then attempts to include alternate values and philosophical positions without disturbing the overall dominant paradigm. Section 4.4 will further my argument in two ways. First, I will show how the philosophies exert hierarchical influence in the mechanisms of international wildlife law. Second, I will show that the international wildlife law framework creates a very particular type of anthropocentrism, which promotes the neo-liberal autonomous legal subject over other forms of human and natural existence.

4.4 THE MAKING OF VALUES: A VULNERABILITY PERSPECTIVE

The conflict evident in the theoretical development of international wildlife law has meant that several factors prevent a resilient relationship between people and wildlife. The regime's ineffectiveness is in large part due to the theoretical and practical constraints of its foundation.

Within international wildlife law, competing ideologies are stitched together into a fabric that merely covers underlying anthropocentrism,[75] being the real theoretical basis of international wildlife law. In practice, this means that a conservation ideology is implemented only when it coincides with an anthropocentric ideology (although, as we shall see, this human-focused ideology does not extend to all humans but only a privileged few). But how did this come about? The implementation of human-centred values, at the expense of other individually and collectively held values, was a strategic process and one that has played out over the history of international law itself.

The Harmony with Nature initiative suggests that 'at the core of the current anthropocentric worldview, the Earth is viewed as a source of raw materials to be commercialised, exploited, modified, altered and privatised'.[76] A critique of international wildlife law based on an ecofeminist approach to vulnerability theory shows that the framework was made to be not only anthropocentric but a very particular type of anthropocentrism that promotes the neo-liberal autonomous agent over other forms of human and natural existence. The prioritisation of this form of the legal subject (whether it be the State or an individual) creates hierarchy and categorisation that Rochette terms a

[75] See, for example, Anna Grear, 'Deconstructing Anthropos: A Critical Reflection on "Anthropocentric" Law and Anthropocene "Humanity"' (2015) 26 *Law and Critique* 225.

[76] Harmony with Nature. Available at: www.harmonywithnatureun.org/ (last accessed 14 February 2022).

'paradigm of dominance'.[77] Specifically, as part of the broader international environmental law framework, international wildlife law's 'dominant paradigm is still one where sustained economic growth, capital and economic development are essential to achieving sustainable development' and wildlife protection.[78] This is indeed a human-centred paradigm based on autonomy, but a very selective one. The development and growth being implicitly promoted in the framework operate in a way that only includes those already within and who benefit from the legal and economic systems in which the framework operates and promotes. That is to say, international wildlife law has struggled to move outside a legal paradigm that is the foundation of and continues to serve a particular political economy, that benefits particular 'liberally autonomous' individuals.[79] Sections 4.4.1–4.4.3 will show just how this has eventuated as the underlying foundational ideology of international wildlife law and is persistently maintained.

4.4.1 *Autonomy and the 'Rights' Paradigm*

International law is not a modern construct by any means,[80] but the system as we know it today is often traced back to the development of the 'concept' of the nation-state and the *Treaty of Westphalia*, leading to the modern system reflected by the UN Charter.[81] Given the sovereignty of States,[82] the premise of international law has been to govern the relationship of and between States and not to impose rules on a State's ability to govern its own land and the people in it. While international law has historically demonstrated an intermittent ability to address human rights issues within a sovereign state's borders,[83] the UN system initiated after World War II solidified this ability and created human rights norms that regulated the way people were treated

77 Note the phrase is an iteration of Warren's 'logic of domination' in her 'oppressive conceptual framework'; Annie Rochette, 'Transcending the Conquest of Nature and Women: A Feminist Perspective on International Environmental Law', in Doris Buss and Ambreena Manji (eds.), *International Law; Modern Feminist Approaches* (Hart Publishing, 2005) 203.

78 Rochette, 'Transcending the Conquest of Nature and Women', 228.

79 Although of course we know that no one is truly autonomous, there are some who benefit from a legal system that promotes that type of autonomy, as discussed in Chapter 2.

80 See Alexander Orakhelashvili, *Akehurst's Modern Introduction to International Law*, 8th ed. (Routledge, 2018), chapter 2.

81 Orakhelashvili, Akehurst's Modern Introduction to International Law, 18.

82 State sovereignty is said to be the founding principle of the international legal system and ensures that States govern within their Territories without external interference (although there are limited exceptions, primarily concerning grave human rights abuses).

83 Such as the series of nineteenth century treaties aimed at abolishing the slave trade and the creation of the international labour standards in 1919.

within State borders. Dinah Shelton suggests that international law is yet to make the leap for wildlife that it did for people after WW2.[84] Before the advent of the UN, treatment of individuals was solely a matter of state jurisdiction. Domestic laws are no longer the sole source of laws on the treatment of individuals since the formation of the UN and the human rights treaties that accompanied it. The concept of human rights further entrenched a paradigm of anthropocentrism that international wildlife law has not been able to overcome.

It was over this system based on State sovereignty and then human rights that environmental law and subsequently wildlife law were framed. Early wildlife agreements concerned the conservation of wildlife as a result of conflicts over their use as a resource.[85] Wildlife law and environmental law more generally had to be superimposed onto a system that was not suited for dealing with long-term global issues but instead for moderating economic and security relations between States and ensuring individual autonomy from improper State interference. The development of wildlife law was initially a response to a very particular resource issue – the purposes of sustained human use, not an ecological or philosophical premise of protection of the environment for its own sake.

This history of human use and the human rights basis of the international system continues to dominate environmental discourse and supports the notion that the dominant philosophy espoused by international wildlife law is that of anthropocentrism. However, the human-centred approach in international law is a very particular kind of anthropocentrism that does not extend to all humans, all of the time. Instead, the anthropocentricity is defined by the promotion of liberal autonomy as described by vulnerability theory in Chapter 2. It is imperative to note that the human rights discourse cannot be disconnected from the liberal system that created it. The framework was not created in a vacuum. In this sense, the institutional promotion of autonomy, as described by Fineman at the domestic level, is equally applicable to the international sphere.

Anna Grear eloquently demonstrates these connections. She argues that the process of *disembodiment* in law, wherein human bodies are seen as external to the rational mind, has reduced the legal personality to one that is aligned

[84] As cited in Rachelle Adam and Joan Schaffner, 'International Law and Wildlife Well-Being: Moving from Theory to Action' (2017) 20(1) *Journal of International Wildlife Law & Policy* 1, 17.

[85] See, for example, the *International Convention on the Regulation of Whaling*.

with those concepts on the 'rational' side of the feminist dichotomies.[86] She argues that international human rights instruments and specifically the *Universal Declaration of Human Rights* 'grants an order of rights to the abstract universal identifiable in the foundations of liberal legal subjectivity'.[87] As evidence, she provides the 'very need for the proliferation of treaties specifying the rights of women and other minorities'.[88]

Kapur and Fineman have also both argued that the pursuit of liberal autonomy is central to the pursuit of human rights.[89] Specifically, Kapur argues that liberalism, autonomy and international human rights have a 'symbiotic' relationship, where human rights represent a modern attempt to formalise the relationship with liberal values by removing interference by the State, where autonomy is integral to both.[90] The histories, processes and unequal relationships surrounding the advent of international law informs the 'symbiotic relationship' and that history has manifested as a form of 'muscular liberalism' in the international human rights discourse. Kapur states;

> Human rights emerge as part of the mode of governance wherein rights-enabled 'freedom' is the outcome of a regulatory endeavour that is increasingly articulated in terms of the neoliberal market, and which discursively constitutes the subject of rights. This endeavour establishes a discriminative hierarchy of who counts and who does not among the subjects constituted. In the process, the central features of liberal freedom – as an aspiration and as an external pursuit by the autonomous subject with rational capacities – are revealed as being thoroughly embedded within relations of power: constrained, confined, and managed from within the liberal fishbowl, and producing unfreedom.[91]

The purpose of human rights in international law is to eliminate State abuse of the person by ensuring each person is their own liberally autonomous being,[92] within a liberally autonomous State. Therefore, liberal promotion

86 Anna Grear, 'Challenging Corporate "Humanity": Legal Disembodiment, Embodiment and Human Rights' (2007) 7(3) *Human Rights Law Review* 511, 522.

87 Grear, 'The Vulnerable Living Order', 36.

88 Grear, 'The Vulnerable Living Order'.

89 Although note that Kapur uses the word 'freedom' in place of 'autonomy', with the same underlying meaning of autonomy as described in Chapter 2. Ratna Kapur, *Gender, Alterity and Human Rights; Freedom in a Fishbowl* (Edward Elgar Publishing Limited, 2018); Fineman, 'Reasoning from the Body', 25–26.

90 Kapur, Gender, Alterity and Human Rights, 28.

91 Kapur, *Gender, Alterity and Human Rights*, 29.

92 Hilary Charlesworth and Christine Chinkin, *The Boundaries of International Law: A Feminist Analysis* (Manchester University Press, 2000), 208; 'For example, at the Vienna conference on

of autonomy in both the individual and the State is a core feature of the regime. Whilst State sovereignty is protected in relations with other States, so is individual sovereignty from interference by the State (representing one of Fineman's two-pronged definition traits of individual autonomy).[93] But, more than this, the liberal regime is currently running in conjunction with an increased neo-liberal economic discourse. Whilst the two are theoretically separate entities and human rights are stated to be 'indivisible' no matter the economic paradigm,[94] there remains a link in how the human rights regime is implemented so that it itself is becoming increasingly neo-liberalised. Grear is at pains to show that the liberal legal subject emerges as a construct that bears remarkable similarities to the corporate form.[95] It might be useful at this point to more clearly define the concept of neo-liberalism, even though it is a concept with a contested meaning depending on the discipline and user of the term. Having said that, the neo-liberal agenda is most often associated with the reduction of the role of the State, the liberation of the economy from State influence and increased privatisation.[96] What that means, in reality, is that all needs, rights and interests are to be moderated and provided by the market and liberal economic system. For wildlife, this means that conservation is left to the private realm and free-markets. Conservation laws promote privatisation of the 'resource' and do not interfere in the autonomous operation of those that purport to promote the stated goal of conservation. Similarly, it means the most effective way of ensuring human rights is to 'reduce the role of the state, liberate entrepreneurial energy, achieve economic efficiency, and promote faster economic growth'.[97]

As stated by Diane Elson; '(a)ll human rights require resources for their fulfilment'.[98] She states: 'Enjoyment of so-called negative freedoms depends on well-resourced systems of law and order, financed by taxation, just as much as enjoyment of so-called positive freedoms, such as the right to education,

HR in 1993, a number of Asian states claimed that human rights as interpreted in the West were based on a commitment to individualism and were at odds with the Asian tradition of concern with the community.'

93 See Section 2.4.1.

94 United Nations, *Universal Declaration of Human Rights*, GA Res 217A (III), UN GAOR, UN Doc A/810 (1948), preamble.

95 Grear, 'The Vulnerable Living Order', 29.

96 See, for example, Stephanie Lee Mudge, 'The State of the Art: What Is Neo-Liberalism?' (2008) 6 *Socio-Economic Review* 703, 705–6.

97 Diane Elson, 'Gender Justice, Human Rights, and Neo-Liberal Economic Policies', in Maxine Molyneux and Shahra Razavi (eds.), *Gender Justice, Development, and Rights* (Oxford University Press, 2002) 78, 80–81.

98 Elson, 'Gender Justice, Human Rights', 79.

depends on well-resourced educational systems, financed by taxation.'[99] The neo-liberalisation of human rights then entails an assumption that the neo-liberal economic system of resource allocation will lead to an increase in human security, prosperity and human rights.[100] The problem is that there is plenty of evidence to suggest that this has not been the case,[101] yet the language of human rights remains decidedly neo-liberal. Although human rights are 'universal' and 'indivisible', they are at the same time subject to the economic policies of the day and this is acknowledged in the UNDHR itself. Elson argues that this is evident in the way that human rights are not immediate but developed as progressive measures and policies are put in place.[102]

The problem though lies not solely with the ideology of neoliberalism but the already existing power structures that it props up. Primarily, the neo-liberalisation structures in international law were constructed by the 'already elites'. Elson describes this process via analysis of the role of the World Bank and IMF in promoting the neo-liberal economic order and 1980s debt crisis.[103] The structure then maintains the power over conceptions of power and privilege, as noted by Warren,[104] that have become part of the dominant paradigm, supported by the reliance on neo-liberalism and not challenged by the human rights paradigm. Arguably then, the symbiotic relationship described by Kapur is no longer one of liberalism, autonomy and human rights but one of neo-liberalism, autonomy and human rights. Thereafter, the kind of autonomy being promoted by human rights moves from liberal autonomy to neo-liberal autonomy.

In effect, this means that the human rights regime denounces the effects of power while at the same time shoring up that power. Paul O'Connell argues that, because of this, human rights advocates are 'faced with a choice . . ., between acquiescence in a process which is inherently inimical to the protection of human rights, or utilising human rights to challenge and overcome the dominant model . . .'.[105]

99 Elson, 'Gender Justice, Human Rights', 79.
100 For a different perspective on this argument, see Paul O'Connell, 'On Reconciling Irreconcilables: Neo-liberal Globalisation and Human Rights' (2007) 7(3) *Human Rights Law Review* 483.
101 For an overview of some of this evidence see both O'Connell, 'On Reconciling Irreconcilables', and Elson, 'Gender Justice, Human Rights'.
102 Elson, 'Gender Justice, Human Rights', 80.
103 Elson, 'Gender Justice, Human Rights', 79–85.
104 See Section 2.3.2.
105 O'Connell, 'On Reconciling Irreconcilables', 483–84.

The increasing neo-liberal articulation of the human rights regime is relevant to the international wildlife law framework because the anthropocentric philosophy embedded in international wildlife law is superimposed over the human rights basis. This means that the human-centred focused of international wildlife law is not supportive of increased human security for all, but only those that fit within the paradigm of dominance established across all international law, as found by Kapur, Rochette and other critical theorists. In other words, the domination of the environment in international law is not for the benefit of humankind, but only those who benefit from already existing power structures that are not questioned by international human rights law. This is consistent with ground-level management decisions in situations of conflict and distribution of ecosystem service benefits and costs, as we saw in Chapter 3. More generally, it supports the problematic nature of the neo-liberal style of conservation that we are increasingly seeing. Neo-liberal policies are not adequately equipped to deal with non-monetary costs and benefits of any kind and this becomes very prominent when considering the plethora of non-monetary costs and benefits associated with wildlife and human–wildlife conflict.[106] A further relevant critique on this point of autonomy and human rights is that the very notion of individualised human rights has been criticised by various members of the global south for not only ignoring the collective approach of other cultures but actively oppressing it.[107] Similarly, Kapur argues that the liberal pursuit of rights excludes non-liberal 'Others'.[108]

An emphasis on a neoliberal version of autonomy is reflected in the reliance on the individual in conflict decision-making at the ground level. A group of people furthering their own autonomy typically make the decisions, even though the decision rarely affects just that group. However, our understanding of autonomy and its abuse in situations of conflict is not merely linked with individual rights but is also subsumed by the overarching principle of State Sovereignty in international law. States can no longer abuse human rights with no consequences under international law and failure to comply with

[106] See Allison L. Mayberry, Alice J. Hovorka and Kate E. Evans, 'Well-Being Impacts of Human–Elephant Conflict in Khumaga, Botswana: Exploring Visible and Hidden Dimensions' (2017) 15(3) *Conservation and Society* 280; Ogra, 'Human–Wildlife Conflict and Gender', 1408; Bond and Mkutu, 'Exploring the Hidden Costs of Human–Wildlife Conflict', 35–54; Barua, Bhagwat and Jadhav, 'Hidden Dimensions of Human–Wildlife Conflict', 309.

[107] Amanda Russell Beattie and Kate Schick, *The Vulnerable Subject: Beyond Rationalism in International Relations* (Palgrave Macmillan, 2013) 2.

[108] Kapur, *Gender, Alterity and Human Rights*, 29.

human rights conventions can affect recognition of Statehood.[109] Yet environmental law is still an opt-in framework, with more and more States opting out for individual nationalist and political reasons.[110] There is a retraction from global thinking and global problem-solving when it comes to individual state responsibility and that responsibility is inconsistent with the economic autonomy of the State.

In this way, autonomy is seen as non-interference by the State. At the international level this might mean autonomous institutions acting outside State control, such as environmental NGOs, or the promotion of individual autonomy such as in international human rights law. But there is a third kind of autonomy in international law and that is autonomy of the State itself. So while international law attempts to moderate the State as an institution and impose human rights obligations on them (and in doing so liberates people from certain oppression that may be imposed by the state, making those people more 'autonomous'), the State can simultaneously push back and fight for its own institutional autonomy from international law. We see this often in international wildlife law and this is why environmental issues are often framed as human rights issues, as individual human rights are tangible and create autonomy from the State, while environmental issues have not yet escaped the overarching principle of State autonomy. Breaches of human rights provide a more legitimate avenue of questioning a State's environmental policies[111] and this approach has been taken several times in recent years.[112] Related to this reliance on human rights in the environmental sphere, there

[109] Orakhelashvili, *Akehurst's Modern Introduction to International Law*, 100.

[110] See, for example, Yong-Xiang Zhang et al., 'The Withdrawal of the U.S. from the Paris Agreement and its Impact on Global Climate Change Governance' (2017) 8(4) *Advances in Climate Change Research* 213 (although note the Biden administrations decision to re-join four years later); Chie Kojima, 'Japan: Japan's Decision to Withdraw from the International Convention for the Regulation of Whaling' (2019) 4(1) *Asia-Pacific Journal of Ocean Law and Policy* 93.

[111] For this reason of autonomy but also because the human rights systems are well established with individual complaint mechanisms that do not exist in international environmental law. See, for example, Svitlana Kravchenko 'Right to Carbon or Right to Life: Human Rights Approaches to Climate Change' (2008) 9(3) *Vermont Journal of Environmental Law* 513, 516.

[112] See, for example, *Juliana* v. *United States*, 339 F. Supp. 3d 1062; *Petition To the Commission on Human Rights of the Philippies Requesting the Investigation of the Responsibility of the Carbon Majors for Human Righs Violations or Threats of Violations Resulting from the Impacts of Climate Change*, Submitted by Greenpeace Southeast Asia and Philippine Rural reconstruction Movement. Available at: www.greenpeace.org/philippines/press/1237/the-climate-change-and-human-rights-petition/ (last accessed 16 February 2022).

has been a sustained argument for the 'human right to a healthy environment' as a more legitimate avenue of providing environmental protection.[113]

This struggle between individual autonomy and State autonomy in international law means that conflict between the State and the individual is amplified in situations of human–wildlife conflict, as we saw in Chapter 3. As stated by Charlesworth and Chinkin, autonomy in the international realm 'should be understood as dependant on international society, rather than in conflict with it'.[114] Autonomy in international wildlife law removes the focus on the relationships that modern international law was designed to promote.[115] A relational take on International Law would likely appease this conflict.

On the other hand, attempts to move the focus away from people and individual autonomy and to the environment are sometimes critiqued for not including a human perspective or enough of a human perspective and, in this way, human rights can be used to argue *against* a more biocentric approach. As an example, Louka discusses the absence of any emphasis on human rights in the in-situ conservation provisions of the CBD, arguing that complete in-situ conservation often means removing people who inhabit protected areas. She states that because of this approach it would 'have been desirable if the provision on in situ conservation includes a clause that ensured [it] . . . will not be pursued by violating human dignity and human rights'.[116] Louka makes a legitimate point, as we saw in Chapter 3, that conservation displacement is a real threat to human security and resilience in certain situations of human–wildlife conflict. However, the positions are often posed as an either/or situation both within international wildlife law and those who commentate on it; in the case of Louka, in-situ conservation vs the security of local people. A provision such as that suggested by Louka would not provide a basis for both things to occur simultaneously or provide any meaningful guidance on how to resolve a conflict between them were it to occur. It instead requires the kind of hierarchical decision-making that creates further conflicts and dichotomises the options, in this case, human rights over in-situ conservation. Practically

[113] See, for example, Jan Hancock, *Environmental Human Rights: Power, Ethics and Law* (Routledge, 2019). See also the work of the UNHCR's Special Rapporteur on Human Rights and the Environment, in particular, Human Rights Commission (2019) *Issue of Human Rights Obligations Relating to the Enjoyment of a Safe, Clean, Healthy and Sustainable Environment - Report of the Special Rapporteur*, UNGA 40th Sess, A/HRC/40/55.

[114] Charlesworth and Chinkin, Boundaries of International Law, 169.

[115] *Charter of the United Nations*, opened for signature 26 June 1945 (entered into force 24 October 1945), Article 1.

[116] Elli Louka, *International Environmental Law: Fairness, Effectiveness, and World Order* (Cambridge University Press, 2006) 301.

speaking, there may be other methods of achieving those human rights being put at risk by in-situ conservation and, in reality, complete adherence to the human rights regime as dictated by individuals would result in very little in-situ conservation, except perhaps in areas uninhabited by people. However, it is also not the case that in-situ conservation means relinquishing human rights. Instead, it may be that we can do both, albeit compromising how both those things are achieved.

4.4.2 *Capitalism, Neo-liberalism and Sustainable Development*

The human rights paradigm has embedded neoliberal autonomy further into international law, but it is not the only source or problematic area when it comes to international law's dominant paradigm. Constructions of 'development' operate in international law to promote 'the neoliberal agenda that was enshrined in the establishment of the WTO in 1995'.[117]

The western concept of development and the resulting avalanche of trade laws promote a certain kind of environmental dominance, based on capitalist concepts of use and value. This is reflected by the use of monetary *value* (such as in trade for wildlife components) and monetisation of *held values* (that is, deciding the value of wildlife by asking people of their 'willingness to pay'[118]) in international wildlife law and in the attempt to link the western forms of development with environmental protection, through the concept of 'sustainable development' and by other means.

The concept of sustainable development in international environmental law was an attempt to demonstrate the need to address both human security and the increasing prevalence of poverty, together with environmental conservation. It was developed as, and remains, the dominant concept in international environmental law.[119] Sustainable development acknowledges that there is a balancing act to be undertaken between conservation of the natural environment and the need for human and economic development. It has been evolving in international environmental law for decades and the core

[117] Rochette, 'Transcending the Conquest of Nature and Women', 231.

[118] See, for example, Johan Anderson, Dan Vadnjal and Hans-Erik Uhlin, 'Moral Dimensions of the WTA–WTP Disparity: An Experimental Examination' (2000) 32(1) *Ecological Economics* 153–62.

[119] There remains some debate concerning whether sustainable development is a principle of international law; Philippe Sands et al., *Principles of International Environmental Law*, 4th ed. (Cambridge University Press, 2018) 217–20. Therefore, this book will refer to it as a 'concept' of international law rather than a principal, although acknowledge the arguments on both sides.

ideas have been ruminated on since at least the Fur Seal arbitration.[120] However, the terminology was popularised by the 1987 Brundtland Report, leading to its elucidation in Agenda 21 produced by the United Nations Conference on Environment and Development.[121]

The concept itself, like most others in international environmental law, lacks precise meaning.[122] The Brundtland Report defines it as 'development that meets the needs of the present without compromising the ability of future generations to meet their own needs'.[123] The Report goes on to states that it contains two key concepts:

1. The concept of 'needs', in particular the essential needs of the world's poor, to which overriding priority should be given; and
2. The idea of limitations imposed by the state of technology and social organisation on the environment's ability to meet present and future needs.[124]

The practical requirements distilled by the principle and the impact on wildlife conservation remain somewhat of a mystery. The different wording expressed in the various wildlife agreements makes definition elusive. What exactly does 'sustainable use' (the common expressed form of sustainable development in wildlife law) mean for wildlife? To what extent are species allowed to be removed? These questions are more difficult than they first appear. For example, should the risk be only at the population level or do sub-populations also deserve individual protection? Species or sub-species? Such questions are important to consider as genetic variations between populations reduce in-breeding and sustain the species over the long-term.[125] Unfortunately, the formulations of the concept within international wildlife law do not provide any real guidance on such specifics. For example, the CBD states in Article 2 that sustainable use is 'the use of components of biological diversity in a way and at a rate that does not lead to the long-term decline of biological diversity, thereby maintaining its potential to meet the needs and aspirations of present and future generations'. Article 2 does define

[120] As noted in Philippe Sands et al., *Principles of International Environmental Law*, 3rd ed. (Cambridge University Press, 2012) 206.
[121] Sands et al., Principles of International Environmental Law, 3rd ed., 206.
[122] Jutta Brunnée, Daniel Bodansky and Ellen Hey (eds.), *The Oxford Handbook of International Environmental Law* (Oxford University Press, 2007) 443.
[123] *Brundtland Report*, para 1.
[124] *Brundtland Report*, para 1. See also the expanded definition in Sands et al., *Principles of International Environmental Law*, 3rd ed., 207.
[125] Conover, *Resolving Human–Wildlife Conflicts*, 161–62.

biological diversity as including 'variability among living organisms' and 'diversity within species' but as a definition provision does not carry substantive weight. In contrast, the in-situ conservation provision only mentions 'viable populations' (with this not being defined) and focuses on establishing protected areas, something which demonstrably reduces genetic diversity within species. The Conference of the Parties, acknowledging the debate surrounding the concept of sustainable use, drafted the *Addis Ababa Principles and Guidelines for the Sustainable Use of Biodiversity* in 2004.[126] The document suggests that sustainable use is possible if 'ecological processes, species and genetic variability remain above thresholds needed for long-term variability'.[127]

The concept of sustainable development warrants particular discussion as it is particularly pertinent to wildlife conservation and human–wildlife conflict. Interestingly, the term suggests that the two things can be achieved simultaneously, but more than that, they are interdependent. That is to say, development and human security are dependent on the environment, whilst protection of the environment is dependent on appropriate economic development. Yet, in reality, the concept of sustainable development rarely plays out in a way where there is a win/win situation for both the wildlife and people concerned in direct conflict and this is reflective of the broader problems associated with the nature of the concept and its development, together with its associated definition and implementation into law.[128] Instead, sustainable use in practice perpetuates the autonomy myth and separates people and the environment. Further, the concept itself is representative of the way that human–wildlife conflict (and broader environmental conflicts) is addressed (or ignored) in international wildlife law. That is because the primary tensions in human–wildlife conflict, being a struggle between human autonomy and habitat or species vulnerability, is reflected in the principle itself, whilst the language of the principle denies the reality of

[126] Conference of the Parties, *United Nations Convention on Biological Diversity, Decision Adopted by the Conference of the Parties to the Convention of Biological Diversity, at its Seventh Meeting*, held in Kuala Lumpur, 9–20 and 27 February 2004, CBD Decision VII/12, Agenda item 19.5.

[127] Secretariat of the Convention on Biological Diversity, *Addis Ababa Principles and Guidelines for the Sustainable Use of Biodiversity (CBD Guidelines)*, (2004, Montreal, Secretariat of the Convention on Biological Diversity), Paragraph 8(a).

[128] For further discussion on this point see, for example, Helen Kopnina, 'The Victims of Unsustainability: A Challenge to Sustainable Development Goals' (2016) 23(2) *International Journal of Sustainable Development & World Ecology* 113; Albert A. Bartlett, 'Reflections on Sustainability, Population Growth, and the Environment' (1994) 16 *Population and Environment* 5.

conflict. Once again, the principle seeks to address the problem by using the language that contributed to the problem in the first place.

Similarly, the problem with the concept is not the motivation for creating the norm. Indeed, human–wildlife conflict is a perfect example of the need to address all aspects of the human relationship with the environment. However, there is an issue with the theoretical premise on which the norm was created. A critical analysis reveals the inherent difficulties with the concept, its various definitions within international wildlife law and its implementation by international organisations. There are four parts to this critique.

First, the emphasis on the mutual dependence of development and environmental protection ignores the role of capitalism, development and commodification in the loss of biodiversity and environmental destruction. Instead of acknowledging the role of these things, it posits them as the way out of the environmental problems they have created. For example, the *World Heritage Convention* is premised on the contention that protection of heritage areas 'often remains incomplete because of the . . . insufficient economic, scientific and technological resources of the country'.[129] This premise links the use and promotion of resources with a failure to protect them. In other words, we are failing to protect resources because we are not using them enough or we do not have enough access to them.

Second, it assumes westernised conceptions of development as being inherently good and the way to reduce poverty and increase human security, whilst again ignoring their role in the conflict. *The Declaration on the Right to Development* positions the notion of development as a human right[130] and makes the human person the central subject of development.[131] This focus minimises the relationality often associated with global south cultures (and the evidence that a relational approach is optimal in addressing specific instances of human–wildlife conflict) and places the focus back on western liberal ideology and individual autonomy. Similarly, the preamble of the *World Heritage Convention* links a failure to protect the environment with insufficient access to economic, scientific and technological resources, as mentioned earlier in this section. All of these things emphasise the westernisation of environmental protection and represent continued colonisation of the environment. At the same time, it has become evident that these factors contribute to ongoing human–wildlife conflict because of differing

[129] *Convention Concerning the Protection of the World Cultural and Natural Heritage*, preamble.
[130] UN General Assembly, *Declaration on the Right to Development*, Resolution adopted by the General Assembly on 4 December 1986, A/RES/41/128, Article 1.
[131] *Declaration on the Right to Development*, Article 2.

values, governance approaches and ongoing interference by high-income countries.

In addition to posing a problem in low-income countries, the factors contribute to conflict in high-income countries, where the different relational approaches to conflict are not able to fit within the structures created by the promotion of these ideologies. As demonstrated, the western liberal ideology surrounding the promotion of the individual is inherently flawed. Making the human person the central subject of development results in development for the individual and ignores the embedded vulnerabilities that accompany that individual. It ignores the fact that the individual is vulnerable to western concepts of conservation and institutions that promote it. Further, it ignores the fact that those institutions themselves are vulnerable and promote that westernised conception precisely because of that vulnerability.

Third, the concept of sustainable development bases itself firmly within economics, once again demonstrating that the law has been unable to move outside of this paradigm. Despite protestations to the contrary, it has become a neo-liberal concept. It is often defined in international law as an 'economic tool'[132] and the purpose of that economic tool is to promote the freedom and autonomy of the neo-liberal individual. In some cases, this might be achieved through environmental conservation but only when an economic analysis deems it be so. Indeed, the neo-liberal perspective has seen the inclusion and promotion of market-based approaches in international wildlife treaties.[133]

The common problem within these conventions then appears to be that the conservation philosophy prioritises economic methods over others. This critique plays out very specifically when it comes to wildlife. For example, international wildlife laws only protect species when they are on the brink of extinction or have demonstrated increased value some other way. Their value becomes high enough to engage market forces and compensate for the heavy discounts associated with the needs of future generations.[134] Thereafter, the implementation of international wildlife law manifests in a reliance on payment for ecosystem services. As discussed in Chapter 3, the reliability of such a conservation method is contentious at best. Because of this process, even intrinsic value is ultimately converted to economic value in the conventions. Otomo argues that CITES and the CBD function to facilitate the

[132] Secretariat of the Convention on Biological Diversity.

[133] See, for example, *United Nations Convention on Biological Diversity*, Art 11.

[134] See Raymond Rasker, Michael Martin and Rebecca Johnson, 'Economics: Theory versus Practice in Wildlife Management' (1992) 6(3) *Conservation Biology* 338–49. While conservation efforts are ideally aimed at improving future as well as current conditions, economic interests usually discount future benefits and costs in favour of present consumption.

consumption of a nature that has intrinsic value.[135] She does so by suggesting the conventions take certain things outside of human trade, by allocating them a 'pricelessness' based on the intrinsic value and irreplaceable quality and 'placing them within a logic of scarcity (the market), and then granting dispensations so as to make them available for trade and consumption'.[136]

The process of marketising wildlife then means that market-based approaches essentially involve moving conservation from the public arena to the private. This privatisation is a mechanism of autonomy. As noted by Fineman;

> On a political level, autonomy restrains the state from acting in any way that can be characterized as either a constraint on freedom of action or some form of wealth or power redistribution. Its role is primarily that of facilitating private competitiveness in an asserted meritocracy that, it is promised, will duly reward individual initiative and talent if only left free to do so.[137]

However, in this case, the reward is the conservation of species that benefit the neo-liberal individual. In much the same way that we have not been able to create real and lasting equality through privatisation (see the discussion in Chapter 2), we have yet to see any real improvement in our relationship with wildlife through privatisation.[138] That is not to say that all private conservation initiatives are inherently flawed. Some are showing particular progress in limited situations of human–wildlife conflict.[139] However, even when private conservation initiatives are successful in engaging the community and reducing conflict, there are still invariably issues associated with the distribution of the burdens and benefits associated with coexistence. Equality of distribution is just not what capitalism is made for. This discrepancy is also evidenced by the capitalist formation of international wildlife law.

Further, the inclusion of other non-economic forms of value in international wildlife law does not lessen the abandonment of wildlife to a

[135] Otomo, 'Species, Scarcity and the Secular State', 171.

[136] Otomo, 'Species, Scarcity and the Secular State', 171.

[137] Fineman, 'Vulnerable Subject', 259.

[138] For example, in Botswana, private conservation parks have been referred to as apartheid parks because of their lack of diversity; Parakh Hoon, 'Elephants are Like Our Diamonds: Recentralizing Community Based Natural Resource Management in Botswana, 1996–2012' (2014) 15(1) *African Studies Quarterly* 55, 57.

[139] Although they do not necessarily translate to benefits to local communities. The most well-known community-based conservation program is CAMPFIRE in Zimbabwe; see Charles Perrings et al., 'The Economics of Biodiversity and Ecosystem Services', in Shahid Naeem et al. (eds.), *Biodiversity, Ecosystem Functioning and Human Wellbeing: An Ecological and Economic Perspective* (Oxford University Press, 2009) 230, 236.

neoliberal economic order but instead creates new forms of commodification that expand the neo-liberalisation of wildlife. Moore provides an example of commodifying elephants through imagery.[140]

The fourth and final part to this critique of sustainable development is the emphasis it places on the 'base of rationality' associated with international law and critical thinking more generally. Within the neo-liberal agenda, numbers, values and statistics are hard lines of evidence that comprise the capitalist approach, this is in line with enlightenment philosophy that reason is the basis of knowledge and so decision-making. This plays out not only in monetary values but the basis of science as THE decision-making tool.

The relationship between science and law, particularly international law, is anything but simple. The use of science as a means of making law and deciding conflicts under and within the law is not always clear cut. There are two primary sides to this issue. The first is that the science itself is often not as 'factual' and impartial as is often assumed. Science as an entity is brought into existence and so mandated by societal institutions, the legitimacy of which is defined by the state. Science itself has not been successful in advocating for conservation or preservation because science is not, somewhat controversially, an autonomous institution (it is not that science itself is necessarily impartial but that the institutions surrounding science are not autonomous). Fineman presents the vulnerability as follows: 'The state brings these entities into existence as legitimate institutions. The law both assigns and enforces content and consequences, and by doing this, the state asserts it has a monopoly over legitimate means of coercion. This exercise of power is one way in which the state constitutes not only its institutions, but also itself.'[141] The embedded vulnerability of the state and its institutions is transferred to the scientific endeavours that it seeks to achieve.[142] When it comes to wildlife, the formulation of science is also embedded in the politics of relationships between institutions and the state. Conservation funding, for example, is decided by scientifically defined priorities around the highest risk species

[140] Lorraine Moore, 'The Neoliberal Elephant: Exploring the Impacts of the Trade Ban in Ivory on the Commodification and Neoliberalisation of Elephants' (2011) 42(1) *GEOFORUM* 51, 52.

[141] Martha Albertson Fineman, 'Injury in the Unresponsive State: Writing the Vulnerable Subject into Neo-Liberal Legal Culture', in Anne Bloom, David M. Engel and Michael McCann (eds.), *Injury and Injustice; The Cultural Politics of Harm and Redress* (Cambridge University Press, 2018) 50, 67.

[142] See, for example, the medical examples given in Janet A. Kourany, *Philosophy of Science after Feminism* (Oxford University Press, 2010); Aziza Ahmed, 'Rugged Vaginas and Vulnerable Rectums: The Sexual Identity, Epidemiology, and Law of the Global HIV Epidemic' (2013) 26 *Columbia Journal of Gender and Law* 1.

and whether the species is a keystone species (which in itself is an embedded scientific process). These considerations are not irrelevant, but when used alone can exclude other vulnerabilities such as that of cultures and place meanings. Further, the formulation of science as above reproach and autonomous to outside influence has seen its inclusion in wildlife agreements as uncontroversial. There are scientific exceptions to 'taking' of threatened wildlife in the *Convention on Migratory Species* and the *International Convention on the Regulation of Whaling*, amongst others. Scientific advisory bodies are mandated by many international agreements and have a large role in the making of decisions under those agreements (sometimes they are the only entity responsible for decisions).

In addition to the vulnerability of science as an institution, the second aspect of the issue is that scientific evidence, once found, and whether impartial or not, can be inappropriately moderated by other institutions, including lawmakers. That is, science is vulnerable to the way it is used by institutions. By way of example, in 2012 North Carolina's lawmakers legislated against the use of particular scientific predictions on sea-level rise.[143] The ban meant that planning policies could not use the available science to mitigate the predicted effects of climate-induced sea level rises. Naturally, the law was backed by economic development groups and real estate developers.[144] As noted by Fineman, here 'the law both assigns and enforces content and consequences'.[145] So, although legal decisions within wildlife conservation are often asserted to be based on the science of, say, population dynamics or genetic variance, the use of that science is vulnerable to the influence of other institutions.

Having been formed based on rationality, the dominant paradigm of international wildlife law largely ignores emotion, community, history and vulnerability, despite these things often playing into environmental decision-making. Some even argue that these things are not just ignored by international law, but actively opposed.[146]

[143] The ban was passed particularly in response to an estimate by the state's Coastal Resources Commission. See Alon Harish, *New Law in North Carolina Bans Latest Scientific Predictions of Sea-Level Rise* (2 August 2012) abcNews. Available at: https://abcnews.go.com/US/north-carolina-bans-latest-science-rising-sea-level/story?id=16913782 (last accessed 14 February 2022).

[144] Wade Rawlins, 'North Carolina Lawmakers Reject Sea Level Rise Predictions', Reuteurs (4 July 2012). Available at: www.reuters.com/article/us-usa-northcarolina/north-carolina-lawmakers-reject-sea-level-rise-predictions-idUSBRE86217I20120703 (last accessed 14 February 2022).

[145] Fineman, 'Injury in the Unresponsive State', 67.

[146] Beattie and Schick, Vulnerable Subject, 2.

4.4.3 *Categorisation and the Lack of Wild Animal Welfare Provisions*

The focus of autonomy in international wildlife law has meant that wild animal welfare has not been a core focus or concern to date and this has resulted in the individual animal being placed at the bottom of the hierarchy in wildlife decision-making. Yet, a vulnerability paradigm warrants inclusion of consideration of the vulnerability of wildlife species, as discussed in Chapter 2. Within international wildlife law there is a lack of any meaningful animal welfare provisions that extend beyond a certain species or kill methods, although the issue is gaining increased international attention.[147]

The language of international wildlife law is focused on conservation, rather than animal welfare. The regime itself was set up to facilitate long-term conservation of species to give longevity to our ability to use them as a resource. As addressed in Chapter 2, the fundamental theoretical premises of conservation and animal welfare are historically at odds. In conservation, the welfare of the individual is of less concern than the survival of a species.[148] From the outset then, international wildlife law has limited space available for animal welfare provisions. This place is limited to welfare only as it fits within this theoretical conservation premise and does not disturb the overall liberal autonomy paradigm. The specific (limited) examples of welfare provisions in international wildlife law are evidence of this.[149]

More fundamentally, these types of provisions are incidental to human use and conservation priorities, not because of a general recognition of animal suffering or their intrinsic value. The treaties themselves are fundamentally anthropocentric and concern conservation principles as a method of sustaining prolonged human use, as discussed in Sections 4.3.1–4.3.3. Where welfare requirements are provided, they are often at the bottom of the list of required considerations. For example, the Addis Ababa principles promote 'more efficient, ethical and humane use of components of biodiversity'.[150] As a matter of interpretation, efficiency is prioritised higher than welfare considerations. The suggestion is not a principle itself, but an operational guideline for principle 11, which states: '(u)sers of biodiversity components should seek to minimize waste and adverse environmental impact and optimize benefits

[147] Bowman, Davies and Redgwell, *Lyster's International Wildlife Law*, 698.
[148] Although there are movements within the conservation discipline to change this. See, for example, the Compassionate Conservation movement; Marc Bekoff (ed.), *Ignoring Nature No More: The Case for Compassionate Conservation* (The University of Chicago Press, 2013).
[149] As discussed in Section 4.3.3.
[150] Secretariat of the Convention on Biological Diversity, practical principle 11 of the operational guidelines, p 18.

from uses'. The principle, given priority, concerns efficiency and the whole of the environment, with welfare a consideration that may further those goals. In addition, the mention of ethical and humane use is coupled with 'use of components', a phrase that breaks the individual into commodifiable parts and ignores the vulnerability and intrinsic value of the animal itself.

There are more promising interpretations of welfare within certain international agreements. For example, Article 13 of the consolidated Treaty on the Functioning of the European Union states:

> In formulating and implementing the Union's agriculture, fisheries, transport, internal market, research and technological development and space policies, the Union and the Member States shall, *since animals are sentient beings, pay full regard to the welfare requirements of animals*, while respecting the legislative or administrative provisions and customs of the Member States relating in particular to religious rites, cultural traditions and regional heritage.[151]

This provision is promising for several reasons, the first of which is the recognition of animal sentience. It also warrants attention outside of specific taking methods or species due to the nature of the requirement itself: State members need regard animal welfare in *all* agriculture, fisheries, transport, internal market research and technological development and space policies. Whilst not requiring universal consideration of the sentience and welfare of animals, this is arguably as broad-ranging a hard provision of international law as has come to date. Finally, there is an argument to be made that the wording of the provision gives credence to animal care theory, paying regard to the welfare requirements of animals. This suggests we must listen to their requirements, not impose sub-standard requirements on them. However, again we must recognise that the provision is still related to the use of animals and the welfare is subsequent to that use.

The failure to implement effective intrinsic value and animal welfare provisions in international wildlife law means that the currency of such language used in the framework has not been able to minimise the damage done by the very particular brand of autonomy that international wildlife law promotes. We still put value into categories and welfare as a stand-alone value is not really considered in any detail at all. These components of the framework add up to an in-built permanent hierarchy that creates and perpetuates human–wildlife conflict while preventing it from being further addressed.

[151] *Consolidated Version of the Treaty on the Functioning of the European Union*, opened for signature 26 October 2012, OJ L. 326/47-326/390, Article 13 (emphasis added).

4.5 RESPONDING WITH VULNERABILITY

Autonomy is the reason that conflict cannot be brought to the centre of international law. It prioritises a value that supports economic valuation and individual pursuit of wealth and minimises other relational values that are present in many human–wildlife conflicts. However, other values could underlie the law.

To start, many of the themes that emerged in the vulnerability analysis in Chapter 3 are being implemented, or at least discussed, in the international realm. These include gender equality, the inclusion of emotion, history and alternative bases for decision-making, devolution of decision-making power and increased community participation, increasing environmental education, and, as discussed in this section, the inclusion of animal welfare. Indeed, the progress being made within international law on each of these factors is too great to detail here, but some examples will follow.

Gender equality has been an issue in the periphery of international law for some time. Principle 20 of the 1992 *Rio Declaration* describes women's role in environmental governance as 'vital' and claims that 'their full participation is therefore essential to achieve sustainable development'.[152] Agenda 21 considers that its success is dependent on the elimination of discrimination against women and an increase in the proportion of women in environment and development fields.[153] Both the CBD and the *Convention to Combat Desertification* affirm the importance of female participation in both policy-making and implementation.[154]

Whilst gender equality has gained prominence, the mode of equality iterated in the agreements does not represent a vulnerability approach. As discussed in Chapter 2 and argued by Fineman, equality demands more than increased representation, which works to shift the responsibility to the already marginalised. It is also known that equality goes beyond dichotomous genders and the concept of equality in international environmental law needs to extend to the vulnerability of other races and minorities.

[152] *Rio Declaration on Environment and Development*, concluded 13 June 1992, UN Doc. A/CONF.151/26 (vol. I), Principle 20.

[153] UNCED, *Agenda 21: Programme of Action for Sustainable Development*, UN Doc A/Conf.151/26 (1992), 24.1–24.2.

[154] *United Nations Convention on Biological Diversity*, preamble; *United Nations Convention to Combat Desertification in Countries Experiencing Serious Drought and/or Desertification, Particularly in Africa*, opened for signature 17 June 1994, 1954 UNTS 3 (entered into force 26 December 1996), Art 19(1)(a).

Some progress has been made recently, with Indigenous knowledge and participation being prioritised by the Intergovernmental Panel on Biodiversity and Ecosystem Services in their Global Assessment Report.[155] Generally, the inclusion of compassion and alternate epistemologies and epistemic communities in international wildlife law still has a long way to go.

Stakeholder involvement is something that has been encouraged in international wildlife law, particularly in implementation and enforcement (negotiation of the actual agreements is still primarily state-led). The *Ramsar Convention* and the *WHC* both encourage stakeholder involvement.[156] The Rio Declaration highlights the importance of promoting the role of local communities in environmental governance.[157] The Revised African Convention has participation arrangements that include Indigenous and local communities and encourages species management projects, such as CAMPFIRE in Zimbabwe, that have had some success in seeing equitable distribution of costs and benefits of conservation activities to local communities.[158] Community involvement is also supported in the access to information provisions in the *Aarhus Convention*.[159]

Community decision-making in wildlife governance has also been recently encouraged by the United Nations Environment Program.[160] They recommend community programmes that build trust, move slowly and allow 'the long timescales necessary to develop cooperative relationships and understand community needs and priorities'.[161] They suggest that 'local voices should be the loudest voices'.[162]

An interesting development is the increasing attention being given to the role of international customary law in promoting a connection between legal norms and a local population.[163] A groundswell of support for wildlife laws

155 IPBES, *Global Assessment Report on Biodiversity and Ecosystem Services of the Intergovernmental Science – Policy Platform on Biodiversity and Ecosystem Services*, IPBES Secretariat (2019).

156 *Ramsar Convention*, Resolutions VIII.19 and IX.21 and Strategy 4.1.iii of the current Strategic plan for 2009–2015; *Convention Concerning the Protection of the World Cultural and Natural Heritage*.

157 *Rio Declaration on Environment and Development*, Principle 22.

158 Bowman, Davies and Redgwell, *Lyster's International Wildlife Law*, 287.

159 *Convention on Access to Information, Public Participation in Decision-Making and Access to Justice in Environmental Matters*, opened for signature 26 June 1998, 2161 UNTS 447 (entered into force 30 October 2001).

160 See UNEP, *Wildlife, Wild Livelihoods*.

161 UNEP, *Wildlife, Wild Livelihoods*, 57.

162 UNEP, *Wildlife, Wild Livelihoods*, 59.

163 Kirk Junker, 'A Strong Role for Custom in International Wildlife Legislation', (2014) 17 *Journal of International Wildlife Law and Policy* 32–61.

and ecological values may be sufficient to instigate normative change at the national level that may then meet the elements of customary law at the international level.[164] Alternatively, there are arguments that values such as animal welfare may be recognised as a general principle of international law under Article 38(1)(c) of the *Vienna Convention on the Law of the Treaties*.[165]

Environmental education is also evident in many international wildlife agreements. The *Bern Convention* requires parties to promote education and disseminate general information on the need to conserve species and their habitats.[166] *Ramsar* perhaps has the most comprehensive educational recommendations, with a focus on raising the awareness of wetland values through the use of nature reserves and formal outreach programmes.[167]

However, the real gain to be made in international wildlife law (and to international environmental law and beyond) is to bring each of these components together via the inclusion of vulnerability as an interrelated human, species and ecological condition. A focus on interconnected vulnerabilities in international wildlife law would include deeper and more consistent references to the human place within the living world, our reliance on it and the intrinsic value of every component of the environment, all species included.

4.6 CONCLUSION; REASSESSING THE DOMINANT PARADIGM

International wildlife law is not equipped to deal with human–wildlife conflict as the regime itself is an embodiment of the values conflicts that often manifest in individual instances of human–wildlife conflict. Human security clashes with conservation and ecological holism and both are often inconsistent with the protection of the welfare of individual wild animals.

Overall, conflict has been swept aside in the discourse of international wildlife law, so conflict becomes difficult to address directly. The system is anthropocentric, even if it does consider future generations and ecosystems for governance purposes. It is used to shore up the concept of autonomy within the institution, and that flows down to the ability to address conflict at the ground level. The system also operates to entrench a very particular type of

[164] *Vienna Convention on the Law of Treaties*, opened for signature 23 May 1969, UNTS 1155 (entered into force 27 January 1980), Art 38(1)(b).

[165] *Vienna Convention on the Law of Treaties*; Scholz, Animal Welfare and International Environmental Law, 476–77; Bowman, Davies and Redgewell, *Lyster's International Wildlife Law*, 681.

[166] Art 3(3), although note that progress on the requirement remains minimal: Bowman, Davies and Redgwell, *Lyster's International Wildlife Law*, 301–2.

[167] Bowman, Davies and Redgwell, *Lyster's International Wildlife Law*, 427.

autonomy – referred to within this chapter as the dominant paradigm. That paradigm is based on promotion of the autonomous individual within the autonomous State and this has led to a hierarchy of dominance based on categorisation (between people and wildlife, but also within groups of people), value and use.

This dominant paradigm is not capable of receiving alternate value positions and so is incapable of addressing human–wildlife conflict in any meaningful way. More than that and as was demonstrated via the evidence in Chapter 3, the dominant paradigm can, and often does, exacerbate the conflict and decrease the resilience of those directly involved.

Many feminist and critical scholars suggest that frameworks such as these, with a very specific and damaging dominant paradigm, need to be scrapped entirely and to start anew. However, such a proposition is unworkable from a political perspective. Instead, we can recognise that the base of a vulnerability framework already exists. Equality, education, Indigenous knowledges, collaboration and animal welfare are all gaining prominence in international law and could be used to overrun the dominant paradigm of neo-liberal autonomy. The international framework, although problematic, is redeemable. The system needs to utilise these strengths to address conflict. Chapter 5 will provide evidence of the critique outlined in this chapter through the evaluation of a situational case study: human–dingo conflict on K'gari.

5

Human–Dingo Conflict on K'gari (Fraser) Island

5.1 INTRODUCTION

Dingoes on K'gari, in Queensland Australia,[1] continuously appear in the media due to their negative interactions with people. The issue first gained widespread attention when nine-year-old Clinton Gage was tragically killed by two dingoes on K'gari in 2001. Since then, negative interactions continue to occur, although thankfully there have been no more human fatalities at this stage. However, there have been near misses. In 2019, two dingoes 'broke into' a camper trailer and 'abducted' a toddler. His parents woke to the sounds of his cries getting further and further away and had to wrestle with the dingoes to rescue their child.[2] In 2021, another toddler was mauled after walking away from his holiday home while his parents were sleeping.[3] Dingoes pose a real threat to the safety of people on K'gari.

Yet, the relationship between dingoes and people on K'gari is a long and complex one, as with most instances of human–wildlife conflict. The relevant stakeholders and interest groups are many and varied, with interactions between local people (both Indigenous and non-Indigenous), tourists and

[1] Fraser Island was officially renamed K'gari Fraser Island in 2017, to incorporate the name provided to the Island by the traditional owners, the Butchulla. In 2021, the 'Fraser' was dropped and the island is now known solely as K'gari. This book will refer to the Island as K'gari hereafter.

[2] 'Dad Fights Off Dingoes That Took Toddler from Camper Trailer on Fraser Island off Queensland Coast', *ABC News* (Brisbane), 20 April 2019. Available at: www.abc.net.au/news/2019-04-19/queensland-toddler-attacked-by-dingoes-on-fraser-island/11031828 (last accessed 14 February 2022).

[3] 'Eyewitnesses Urged to Come Forward after Dingo Mauls Toddler on Fraser Island', *The Guardian* (Online), 18 April 2021. Available at: www.theguardian.com/australia-news/2021/apr/18/eyewitnesses-urged-to-come-forward-after-dingo-mauls-toddler-on-fraser-island (last accessed 14 February 2022).

tourism operators, wildlife services, different levels of government and, of course, the dingoes, their habitats and the ecosystem as a whole. The role of international law is particularly pertinent given K'gari is listed as a World Heritage Area under the *World Heritage Convention*.[4] The surrounding discourse is one of autonomy, separation and the maintenance of 'naturalness'. Policies continue to enforce the separation of people and dingoes not only physically, but ideologically. This discourse has limited the availability of responses to the conflict so that any potential response that responds to vulnerabilities and seeks to mend relationships is not entertained. What is called for is a much broader understanding of the history of the relationship, the social context of the conflict and the vulnerabilities in question.

This case study, and the following case study in Chapter 6, represent some of the diversity of circumstances that are central to issues of human–wildlife conflict. An eco-vulnerability approach to an analysis of these case studies demonstrates specific advantages (conceptually and practically) that the model offers for typical contemporary human–wildlife conflict scenarios.

5.2 HUMAN–DINGO CONFLICT ON K'GARI

In April 2001, nine-year-old Clinton Gage was killed by two dingoes on K'gari. Reports suggest that Clinton was playing with his seven-year-old brother when they were approached by a pack of dingoes and was mauled after he tripped and fell while running away.[5] His brother was also bitten. Clinton's tragic death was preceded and followed by countless instances of human–dingo conflict on the island,[6] notwithstanding various attempts by the local and state authorities to address it. At the time of writing, the most recent dingo 'attack' on a person on K'gari occurred in April 2021 when a two-year-old boy

4 *Convention Concerning the Protection of the World Cultural and Natural Heritage.*

5 Patrick Barkham, 'Dingoes Kill Boy, 9, and Maul Brother on Tourist Isle', *The Guardian* (Sydney), 1 May 2001. Available at: www.theguardian.com/world/2001/may/01/patrickbarkham (last accessed 14 February 2022).

6 See Matthew McInerney, 'QPWS Reveals Dingo Incidents on the Rise at Fraser Island', *Fraser Coast Chronicle*, 20 April 2017. Available at: www.couriermail.com.au/news/queensland/fraser-coast/qpws-reveals-dingo-incidents-on-the-rise-at-fraser-island/news-story/c7ddf3121e8ede12cf926679a31a9126 (last accessed 16 February 2022); Carlie Walker, '17 Dangerous Dingo Encounters on Fraser Island', *Fraser Coast Chronicle*, 1 May 2018. Available at: www.couriermail.com.au/news/queensland/fraser-coast/17-dangerous-dingo-encounters-on-fraser-island/news-story/804a01cb79443277676017ffd409ce6a (last accessed 16 February 2022); Rob Appleby et al., 'Human–Dingo Interactions on Fraser Island: An Analysis of Serious Incident Reports' (2018) 40(2) *Australian Mammology* 146.

wandered away from his holiday home and was attacked by a lone dingo.[7] Of course, as demonstrated in the preceding chapters of this book, human–dingo conflicts do not occur as isolated, sporadic events, but are connected to the history, ecology and social politics of the area and beyond. Clinton's death and the more recent incidents are tied to these circumstances. As such, an exploration of these things is necessary to understand the full context of the conflict and ensure the terrible fate of Clinton Gage is not repeated in the future.

The World Heritage-listed K'gari lies off the southeast coast of Queensland in Australia. It is the world's largest sand island and is home to a small permanent population (around 200 people)[8] and a much larger tourist industry of around 400,000 visitors per year.[9] The island was inhabited by Indigenous Australians, the Butchulla people, when the island was given its European name of Fraser Island in 1836.[10] Since then, the island has been a place of typical European settlement. In 1860 it was gazetted as an 'Aboriginal Reserve' and a mission was established. However, the Reserve was revoked only two years later to permit timber harvest and a commercial timber industry commenced in 1863. The Aboriginal mission was completely abandoned in 1904 and the remaining Indigenous population were removed. Around this time, the island was formally declared a forestry reserve. The commercialisation of the island continued in 1950 when sand mining leases were granted. Sand mining and logging continued on the island for the following two decades.[11]

Several changes occurred in the 1970s, largely as a result of the 1971 establishment and subsequent advocacy work of the Fraser Island Defenders Organisation (FIDO). The campaigns for the protection and sustainable use of the island led to part of it being designated as a National Park and thereby coming under legal protection.[12] Further additions to the designation were added in the following years.

7 'Eyewitnesses Urged to Come Forward after Dingo Mauls Toddler on Fraser Island'.

8 Australian Bureau of Statistics, *Fraser Island* (13 December 2018) 2016 Census QuickStats. Available at: https://quickstats.censusdata.abs.gov.au/census_services/getproduct/census/2016/quickstat/SSC31091 (last accessed 16 February 2022).

9 Department of Environment and Heritage Protection, Ecosystem Services, *Fraser Island Dingo Conservation and Risk Management Strategy* (Queensland Government, July 2013) 1.

10 The island was given its European name after Eliza Fraser, when she and her husband, Captain James Fraser, were shipwrecked there.

11 For a further historical account of K'gari, see Stephen Healy, 'Deadly Dingoes: "Wild" or Simply Requiring "Due Process"?' (2007) 37(3) *Social Studies of Science* 443; Jennifer Parkhurst, *The Butchulla First Nations People of Fraser Island (K'gari) and their Dingoes* (Australian Wildlife Protection Council, 2015).

12 *Nature Conservation Act 1992* (Queensland).

Notwithstanding, sand mining and logging continued over the following years. Ultimately, the public backlash against those commercial endeavours resulted in the implementation of the *Environment Protection (Impact of Proposals) Act* 1974 and the commencement of the Fraser Island Environmental Inquiry. That inquiry ultimately recommended the island be listed as a World Heritage site. The island was finally declared a World Heritage Protected Area under the *World Heritage Convention* in 1992 and Queensland Parks and Wildlife Service (QPWS) took over management responsibility.

The Butchulla people continued to assert their rights as Native Title holders during this time and in November 2009 a Native Title claim was lodged by nine claimants, on behalf of the Butchulla people, over most of the island as well as some marine and adjacent land. They were legally acknowledged in Australian law as the native title owners of K'gari in 2014, and the Butchulla Registered Native Title Body Corporate (RNBTC) was established.[13]

The island averages 400,000 visitors per year.[14] Tourism on the island has exploded since the World Heritage listing and the figure has increased from around 200,000 at the time the island was listed.[15] Many suggest that the number of tourists visiting the island is way beyond sustainable capacity.[16] Tourists visit the island for day trips, camping, homestays in the limited number of permanent residences or to stay at one of the three resorts on the island.

Many tourists visit to see the island's most iconic fauna, the dingo (*Canis lupus* Dingo).[17] The dingo is Australia's largest predator. It is a wild dog of the *Canis* genus, meaning it is related to wolves, jackals and coyotes, and is a

[13] Kallee Buchanan, Ross Kay and Elaine Ford, 'Fraser Island: Native Title Rights Granted to Indigenous People by Federal Court' (7 November 2014), *ABC News*. Available at: www.abc.net.au/news/2014-10-24/federal-court-rules-on-fraser-island-native-title/5839474 (last accessed 14 February 2022).

[14] Department of Environment and Heritage Protection, *Fraser Island Dingo Conservation and Risk Management Strategy*, 1.

[15] IUCN, *World Heritage Nomination, Fraser Island and the Great Sandy Region (Australia) Advisory Evaluation*, International Union for the Conservation of Nature (March 1992), 12.

[16] See, for example, Angela Wardell-Johnson, 'Future of an Icon: K'gari-Fraser Island, Climate Change and Social Expectations' (2015) 22(2) *Australasian Journal of Environmental Management* 91.

[17] Indeed most of the marketing material for K'gari includes the dingo in some way; see S. Brown, C. Baldwin and L. Chandler, 'Representation of Butchulla Cultural Heritage Values in Communication of K'gari (Fraser Island) as a Tourism Destination' (2015) 22(2) *Australasian Journal of Environmental Management* 163. There is even a tourism operator called 'Cool Dingos'; see www.cooldingotour.com/.

highly social animal who lives in a pack.[18] Dingoes have not always been in Australia but were brought by Indigenous people roughly 4,000–5,000 years ago, who likely used them for hunting.[19] Although dingoes exist in many parts of the country, dingoes on K'gari are thought to be 'special'. For many years, scientists believed that mainland dingoes had interbred with wild and domestic dogs, meaning the mainland population was considered 'hybrid' which, in turn, makes them less worthy of saving in legal terms.[20] Dingoes on the mainland are not legally protected. K'gari dingoes have been deemed the last hope of saving the 'pure' genetic species from extinction.[21] The special status given to K'gari dingoes is mentioned often in official documents.[22]

The population of dingoes on K'gari is not currently known (only dingoes deemed 'problematic' are closely monitored and the remaining dingoes are left alone),[23] but there are an estimated 25–30 stable packs, each containing between 3 and 12 individuals.[24] The dingoes on the island are a tourist attraction and so tourist–dingo interactions are common. Tourists are often seen crowding a dingo for a photo opportunity or directly encouraging them with food. Further, dingoes are drawn to camping and residential areas when tourists do not dispose of rubbish and food scraps appropriately. Whilst most interactions seem to be positive (at least on the human side), there have been many significant negative interactions, for both people and the dingoes. The

[18] Lesley J. Rogers and Gisela Kaplan, *Spirit of the Wild Dog: The World of Wolves, Coyotes, Foxes, Jackals & Dingoes* (Allen & Unwin, 2003) 4–5.

[19] Rogers and Kaplan, Spirit of the Wild Dog, 37. There is some disagreement about whether this makes them 'native' to Australia, see, for example, Karen F. Hytten, 'Dingo Dualisms: Exploring the Ambiguous Identity of Australian Dingoes' (2009) 35(1) *Australian Zoologist* 18; David Trigger et al., 'Ecological Restoration, Cultural Preferences and the Negotiation of "Nativeness" in Australia' (2008) 39(3) *GEOFORUM* 1273.

[20] Note though that this is now being questioned. See, for example, Kylie M. Cairns et al., 'Geographic Hot Spots of Dingo Genetic Ancestry in Southeastern Australia despite Hybridisation with Domestic Dogs' (2020) 21(1) *Conservation Genetics* 77.

[21] Queensland Parks and Wildlife Service Environmental Protection Agency, *Fraser Island Dingo Management Strategy* (Queensland Government, November 2001) 2–3.

[22] See, for example, *Fraser Island Dingo Management Strategy*, 3; L. K. Corbett, *Canis lupus ssp. dingo. The IUCN Red List of Threatened Species* 2008 e.T41585A10484199 International Union for Conservation of Nature and Natural Resources. Available at: http://dx.doi.org/10.2305/IUCN.UK.2008.RLTS.T41585A10484199.en (last accessed 14 February 2022).

[23] Hugh Possingham et al., *Review Steering Committee Report on the Ecosure Pty Ltd Review of the Fraser Island Dingo Management Strategy (December 2012)*, Report to the Department of Environment and Heritage Protection (January 2013). See also B. L. Allen et al., 'Balancing Dingo Conservation with Human Safety on Fraser Island: The Numerical and Demographic Effects of Humane Destruction of Dingoes' (2015) 22(2) *Australasian Journal of Environmental Management* 197.

[24] Department of Environment and Heritage Protection, *Fraser Island Dingo Conservation and Risk Management Strategy*, Strategy 7.

first well-reported human injury occurred in 1988, when a child was 'attacked' by a dingo.[25] Dingo warning signs were installed at two sites in 1989. However, negative interactions continued and the first major cull of dingoes on the island occurred in 1994, when QPWS killed 16 animals. The sporadic killing of dingoes deemed 'dangerous' has occurred since then.[26]

Several more serious incidents occurred in 1998 and prompted the Queensland Government to commission a report on the issue. As a result, the Draft Fraser Island Dingo Management Strategy was developed in 1999.[27] However, tragedy struck before the draft strategy was finalised and there was no formal programme in place when Clinton Gage died. Thereafter, 31 dingoes were killed by QPWS in the weeks following Clinton's death. The draft management strategy was expedited and the first Fraser Island Dingo Management Strategy (FIDMS) was released in November 2001.[28] The management strategy has subsequently been updated in 2006 and 2013,[29] and most recently in 2021.[30]

A contextual analysis of the conflict shows the number of people concerned with and by the dingoes on K'gari and the stakeholders that need to be considered in an appropriate legal framework. These include, but are not limited to, the traditional owners, tourists and visitors, mainland and island locals, island tourism employees and businesses, conservation groups, the government and local councils, the QPWS rangers, scientists and ecologists and, of course, the dingoes themselves. Each of these groups can also have (and have had) stakeholder conflicts with other groups, which can compound the inability to resolve the primary human–dingo conflict.[31] In Section 5.3, I will explore the current legal framework before exploring whether all vulnerabilities of the stakeholders are adequately considered.

25 Jim Thompson, Leslie Shirreffs and Ian McPhail, 'Dingoes on Fraser Island – Tourism Dream or Management Nightmare' (2003) 8(1) *Human Dimensions of Wildlife* 37, 39.

26 Adam J. O'Neill et al., 'Managing Dingoes on Fraser Island: Culling, Conflict, and an Alternative' (2017) 23(1) *Pacific Conservation Biology* 4, 5.

27 Queensland Parks and Wildlife Service, *Draft Fraser Island Dingo Management Strategy* (Queensland Government, Environmental Protection Agency, 1999).

28 *Fraser Island Dingo Management Strategy*.

29 Queensland Parks and Wildlife Service, *Fraser Island Dingo Management Strategy – Review* (Queensland Government, December 2006); Department of Environment and Heritage Protection, *Fraser Island Dingo Conservation and Risk Management Strategy*.

30 Note the 2021 Policy was released while this book was in production, and so is not discussed in any detail here.

31 See, for example, the discussion of the conflict between on-the-ground managers and scientists in Angela Wardell-Johnson, Clare Archer-Lean and Jennifer Carter, 'Dingo Singing: The Howl of the Advocate' (2018) 25(1) *Pacific Conservation Biology* 37.

5.3 THE K'GARI–DINGO LEGAL FRAMEWORK

Australia is a federation of seven states and two territories and has a common law system. The legal position of human–dingo conflict on K'gari thus encompasses international conventions, national legislation and case law implemented by the Commonwealth of Australia, state legislation and case law implemented by the State of Queensland and the local laws and policies of the two councils under which the island falls: Maryborough Council (with control over the Southern end of the freehold areas of the island) and Hervey Bay Council (with control over the Northern end of the freehold areas of the island).

Dingoes are protected on the island, due to the national park and world heritage status of the area. Wardell-Johnson et al. suggest that the dingoes have earned their iconic status on K'gari as 'apex predators within the ecology of the island and through deep-time associations with the Butchulla . . . The perception of their status as symbols of "wild Australia" holds cultural significance to visitors . . .'.[32] Elsewhere in Australia, they are treated as a pest species, with some states even describing them as such.[33] They are persecuted by farmers and pastoralists and they have been subjected to council supported bounties.[34] The conflict that arises on mainland Australia outside of national parks involves different stakeholders and evokes several different values and is outside the scope of this case study.

The *World Heritage Convention* and the *Convention on Biological Diversity* are the two primary international conventions that are relevant to the governance of the human–dingo conflict on K'gari. Also, the International Union for the Conservation of Nature (IUCN) placed the species on the Red List as 'vulnerable to extinction' in 2008, due to the threat of hybridisation with domestic dogs.[35] The island was listed under the WHC because of its 'significant on-going geological and biological process' and its 'superlative natural features and exceptional natural beauty'.[36] The listing requires the Australian government to ensure no deliberate measures are taken which 'might damage

[32] Wardell-Johnson, Archer-Lean and Carter, 'Dingo Singing', C.

[33] This is also the case for Queensland outside of National Parks. See *Biosecurity Act 2014* (Queensland), where dingoes are listed as an invasive animal in Schedule 2.

[34] See, for example, Agriculture-Victoria, *Fox and Wild Dog Bounty*. available at: https://agriculture.vic.gov.au/biosecurity/pest-animals/victorian-fox-and-wild-dog-bounty (last accessed 16 February 2022).

[35] Corbett, *Canis lupus ssp. dingo*. But contrast this with Cairns et al., 'Geographic Hot Spots'.

[36] IUCN, *World Heritage Nomination*, 21.

directly or indirectly the cultural and natural heritage' of the island.[37] It also provides several positive obligations to protect and conserve the area, including giving the area a function in the life of the community and integrating it into comprehensive planning programmes, developing scientific and technical studies to counteract the threats to the area and fostering training in the protection, conservation and presentation of the area.[38] Although the dingoes themselves were not explicitly discussed in the WHC decision, the unique status of the dingoes and their ecological role was one basis for the nomination.[39] Subsequently, the Federal Court of Australia found that dingoes are a part of the World Heritage values associated with K'gari.[40]

In addition to the WHC, Australia is a party to the CBD, which requires it to ensure the conservation of biological diversity on K'gari and beyond. The vulnerability of the CBD as an institutional arrangement is exemplified by the varying degrees of implementation across the world. In this case, the national implementation of the CBD has been undertaken via the Commonwealth *Environmental Protection and Biodiversity Conservation Act*.[41] In practice though, the Queensland State Government is responsible for the management of the island, with national approval only being required for activities that would have a 'significant impact' on the World Heritage area.[42] So, although the Commonwealth government holds responsibility for Australia's obligations under the WHC, the management of such is not their concern. This can be problematic as the Australian States do not hold the same obligations to uphold international conventions and States have legislated in a way that is inconsistent with those conventions.[43] The relevant State legislation here is the Queensland *Nature Conservation Act 1992*.[44] It grants K'gari status as a 'protected area' as a result of it being a National Park.[45] The Act

37 *Convention Concerning the Protection of the World Cultural and Natural Heritage*, Art 6(3).

38 *Convention Concerning the Protection of the World Cultural and Natural Heritage*, Art 5.

39 Chris McGrath, 'The Fraser Island Dingo Case' (2001) 18(3) *Environmental and Planning Law Journal* 269, 270.

40 *Schneiders* v. *The State of Queensland and Jones* v. *The State of Queensland* [2001] FCA 533.

41 *Environment Protection and Biodiversity Conservation Act 1999* (Cth).

42 *Environment Protection and Biodiversity Conservation Act 1999* (Cth), s12. Note though that there is a precedent for the proposition that a dingo cull on the island would qualify as a 'significant impact'; see *Schneiders* v. *The State of Queensland and Jones* v. *The State of Queensland* [2001] FCA 533.

43 For a thorough discussion of the relationship between the Commonwealth and State governments on this issue, see Brendan Mackey et al., 'Assessing the Risk to the Conservation Status of Temperate Rainforest from Exposure to Mining, Commercial Logging, and Climate Change: A Tasmanian Case Study' (2017) 215 *Biological Conservation* 19, 24–26.

44 *Nature Conservation Act 1992* (Queensland).

45 Part 4 Division 1.

specifies management principles for National Parks, including the provision of permanent preservation of the area's natural condition, ensuring that the only use of the area is nature-based and ecologically sustainable, and the provision of opportunities for ecotourism in a way consistent with the area's natural and cultural resources and values.[46] It also makes unlawful the taking of a natural resource from a protected area[47] and allows for the drafting of specific management plans.[48]

The first FIDMS was released in 2001 and was prepared mainly from QPWS files, staff information and a scientific report from Laurie Corbett.[49] Although public submissions were taken (they were only taken before the death of Clinton Gage), none are referred to in the management plan itself. The FIDMS had five objectives which include ensuring the sustainable conservation of the dingoes, reducing the risk to people and eliminating the deliberate and inadvertent feeding of the dingoes by the people on the island.[50]

Those objectives provided the basis for seven strategies that centre on research and monitoring, awareness programmes, prohibition of dingo feeding, modification of dingo behaviour and euthanising and/or culling dingoes if deemed necessary.[51] These objectives and strategies are based on a very particular perspective on the cause of ongoing human–dingo conflict (although unsurprisingly the strategy itself appears to limit human–dingo conflict to dingo attacks on humans). That perspective, based on the report of Corbett, is 'Attraction → Habituation → Interaction → Aggression'.[52] It is assumed that dingoes are attracted to densely populated areas because of the association with food, they then lose any natural fear of humans because of regular, beneficial contact (feeding). Their habituation encourages further human interaction, with many tourists trying to get close for photo opportunities and the like. This can lead to dingo aggression when the favourable stimulus (food) is not presented. The management plan does not address conflict in any way other than the suggestion that feeding leads to aggression, even though conflict does not in itself only equate to an increase in aggression.

The management strategy was updated in 2006[53] and was amended to the 'Fraser Island Dingo Conservation and Risk Management Strategy'

[46] s 17(1).
[47] s 62.
[48] Part 7.
[49] Queensland Parks and Wildlife Service, *Fraser Island Dingo Management Strategy*, 7.
[50] Queensland Parks and Wildlife Service, *Fraser Island Dingo Management Strategy*.
[51] Queensland Parks and Wildlife Service, *Fraser Island Dingo Management Strategy*, 2.
[52] Queensland Parks and Wildlife Service, *Fraser Island Dingo Management Strategy*, 5.
[53] Queensland Parks and Wildlife Service, *Fraser Island Dingo Management Strategy – Review*.

in 2013.[54] As the name suggests, the 2013 strategy put a heavier focus on the welfare and conservation status of the dingoes. By way of example, systematic hazing, encouraged in the 2001 strategy, was suspended, with the 2013 strategy noting its potentially negative effects.[55] The causal assumption was also downplayed and instead changed to regular notation that human feeding 'may lead to habituation and potentially negative human interactions which may ultimately compromise the dingoes long-term survival chances'.[56] The 2013 strategy noted that human–dingo conflict and the euthanisation of dingoes had been reduced and that dingo-safe behaviour was being more consistently practised. It noted a 'meaningful adaptive management system of monitoring, reporting, evaluation and review is facilitating continuous improvement of outcomes for both dingo conservation and human safety on Fraser Island'.[57]

The practical effect of the management plan is not known. While the 2006 strategy suggests a reduction of dingo sightings at major visitor nodes, there is no objective evidence that conflicts had reduced. Dingoes continue to be killed, with 110 dingoes euthanised by the end of 2012.[58] Further, people continue to perceive dingo aggression and serious incidents still occur annually.[59] News reports suggest that incidents increased in 2017[60] and that 17 'threatening interactions' had occurred between January and May 2018.[61] Three serious injuries occurred within two months in early 2019,[62] after which

54 Department of Environment and Heritage Protection, *Fraser Island Dingo Conservation and Risk Management Strategy*.

55 Systematic hazing involves 'harassing dingoes by way of irritation' in order to modify their behaviour. Common techniques include firing non-lethal weapons, spray bottles containing irritating substances, ultrasonic devices, stock whips and aversive baiting that makes the dingo physically ill. See Department of Environment and Heritage Protection, *Fraser Island Dingo Conservation and Risk Management Strategy*.

56 Department of Environment and Heritage Protection, *Fraser Island Dingo Conservation and Risk Management Strategy*, 7.

57 Department of Environment and Heritage Protection, *Fraser Island Dingo Conservation and Risk Management Strategy*, 7.

58 Appleby et al., 'Human–Dingo Interactions on Fraser Island', 147. Unfortunately, more recent numbers are not made publicly available, although it is clear that the lethal programme is continuing.

59 Appleby et al., 'Human–Dingo Interactions on Fraser Island', 147.

60 McInerney, 'QPWS Reveals Dingo Incidents on the Rise at Fraser Island'.

61 Walker, '17 Dangerous Dingo Encounters on Fraser Island'.

62 'Toddler Dragged by Dingo from Fraser Island Campsite has Fractured Skull', *The Guardian* (Queensland), 19 April 2019. Available at: www.theguardian.com/australia-news/2019/apr/19/toddler-rescued-after-dingo-drags-him-from-fraser-island-campsite#:~:text=A%20toddler%20is%20in%20hospital,bed%20on%20Queensland%27s%20Fraser%20Island.&text=Paramedic%20Ben%20Du%20Toit%20said,him%20away%20into%20the%20bush (last accessed 16 February 2022).

the Queensland Environment Minister released a statement suggesting that three key policy measures were being increased: (1) The number of fenced camping areas would be increased; (2) There would be higher penalties for feeding dingoes and inappropriate behaviour towards dingoes; and (3) A new Butchulla community education ranger position would be created to help educate tourists.[63] Separately, news reports suggest that dingoes on the island have had to be euthanised due to illness arising from intentional poisoning.[64] Human–dingo conflict continues at concerning rates. In Section 5.4, I consider why this might be the case.

5.4 HOW DO DINGOES INFORM THE HUMAN–WILDLIFE RELATIONSHIP? AN ECO-VULNERABILITY ANALYSIS

The case of human–dingo conflict on K'gari highlights some of the constructs and themes that not only inform our relationship with wildlife, but also influence our held values and attitudes concerning wildlife. Those themes include the use of autonomy and separation to promote a construct of 'naturalness', autonomy and hierarchy, sequestration of institutional vulnerability, and liberal capitalism and related commodification.

5.4.1 *Autonomy, Separation and 'Naturalness'*

The human idea of our autonomy from the environment requires separation and this separation has been central to the building of wildlife law for some time.[65] Separation continues to drive various wildlife governance policies like the Fraser Island Dingo Management Strategy. Some of the more pro-dingo attitudes displayed on the island are defined by this human construction. The separation works to not only present a façade of the autonomy of humans *from*

[63] Minister for Science and Minister for the Arts, Minister for Environment and the Great Barrier Reef, The Honourable Leanne Enoch, 'Government Announces New Measures to Promote Safety on K'Gari' (Media Statement, Friday, April 26, 2019). Available at: https://statements.qld.gov.au/statements/8720 (last accessed 16 February 2022).

[64] Amy Mitchell-Whittington, 'Six Dingoes Found Dead at Fraser Island after Poisoning', *Brisbane Times* (Brisbane), 21 June 2016. Available at: www.brisbanetimes.com.au/national/queensland/six-dingoes-found-dead-at-fraser-island-20160621-gpoihr.html (last accessed 14 February 2022).

[65] For example, protected areas are built around the notion of separation. The idea of separation has been taken to a new realm with publications such as Edward O. Wilson, *Half-Earth; Our Planet's Fight for Life* (W.W Norton & Company, 2016); Helen Kopnina, 'Half the Earth for People (or More)? Addressing Ethical Questions in Conservation' (2016) 203 *Biological Conservation* 176.

the environment but also the autonomy *of* the natural environment, where such separation fits within the dominant paradigm discussed in Chapter 4. However, the idea of what is 'natural' is a contested one, both generally and concerning the human relationship with dingoes on K'gari.[66] The law and other institutions promote autonomy from the environment by giving it a status separate from people, defining untouched areas as 'pure', 'pristine', and 'natural' and so elevating their protection. This separation is described as maintenance of the 'natural state', at least in the sense it is used in conservation, the *World Heritage Convention*, the FIDMS and subsequent plans.

To start, it must be stressed that the dingoes on K'gari are given a different status to mainland dingoes because of their inclusion in a National Park and World Heritage Area, but also because of their genetic 'purity'. In essence, they are seen as more natural than their mainland relatives. Many of the official documents and policies highlight this genetic blessing and the perceived need to conserve it.

For example, one of the principles underpinning the 2001 Management Strategy states: 'With hybridisation threatening to bring about the eventual extinction of pure dingoes on the Australian mainland, preservation of the Fraser Island dingo population represents a unique opportunity to conserve the species in a near-natural environment.'[67] The purity of the dingoes also leads to the suggestion that 'their conservation is of national significance'.[68] The 2013 Strategy also includes references to observing dingoes in their 'natural state' but does not detail the conservation significance in as much detail.[69] Tourism material tends to focus on the 'pristine' environment and natural values associated with the island[70] and the main community conservation group, the Fraser Island Defenders Organisation (FIDO), supports the QPWS approach of maintenance of the 'wilderness'.[71]

The human construction of a 'natural' and 'wild' environment was also central to the heritage listing process and the arguments made to fit that construction have been detailed in various papers.[72] The central premise is

66 See, for example, K. J. Willis and H. J. B. Birks, 'What Is Natural? The Need for a Long-Term Perspective in Biodiversity Conservation' (2006) 314(5803) *Science* 1261.

67 Queensland Parks and Wildlife Service, *Fraser Island Dingo Management Strategy*, 6.

68 Queensland Parks and Wildlife Service, *Fraser Island Dingo Management Strategy*, 2.

69 Department of Environment and Heritage Protection, *Fraser Island Dingo Conservation and Risk Management Strategy*, 9.

70 See Brown, Baldwin and Chandler, 'Butchulla Cultural Heritage Values', 171.

71 Healy, 'Deadly Dingoes', 449.

72 See, for example, Karen F. Hytten and Georgette Leah Burns, 'Deconstructing Dingo Management on Fraser Island, Queensland: The Significance of Social Constructionism for Effective Wildlife Management' (2007) 14(1) *Australasian Journal of Environmental*

the link between human understandings of 'conservation' as a means of maintaining the natural state of the area and ultimately promoting liberal autonomy through sustainable utilisation of resources. The link between separation, the WHC, and autonomy/vulnerability is worth exploring. Importantly, the WHC itself does not give a precise definition of our relationship with wildlife but defines our relationship with the natural world based on social-cultural, ecological and conservation values.[73] This mix of values would theoretically be well placed to deal with human–wildlife conflict, given the need to incorporate a social response to the issue. However, the focus on maintaining a particular state of separation has reduced the ability to incorporate social and cultural values that do not fit within that definition. Further, this need to maintain a 'natural state' for the benefit of WHC listing impacts the ability to address the conflict at the ground level. For example, QPWS rejected many of the governance proposals offered by community groups, such as feeding stations (also known as diversionary feeding) as being inconsistent with the management intent of a World Heritage area.[74] Hytten and Burns similarly suggest that dingo pup training was rejected for this reason.[75] While these suggestions may or may not be appropriate, they are a practical example of the inability of the law to address conflict, by ignoring the language and causes of the conflict itself. This matches with the reason for protecting the dingo in the first place – its representation of a natural strain in a near-natural environment, free from hybridisation.

It is also arguable that the Convention does not pay due regard to the vulnerability of the environment within the site and its relationship to the construct of 'naturalness' that listing tends to imply. There is ample literature suggesting that World Heritage listing of a site can increase tourist numbers (this was indeed the case with K'gari), thereby reducing the resilience of the site itself.[76] Yet, the WHC does not consider the vulnerability of the sites to the institutional influences the listing process creates or that there may be a negative effect on species that are involved in the conflict, such as the dingo.

Management 48; Healy, 'Deadly Dingoes'; Brown, Baldwin and Chandler, 'Butchulla Cultural Heritage Values'.

73 *Convention Concerning the Protection of the World Cultural and Natural Heritage*, preamble.

74 Department of Environment and Heritage Protection, *Fraser Island Dingo Conservation and Risk Management Strategy*, 7.

75 Hytten and Burns, 'Deconstructing Dingo Management', 54.

76 Although note that this trend does not apply across all World Heritage areas. See Ralf Buckley, 'The Effects of World Heritage Listing on Tourism to Australian National Parks' (2004) 12(1) *Journal of Sustainable Tourism* 70; C. Michael Hall, 'Implementing the World Heritage Convention: What Happens after Listing?', in Anna Leask and Alan Fyall (eds.), *Managing World Heritage Sites* (Elsevier, 2006) 20.

The current approach of conserving 'natural' states is certainly not holistic, in the ecofeminist sense of the word. The idea of a natural environment is a relatively new one in human history.[77] The construction of 'natural' distances the conservation of the area and the species within it from the history, social circumstances, human and wildlife vulnerabilities (and dingo agency) and the vulnerability of the area around it. Assumptions about what is 'natural' are directing rules and behaviour and working to separate people from the island's dingoes. Hytten and Burns, for example, talk about three assumptions concerning 'natural' dingo behaviour that is evident in the management policies:[78] (1) The dingo should not frequent human-occupied areas; (2) That aggression towards humans is unnatural; and (3) That dingoes should have a natural fear of people. However, all those assumptions are contested in the literature and through an analysis of the historical relationship between people and dingoes, including the Butchulla and other Indigenous people.[79] By way of example, dingoes have a long history of visitation and proximal residency with Aboriginal people.[80] The relationship has been described as one of 'mutual exploitation', as there were various advantages to both the dingoes and the Aboriginal people in being associated with each other.[81] If these historical behaviours and connections are ignored, dingoes are placed into the human world of autonomy and disconnect, rather than situating people within theirs. The concept of separation based on purity and naturalness is therefore not one that has been given a holist perspective but instead is situated in a very specific time, place and conservation culture.

Separation also denies the dingo agency and creates a hierarchy of morality. The standards we have for human agency and welfare are vastly different from those given to the dingoes. Dingoes are killed on K'gari to protect their purity; dingoes that are not pure are killed so they cannot breed.[82] This differentiation

77 Paul Warde, Libby Robin and Sverker Sorlin, *The Environment: A History of the Idea* (John Hopkins University Press, 2018).

78 Hytten and Burns, 'Deconstructing Dingo Management', 50.

79 See, for example, Jennifer Carter, 'Displacing Indigenous Cultural Landscapes: The Naturalistic Gaze at Fraser Island World Heritage Area' (2010) 48(4) *Geographical Research* 398.

80 J. Carter, A. Wardell-Johnson and C. Archer-Lean, 'Butchulla Perspectives on Dingo Displacement and Agency at K'gari–Fraser Island, Australia' (2017) 85 *GEOFORUM* 197, 197; Parkhurst, Butchulla First Nations People.

81 Carter, Wardell-Johnson and Archer-Lean, 'Butchulla Perspectives on Dingo Displacement'.

82 Queensland Parks and Wildlife Service, Fraser Island Dingo Management Strategy – Review, 13.

in moral standards promotes the autonomy and agency of people over that of wildlife and specifically the dingo. The dingo is forced to perform an idea of 'naturalness' for humans. Any dingo who, through their own agency, chooses not to fit the human construction of 'natural', by hanging around tourist hotspots or getting too friendly with locals, is simply not allowed to continue to exist.[83] The agency of dingoes in this regard has long been reported, especially by the Butchulla people.[84] Yet, paradoxically they are killed in the name of this image of 'naturalness' to which they cannot conform. In this sense, the threat may not come from the dingo but the fragility of the notion of the wild, a notion that is held onto in order to imagine that we can either conquer or conserve, depending on what the dominant paradigm requires at any given point in time. This point leads to the role of autonomy in the construction of naturalness and the wild, which is the topic of the next discussion.

5.4.2 *Autonomy and Hierarchy*

Autonomy plays an integral role in this conflict and our understanding of the constructs that surround it. People are autonomous from nature and so people are autonomous from the dingo and they are autonomous from people. Thus, the 'natural' state of the relationship is one of autonomy. Mutual support by way of feeding, companionship and guarding is not allowed within this paradigm.

Of course, this perceived autonomy is a fallacy. As individual autonomy from society is a myth, so is autonomy from wildlife, including the dingo. The dingo plays an important ecological role on K'gari, one that cannot be separated from ours. Dingoes are thought to regulate ecological cascades.[85] Their presence can help to prevent the extinction of smaller animals within their habitat, while regulating other animals that are viewed as 'problematic', such as invasive species.[86] Unfortunately, as with most species, this ecological

83 For more on the agency of dingoes and their choices surrounding usual pack behavior, see Wardell-Johnson, Archer-Lean and Carter, 'Dingo Singing'.

84 Carter, Wardell-Johnson and Archer-Lean, 'Butchulla Perspectives on Dingo Displacement', 200.

85 An ecological cascade is the term used to describe a series of secondary extinctions or reduction in viability of populations that is triggered by the primary extinction of a key species in an ecosystem; Mike Letnic, Euan G. Ritchie and Christopher R. Dickman, 'Top Predators as Biodiversity Regulators: The Dingo Canis Lupus Dingo as a Case Study' (2012) 87(2) *Biological Reviews* 390, 401.

86 Letnic et al., 'Top Predators as Biodiversity Regulators'.

function can be negatively affected by social disruption, that is, through our presence and 'management'.[87] Thus, people are not actually autonomous from them, as they are vulnerable to the influences of people.

The perceived autonomy of the people directly and indirectly involved in the conflict is also worthy of analysis. Visitors, locals and resort staff continue to act against the formal management policy. Despite countless public and tourist education programmes including signage and ranger outreach, dingoes continue to be fed directly and tourists approach dingoes and coax them for photographs and 'selfies'. These actions are directly linked to a sense of independence or autonomy from the overall governance of dingoes and any greater effect that the action may have on the dingoes and greater ecosystem. Whether or not there is a direct link between increased feeding and dingo aggression, the fact is that if a dingo continually approaches people for food or otherwise and is perceived to act aggressively, there is a chance that dingo will be destroyed. This fact escapes the reality of many people (despite persistent education from rangers and messaging on the island) so that their actions are separated from the larger circumstances. By way of example, there is evidence that Instagram 'selfies' with dingoes actually increased after the incident with the 14-month-old boy in April 2019.[88] People that continue to encourage dingoes may consider themselves to be 'autonomous' from the management plan, the dingo, and the ecosystem. The disconnect from one's own actions to a greater ecological or social effect certainly plays out in these conflict scenarios. The following are quotes taken from a study undertaken by Carter, Wardell-Johnson and Archer-Lean:

FEMALE D: you see one poor dingo coming up the beach and you'll see them all pull up and pile out of their cars, like have 80 people all around the dingoes. It's going to get scared or something and I reckon they'll end up biting someone but they'll get their photo . . .

MALE X: [a ranger has] seen people feeding the dingoes tins of pal and how do you stop that?

MALE Y: You can't stop it. It's human nature.[89]

[87] O'Neill et al., 'Managing Dingoes on Fraser Island', 7.

[88] Phoebe Loomes, 'Tourists on Fraser Island Brag about Getting Close to Dingoes following Attack on Toddler', *news.com.au* (Sydney), 23 April 2019. Available at: www.news.com.au/travel/australian-holidays/queensland/tourists-on-fraser-island-brag-about-getting-close-to-dingoes-following-attack-on-toddler/news-story/2f93cd32fc54e032852b826eee51ab66 (last accessed 14 February 2022).

[89] Carter, Wardell-Johnson and Archer-Lean, 'Butchulla Perspectives on Dingo Displacement', 202.

The question of whether it is human nature to continue to act independently from our surrounds, institutions and each other is one that eco-vulnerability recognises but disputes. Autonomy is what society has taught certain privileged individuals so that it has become their nature when really it is our vulnerability that is an accurate representation of the human condition. That vulnerability though has not been embedded in our sociological structures and institutions and so remains a distant concept to many. Instead, society has situated vulnerability as a negative condition, only to be associated with certain people or groups who cannot support themselves. Society and its institutions do not support the notion of universal vulnerability and this means that many people also do not recognise it.

Again though, the individual autonomy played out here is forced to fit into the particular hierarchy discussed in Chapter 4. Not all individuals are deemed worthy of being 'autonomous' and the ability to make independent decisions concerning the conflict really depends on where you sit within that hierarchy. So, who or what gets to be autonomous in this conflict scenario? Certainly not the dingoes. This is highlighted by Carter, Wardell-Johnson and Archer-Lean who argue that a 'culture of human exceptionalism is reflected in the marketed, wilderness and party atmospheres on K'gari-Fraser Island'.[90] Prioritisation of human safety certainly occurs and is understandable to many people,[91] however, the 'human exceptionalism' extends beyond attempts to avert human injury or death. The neo-capital hierarchy described in Chapter 4 functions to prioritise economic interests and maintain power conceptions between stakeholders on K'gari.

There are also questions concerning the prioritisation of people as a whole, with many Aboriginal people and commentators suggesting that they are also not granted a status that encourages the promotion of autonomy.[92] As noted in Section 5.3, the importance of the dingo to Aboriginal people on K'gari and beyond is not acknowledged or supported in the legal context. They are denied a relationship that had historically existed both before and after colonisation.[93]

90 Carter, Wardell-Johnson and Archer-Lean, 'Butchulla Perspectives on Dingo Displacement', 203.

91 Queensland Parks and Wildlife Service, *Fraser Island Dingo Management Strategy*, 6.

92 Arguments are made along this line with respect to the lives of Aboriginal and Indigenous communities as a whole, although this book is limited to the specific human–wildlife conflict situation. That said, the arguments undoubtedly overlap. For a broader context of institutional racism in Australia, see the memoir of Maxine Beneba Clarke, *The Hate Race* (Hachette Australia, 2016).

93 Carter, Wardell-Johnson and Archer-Lean, 'Butchulla Perspectives on Dingo Displacement', 197 and 200.

They are deemed to be 'autonomous' from one another whilst at the same time denying autonomy to make their own decision regarding the relationship. In this way, the autonomy they are granted is only autonomy to the extent that the dominant paradigm allows, and that maintains the power conceptions already in existence. The colonising discourse was continued with the introduction of the island as a World Heritage Area and the continued representation of the island and its dingoes as 'pure' and 'natural'. By seeking to maintain a particular natural state (whether that natural state be accepted universally or not), the long, historic cultural association of the local people is swept aside. K'gari cultural values are not formally acknowledged in the World Heritage listing, despite the ability of the WHC to do so.[94] This is a stated problem for the Butchulla, who argue that continued culling of their 'camp dingoes' represents a continued attack on their rights and customs.[95] Aunty Marie, a prominent Elder of the Butchulla people, states; 'dispossess the dingoes and you dispossess us'.[96]

In a sense, the listing process and subsequent requirements for governance have meant that the Butchulla people have had to continue assimilation into a white person's conception of 'naturalness'. They have not been granted autonomy in deciding what this means, nor has their vulnerability to the governance practices been considered. Bohensky argues a similar thread, stating that even when Indigenous Ecological Knowledge is incorporated into governance decisions and process, it can first require assimilation so that Indigenous people are made to fit within the dominant paradigm to have their voice heard.[97] Their autonomy is dependent on their ability to fit within the dominant paradigm. This may also be the case with the Butchulla consultation process into the listing and subsequent dingo decision-making. An Indigenous advisory committee was established to provide advice to Australian Ministers before the application for WHC listing.[98] Thereafter, Butchulla members have been invited to sit on a Community Advisory Committee and have taken a greater role in governance, at least on paper. However, even after the latest incidents, the Butchulla people continue to

94 Jane Lennon, 'From K'gari to World Heritage: Reading the Cultural Landscapes of Fraser Island' (2012) 19(1) *Queensland Review* 27, 30.

95 Marie-Louise Sarjeant, Submission to the Fraser Island Dingo Management Strategy Review (2016) 2 [no longer available].

96 Sarjeant, Submission.

97 Erin L. Bohensky, R. A. Butler James and Jocelyn. Davies, 'Integrating Indigenous Ecological Knowledge and Science in Natural Resource Management: Perspectives from Australia' (2013) 18(3) *Ecology and Society* 20.

98 Carter, Wardell-Johnson and Archer-Lean, 'Butchulla Perspectives on Dingo Displacement', 199.

lobby for a greater voice in the decision-making process.[99] Overall it has been noted that many of the Butchulla community 'feel that human privilege is encouraged by the structural enrolment of conservation agencies into global capital bureaucracies as part of the colonial architecture'.[100]

5.4.3 *Tourism Values and Commodification*

The economic value of tourism on the Fraser Coast (including K'gari) is thought to be nearly $425 million per year.[101] Tourists on K'gari are thus given special status when it comes to human–wildlife conflict decision-making.

Tourism is prioritised by both local management and international law. As noted by Gillespie, 'tourism is one of the economic powerhouses of the modern global economy'[102] and so plays a large role in environmental/economic decision-making. Environmental and nature-based tourism continues to grow worldwide,[103] encouraged both by States and international institutions. Gillespie details the role of the Global Environment Facility (GEF) in encouraging nature tourism growth and explains that the GEF had 76 projects containing eco-tourism components, encompassing 542 protected areas worldwide.[104] In 2003, it was estimated that the tourism value of Australia's top eight national parks was over $2 billion per year.

The natural result of this is that where tourism is important to the economy, tourists are placed on the top of the hierarchy and thus their perceived autonomy is deemed to be of higher importance than other stakeholders within the conflict. The promotion of tourism to the island is a prime example of autonomy being prioritised over vulnerability (human, dingo and the environment). By way of example, a result of World Heritage listing under the WHC is that the local economy becomes one primarily concentrated on

99 Carlie Walker, 'Butchulla: "Govt Keeping Us at Arm's Length on Dingo Policy"', *Fraser Coast Chronicle*, 21 April 2019. Available at: www.couriermail.com.au/news/queensland/fraser-coast/butchulla-govt-keeping-us-at-arms-length-on-dingo-policy/news-story/7854032bd71384e060f5d6452ad08fc1 (last accessed 16 February 2022).

100 Carter, Wardell-Johnson and Archer-Lean, 'Butchulla Perspectives on Dingo Displacement', 203.

101 Fraser Coast Tourism & Events, 'Near-Record Number of Visitors Push Spending to Highest Levels' (9 January 2019, Media release). Available at: www.fcte.com.au/Media/Media-Releases/Post/1447/Near-record-number-of-visitors-push-spending-to-highest-levels (last accessed 16 February 2022).

102 Alexander Gillespie, 'An Introduction to Ethical Considerations in International Environmental Law', in Malgosia Fitzmaurice, David M. Ong and Panos Merkouris (eds.), *Research Handbook on International Environmental Law* (Edward Elgar, 2010) 117–37, 126.

103 Gillespie, 'Introduction to Ethical Considerations'.

104 Gillespie, 'Introduction to Ethical Considerations'.

nature-based tourism. UNESCO itself acknowledges this, suggesting that WHC can affect the socio-economics of listed sites, with tourism being the primary example.[105]

A tourism-based economy is not in itself destructive and is certainly preferable to the logging and sand-mining economies that existed on K'gari before it was given World Heritage status. That said, the sustainability of such large visitor numbers in a relatively small area has been repeatedly questioned,[106] including by the Queensland Government,[107] managers on the island and scientists.[108] Further, the 2013 management plan states the island 'is a popular international tourist destination and as visitor numbers increase, the risk to human safety resulting from human–dingo interactions also increases'.[109] Also, the ecological effects of such a high number of annual visitors extend far beyond the impact on dingoes.[110] Yet, serious consideration has not been given to reducing tourist numbers or increasing fees, even when research suggests that visitors are willing to sacrifice some access for improved environmental outcomes and a reduction in crowding.[111] Such suggestions have been specifically rejected by decision-makers and noted within the management plans. The 2001 Management Plan suggested controlling or limiting visitor numbers in particular locations at specific times, such as 'critical periods in dingo biology'.[112] It was suggested that the possibility of limiting tourist numbers should be investigated in consultation with stakeholders, including tour operators.[113] Any intervention to restrict or even measure tourist numbers

105 UNESCO, 'Socio-economic Impacts of World Heritage Listing'. Available at: whc.unesco.org/en/socio-economic-impacts (last accessed 14 February 2022). In fact, UNESCO has a World Heritage and Sustainable Tourism Programme that works to facilitate the management and development of sustainable tourism at World Heritage sites. Available at: https://whc.unesco.org/en/tourism/ (last accessed 14 February 2022).

106 See, for example, Wade Hadwen et al., *Effects of Tourism on Fraser Island's Dune Lakes* (CRC for Sustainable Tourism, 2005); Wade Hadwen and Angela Arthington, *Where Do They Go? Predicting Visitation Intensity at Focal Tourist Sites within Protected Areas* (CRC for Sustainable Tourism, 2008); Christopher M. Fleming, *Rationing Access to Protected Natural Areas: A Case Study*, Discussion Papers, Griffith Business School, Griffith University (2011).

107 The Great Sandy Region Management Plan states that 'existing and predicted use levels exceed the capacity of some visitor destinations at peak times only'; Queensland Parks and Wildlife Service, *Great Sandy Region Management Plan 1994* (Queensland Government, Environmental Protection Agency, September 2005) 84.

108 Wardell-Johnson, Archer-Lean and Carter, 'Dingo Singing'.

109 Department of Environment and Heritage Protection, *Fraser Island Dingo Conservation and Risk Management Strategy*, 4.

110 See for example Wardell-Johnson, 'Future of an Icon', 97.

111 Fleming, *Rationing Access to Protected Natural Areas*.

112 Queensland Parks and Wildlife Service, *Fraser Island Dingo Management Strategy*, 9–10.

113 Queensland Parks and Wildlife Service, *Fraser Island Dingo Management Strategy*, 11.

was rejected by the drafters of the 2013 management policy as 'unnecessarily increasing red tape rather than directly benefit(ing) dingo conservation and risk management'.[114] I do note though that, in the months before publishing this book, the QPWS had shut down campsites where dingoes were whelping. How this decision fits into the larger suggestion of permanently restricting tourist numbers remains to be seen.

The prioritisation of the tourist dollar encourages commodification of the 'natural status' of the island, including its dingo inhabitants. There is little doubt that dingoes are commodified as part of the tourist attraction. They are pictured in most tourist brochures[115] and there is even a tourist company specifically for K'gari called 'Cool Dingos'.[116]

But where does the value of the commodification lie? There is a lack of any substantial visitor fees and it has been suggested that lack of funding related to small visitor fees is one of the reasons the draft management plan took so long to finalise.[117] So although the State and QPWS are not directly benefitting to a great extent, the value in tourism lies within the dollars spent by the tourists overall and the business and employment numbers created for and supported by the industry both on K'gari and in the surrounding areas. That said, the total dollar amount spent annually by tourists on K'gari is not clear, with estimates only encompassing domestic visitors, who account for only one-half of all annual visitors.[118] In any event, the tourism industry itself is benefiting primarily from the commodification and indeed propelling it, rather than the State. This is seen when the industry features the dingo so heavily in their promotional material and continues to encourage dingoes to tourist hot-spots.[119] However, as noted by Burns and Howard, the promotion of positive experiences between tourists and dingoes is inconsistent with the current dingo management policy.[120] Yet, the policies continue, as does the influx of tourism, meaning that the policy is ineffective. Thereby, the autonomy of the State government and their ability to make decisions separate from the tourism industry deserves to be questioned.

[114] Department of Environment and Heritage Protection, *Fraser Island Dingo Conservation and Risk Management Strategy*, 5.

[115] Brown, Baldwin and Chandler, 'Butchulla Cultural Heritage Values'.

[116] See Cool Dingo Tours. Available at: www.cooldingotour.com (last accessed 14 February 2022).

[117] Georgette Leah Burns and Peter James Howard, 'When Wildlife Tourism Goes Wrong: A Case Study of Stakeholder and Management Issues Regarding Dingoes on Fraser Island, Australia' (2003) 24(6) *Tourism Management* 699–712.

[118] See Wardell-Johnson, 'Future of an Icon', 97.

[119] Brown, Baldwin and Chandler, 'Butchulla Cultural Heritage Values'.

[120] Burns and Howard, 'When Wildlife Tourism Goes Wrong', 699–700.

5.4.4 *Sequestration of Institutional Vulnerability*

State governance authorities, political bodies, universities, law and science are institutions that work together to promote autonomy within this conflict scenario. Yet, they are often posited as autonomous from each other in their work, coming together at a crucial juncture to contribute findings and reach a governance output. For example, the institution of science is seen as being factually and empirically driven and so autonomous to outside influence. In reality, there are many instances where the institution of science is vulnerable to other institutions and societal influence, as discussed in Chapter 4.[121] Conservation science is not immune to this discourse. The production of scientific data in the area of conservation is hardly ever neutral, due to larger societal interests and the interests of the researcher themselves.[122] Conservation science is something that is being questioned when it comes to its underlying conservation ethic, and the premise that it is the whole of the ecosystem that gets hierarchical priority.[123] Also, the science itself is selectively understood and promoted by different groups to promote their value-based demands.[124]

This is particularly evident in the context of this conflict within the group of ecologists and conservation biologists that study the dingo populations on K'gari. Of important note, there is no solid agreement on the effectiveness of culls in managing the population or that culls do not adversely affect the population dynamics of the dingoes on the island.[125] Researchers also disagree on the cause of conflict and dingo aggressions, which has direct consequences for the legitimacy of the policies.[126] They even disagree on the proper

[121] See Section 5.4.2.

[122] One example is the ideological differences between varying groups of conservation scientists surrounding animal welfare and intrinsic value. See Arian D. Wallach et al., 'Summoning Compassion to Address the Challenges of Conservation: Compassionate Conservation' (2018) 32(6) *Conservation Biology* 1255; Meera Anna Oommen et al., 'The Fatal Flaws of Compassionate Conservation' (2019) 33(4) *Conservation Biology* 784.

[123] Emily C. Chamberlain, Murray B. Rutherford and Michael L. Gibeau, 'Human Perspectives and Conservation of Grizzly Bears in Banff National Park, Canada' (2012) 26(3) *Conservation Biology* 420, 428–29.

[124] Chamberlain, Rutherford and Gibeau, 'Human Perspectives and Conservation', 429–30.

[125] For example. compare Allen et al., 'Balancing Dingo Conservation', with O'Neill et al., 'Managing Dingoes on Fraser Island', and B. P. Smith and R. G. Appleby, 'Promoting Human–Dingo Co-existence in Australia: Moving Towards More Innovative Methods of Protecting Livestock Rather than Killing Dingoes (*Canis dingo*)' (2018) 45(1) *Wildlife Research* 1.

[126] R. Appleby, 'Dingo–Human Conflict: Attacks on Humans', in B. Smith (ed.), *The Dingo Debate: Origins, Behaviour and Conservation* (CSIRO Publishing, 2015) 103–22; O'Neill et al., 'Managing Dingoes on Fraser Island'.

scientific name for the dingo.[127] This is an example of the vulnerability of the institution of science itself and the way it is used and is an additional reason why science *alone* is not a sufficient basis for a conflict policy. An autonomous institution would consider all available evidence and resolve any conflicts within the premise of scientific rules. Given that a large proportion of alternative evidence was not mentioned in the policy documents, the vulnerability of the policy process and the science behind it ought to be explored.

Although the science itself is no doubt consistent with the conservation ethic of the researchers, the greater problem seems to be the relational pull between those scientists and organisations and the State governments who drafted and implemented the dingo policies. Of course, the State is vulnerable to a great many interests, stakeholders and particular discourses and to lobbying from the industry even when it is not in their own or public interest. For example, there are compellable reasons for fewer tourists; something that would be in the interests of a responsive State. There would be less need to employ additional rangers and improve public tourist facilities. The State hides its vulnerability to outside influence by promoting its reliance on science; how can the State be influenced by lobbies and industry influence when the policy is firmly supported by science? The State appears to have been vulnerable to the political influence of the economics of the tourist industry and as such has ingrained that vulnerability in the policy document itself. As a result, the balancing of embodied vulnerabilities is not undertaken neutrally.

5.5 A VULNERABILITY GOVERNANCE FRAMEWORK

What does this case study tell us about the larger phenomenon of human–wildlife conflict? First, it appears the conflict itself is still too narrowly defined. A large part of the conflict revolves around the commercial utilisation of the 'naturalness' of the World Heritage area, with dingoes included as an integral part of that. Further, the vulnerability of the Island itself has been divorced from the legal listing process; a process that appears to be autonomous from the broader relationship that it has with conservation and sustainable tourism. In this section, I provide some starting points to improve the legal framework.

5.5.1 *Highlighting Vulnerability*

For a law to be based on vulnerability, it must highlight vulnerability, address respective vulnerabilities and seek to increase resilience. First, the policy must

[127] Dyani Lewis, 'An Identity Crisis for the Australian Dingo', UNDark (12 August 2019). Available at: https://undark.org/article/identity-crisis-australian-dingo/ (last accessed 14 February 2022).

outline who and what is vulnerable, including where the vulnerabilities lie and how they are considered by law. In this vein, consideration needs to be given to the people (sub-groups of tourists, locals, Butchulla people, employees), the dingoes, the greater island environment, the industry and business associated with the tourists and the government bodies responsible for managing the conflict and making decisions surrounding the conservation of the island. All these individuals, groups and bodies have inherent vulnerability, either embodied, embedded or both.

There are several vulnerabilities considered in the policy and that is certainly positive and representative of the detail and planning that has gone into the creation of the policy and the review process. The embodied vulnerability of the people visiting or associated with the island is clear. For example, the third objective of the 2013 policy is to minimise the risk posed to people by dingoes.[128] However, as explained in Chapter 2, vulnerability inherent in the human condition goes well beyond our embodied vulnerability. The embedded vulnerability of individual people and groups is also evident in the manifestation of the conflict, but it is not clear in the policy. By way of example, people are vulnerable to decisions taken by the Queensland government and QPWS, past, present and future, and the effect they have had or will have on dingo populations and behaviour. The resilience of individuals and groups though, like resilience in any given situation, is context-dependent. At the least, express notation of the particular vulnerability of tourists staying outside of resorts and fenced camping areas is required.

The dingoes have a vulnerability that is only moderately acknowledged in the laws and policies. Their vulnerability to extinction is noted[129] and this is consistent with the conservation ethic evident in the environmental laws and policies in general. Yet the laws and policies separate dingoes from people as they are viewed as autonomous to people, without being given any individual agency. Dingoes as 'agents' is not considered in governance strategies and public communications.[130] Nor is wildlife agency given any credence within the national and international wildlife laws. The agency to be associated with the individual animals is not related to their choices in attacking or injuring a person, but instead their choices to have an existence beside people. Several

[128] Department of Environment and Heritage Protection, *Fraser Island Dingo Conservation and Risk Management Strategy*.

[129] The first objective of the 2013 policy is to 'ensure the conservation and preservation of a sustainable wild dingo population'; Department of Environment and Heritage Protection, *Fraser Island Dingo Conservation and Risk Management Strategy*.

[130] 'Agency' in this sense refers to the ability to act independently and make free choices.

papers discuss this type of agency.[131] Healy states that it is important to distinguish the habituation perspective from a relational one: 'Whereas the "matter of fact" habituation perspective's behavioural focus stresses specific dingo responses to specific human stimuli, the relational concern is rather with a "change in the terms of engagement" between people and dingoes.'[132]

The argument is that the dingoes themselves are responding to a change in terms of engagement and rebelling against it. Some of the Butchulla people also consider that the dingoes rebel against the naturalisation policy and 'follows his own law, asserting its sovereignty and agency'.[133] This is relevant to an eco-vulnerability analysis and assigning the dingo vulnerability, not merely linking it to ours.

The environmental vulnerability goes well beyond the threat level experienced by the species and that consideration has not been made clear in the policy. Although the policy does note that dingoes are an 'apex predator' that keeps the natural system in balance,[134] the vulnerability of the ecosystem to the removal of dingoes is not considered.

Finally, the eco-vulnerability thesis also demands that the link between the inherent vulnerabilities of people, the dingoes and the greater environment be expressed clearly in the policy. Any human–wildlife conflict policy needs to begin with a statement outlining the overarching relationships that are required to maintain our status on the planet, in order to start with an appropriately neutral base. That is to say, neither anthropocentric concerns nor species/environmental concerns are placed at the top of the hierarchy within the policy but, instead, the relationship between the two is given centre stage to allow for consideration of vulnerabilities on an equal footing. This is necessary as we know that starting with a particular values position can antagonise stakeholders and increase stakeholder conflict before any human–wildlife conflict has even occurred.

5.5.2 *Collaboration*

Collaboration between the state and stakeholders is something that has certainly progressed between the 2001 to 2013 management policies. This is

[131] See, for example, Healy, 'Deadly Dingoes'; Carter, Wardell-Johnson and Archer-Lean, 'Butchulla Perspectives on Dingo Displacement'; and Wardell-Johnson, Archer-Lean and Carter, 'Dingo Singing'.

[132] Healy, 'Deadly Dingoes', 454.

[133] Carter, Wardell-Johnson and Archer-Lean, 'Butchulla Perspectives on Dingo Displacement', 198.

[134] Department of Environment and Heritage Protection, *Fraser Island Dingo Conservation and Risk Management Strategy*, 2.

demonstrated first and foremost by the way in which the policies were created. The 2001 policy contained no mention of alternative stakeholder viewpoints, although public submissions were taken, suggesting that process was public participation lip service and not true collaboration. In contrast, the 2013 policy started with a review process that called for greater collaboration and transparency.[135] The review itself was conducted by independent experts outside of the governance realm of QPWS and was overseen by an external Review Steering Committee.[136] Further, the 2013 policy states that the 'establishment and maintenance of productive partnerships across a variety of stakeholders including the three levels of government, Traditional Owners, local community, business operators, non-government organisations, research agencies and universities to facilitate existing and new initiatives was considered very important to the success of all aspects of the strategy'.[137] Further, the strategy lists all those who have an interest or involvement in the governance of dingoes but states that none of them specifically holistically focus on dingo governance.[138] That is to say, they are all advocacy groups for their particular ethic and are not cross-cutting. To address this issue, it was recommended that an annual collaborative meeting be established through one of the already established advisory networks, to foster productive relationships, strengthen partnerships and progress the approach outlined in the strategy.[139] This collaborative meeting was convened in 2014, although had not occurred since then until 2019 when the Queensland Government sought to review the policy in light of the spate of incidents that occurred early in that year.[140]

The need to engage stakeholders is represented in the relevant environmental legislation. Queensland's *Nature Conservation Act*, which gives power to QPWS to manage the island, states that the Act 'is to be administered, as far as practicable, in consultation with, and having regard to the views and interests of, landholders and interested groups and persons, including Aborigines and Torres Strait Islanders'.[141] The *Recreation Areas Management*

[135] See B. Allen et al., *Fraser Island Dingo Management Strategy Review – Final Report*, Report to Department of Environment and Heritage Protection (December 2012).

[136] Possingham et al., *Review Steering Committee Report*.

[137] Department of Environment and Heritage Protection, *Fraser Island Dingo Conservation and Risk Management Strategy*, 5.

[138] Department of Environment and Heritage Protection, *Fraser Island Dingo Conservation and Risk Management Strategy*, 17.

[139] Department of Environment and Heritage Protection, *Fraser Island Dingo Conservation and Risk Management Strategy*, 17.

[140] See Wildlife Preservation Society of Queensland, 'Fraser Island Dingo Conservation and Risk Management Strategy – April 2014'. Available at: https://wildlife.org.au/fraser-island-dingo-conservation-and-risk-management-strategy-april-2014/ (last accessed 14 February 2022).

[141] *Nature Conservation Act 1992* (Queensland), s 6.

Act requires stakeholder notice and invitation of submissions with respect to any draft management plan.[142] The objectives of the national *Environmental Protection and Biodiversity Conservation Act* include cooperative process to environmental responsibilities and promotion of Indigenous roles and traditional knowledge.[143]

However, none of these legislative requirements detail anything more than a basic participation process and certainly do not require extensive collaboration or devolution of decision-making. Amendments are required to insert a more specific collaborative process at all stages of management and institutionalise proper collaboration to make the State responsive to all the relevant vulnerabilities detailed in Section 5.5.1 and throughout this chapter .

On K'gari the collaborative process remains problematic and not properly entrenched. This is evident by the many requests of the Butchulla people to be more heavily involved in the governance process and their ongoing grievances concerning dingo treatment. For example, submissions by Marie-Louise Sarjeant, a prominent Indigenous elder, suggest that the local Indigenous community are ignored and their cultural rights are eroded through mismanagement of the dingo population on K'gari.[144] The most recent Ministerial statement indicates that collaboration with the Butchulla will increase, suggesting that previous attempts at collaboration have not been enough.[145] Although the policy now is very clear about the need for collaboration, the institutional structures and budgeting have not been created to allow that to happen over the long-term.

There appears to be a lack of any real devolution of power to the locals and collaborative groups. For example, the 2001 FIDMS discusses collaborative efforts as inviting groups to support the already determined strategies and thereafter engaging in regular consultation regarding the implementation of those strategies.[146] This is certainly not reflective of the level of collaboration and devolution necessary to assist in the resolution of the stakeholder conflicts associated with human–wildlife conflict discussed in Chapter 3. There was no active role in the decision-making process, with no power to decide the process before implementation. This does not appear to have been improved

[142] *Recreation Areas Management Act 2006* (Qld), s 19(2)(b).

[143] *Environment Protection and Biodiversity Conservation Act 1999* (Cth), s 3(1)(d)–(g).

[144] Sarjeant, *Submission*, 2.

[145] Minister for Environment and the Great Barrier Reef, 'Government Announces New Measures to Promote Safety on K'gari'.

[146] Queensland Parks and Wildlife Service, *Fraser Island Dingo Management Strategy – Review*, 9.

with the later policies in 2006 and 2013, although the range of stakeholders has been better defined. There remains a lack of any real decision-making power.

It is also problematic that there remains a lack of clear transparency concerning specific actions taken. For example, what is the outcome of the consultative meetings discussed in the 2013 policy? How many dingoes continue to be culled? How many negative interactions are reported annually? What are the outcomes and results of the Fraser Island World Heritage Scientific Committee? A legislative need to increase transparency is required.

5.5.3 *Equality/Diversity*

The Butchulla people were legally recognised as the native title owners of K'gari in 2014.[147] Yet, there continues to be a lack of adequate representation by the K'gari people in the dingo decision-making process and a lack of diversity generally in approaches to decision-making.

Having said that, the policy is not entirely negative. Positive steps have been taken to ensure an appropriate level of diversity within the interest groups, including the island's rangers. This includes the creation and participation of the Fraser Island Natural Integrity Alliance (FINIA), a collaboration of government agencies and non-government groups, formed to protect the natural values of Fraser Island. The Butchulla people are one member group in this alliance, with representation from each Butchulla clan group.[148] Also included in the alliance are Conservation Volunteers Australia, the local council and Queensland Government, Fraser Island Defenders Organisation and the University of the Sunshine Coast. FINIA has an influence on the governance of the island but has no legal right to intervene in it.[149]

However, further steps are required. It is important to start at the top of the governance process and recognise the cultural significance of K'gari within the World Heritage Listing. There was some Indigenous input during the initial national consultation process concerning the possibility of World Heritage listing. Initially, there were three advisory committees – an Indigenous, a Community and a Scientific Committee. The Indigenous Committee was incorporated with the Community committee and so did

147 PBC, 'Butchulla Aboriginal Corporation RNTBC'. Available at: www.nativetitle.org.au/find/pbc/8107 (last accessed 14 February 2022).

148 FINIA, 'The Butchulla People'. Available at: https://finia.org.au/the-butchulla-people/ (last accessed 14 February 2022).

149 Carter, Wardell-Johnson and Archer-Lean, 'Butchulla Perspectives on Dingo Displacement', 199.

not have an independent voice[150] and this is reflected in the fact that the cultural heritage of the island was not part of the formal reasoning for the listing.[151] The island should be recognised as both a place of cultural significance for the Butchulla, as well as a place of outstanding natural beauty and significance. Carter suggests that the Butchulla people are fighting for such recognition.[152] Such recognition is a necessary institutional step in the full recognition of the vulnerability of the local Indigenous communities. The inclusion of cultural heritage will provide a further basis for increasing the resilience of the Butchulla, as the implementation of the Convention will need to take that culture into specific consideration.

Further, although the Butchulla have Native Title, that in itself remains problematic in that national and local laws do not yet grant full legal rights. Native Title in Australia provides various rights and interests to Indigenous title holders, according to their 'traditional' laws and customs. That is to say, Native Title rights do not extend beyond the content of traditional laws and so cannot displace existing legal rights or be provided with a type of title that can be legally transferred. In effect, they remain only a 'voice' that can contribute to the debate concerning future developments and policies, but do not have the right to intervene and stop a particular course of action (in this case the Butchulla do not have joint management rights over the island and so, for example, cannot stop the cull of their camp dingoes).

The structural laws surrounding the policy need to be amended to allow the Butchulla people, via the Registered Native Title Body Corporate (RNBTC), a real seat at the collaborative governance table. This might require a challenge to the national Native Title rights or specific devolution of State power in specific situations where it is required, such as under the *Nature Conservation Act*.[153] Further, the importance of the community and their culture needs to be expressed to visitors to the Island. A recent study of the discourse and literature that informs and attracts tourism at K'gari indicates there is a minimal acknowledgement of the Indigenous culture and connection with the Island, and the absence of such a connection in the tourism material acts to continually marginalise Indigenous values.[154] The tourism industry, as an institution, need to formally acknowledge the Indigenous connection and their participation in the governance of the Island.

150 Carter, Wardell-Johnson and Archer-Lean, 'Butchulla Perspectives on Dingo Displacement', 199.
151 Lennon, 'From K'gari to World Heritage'.
152 Carter, 'Displacing Indigenous Cultural Landscapes', 405.
153 *Nature Conservation Act* 1992 (Queensland).
154 Brown, Baldwin and Chandler, 'Butchulla Cultural Heritage Values', 15.

5.5.4 *Emotion and Other Forms of Knowledge*

Allowing a greater voice for Indigenous Australians would bring the benefit of the inclusion of traditional knowledge. Specifically, greater weight would be given to their understanding that dingoes on K'gari have never been 'truly wild'[155] and, as a result, the current naturalisation policy is a fallacy. They know dingoes as 'Wongari' and consider them to be important to the island's cultural, ecological and conservation values.[156]

However, an eco-vulnerability approach would need to recognise not only the traditional knowledge of the Butchulla people but also incorporate the cultural and emotional connection that they and others have with dingoes. Both Indigenous and non-Indigenous residents on or near the Island view the dingoes as pets, 'camp animals' or 'revered symbols of the wild'.[157] Ignoring the cultural and emotional connection between Indigenous people, other members of the community and the dingoes decreases the resilience of all parties, including the dingoes. It increases and perpetuates the historical colonial-type rule wherein a particular discourse is imposed on all parties regardless of their knowledge and consent, which decreases their autonomy and affects their resilience to their specific embedded vulnerability.

Similarly, compassionate emotional reactions to dingo culls and to dingo attacks should not be discounted. The stakeholder conflict is only intensified if appropriate emotional responses are dismissed as being irrelevant or inconsistent with science and/or policy, as discussed in Chapter 3.[158] Such an approach would recognise that, by removing the dingoes, the resilience of the community is decreased.

In this vein, the emotional connection associated with positive dingo encounters ought to be further explored. Most interactions between dingoes and people on the island are thought to be positive. For example, a study was undertaken by Appleby and others of all reported serious dingo encounters over the period 2001–15, which found that '... dingoes rarely seriously injure even the most vulnerable of people, despite the opportunity to do so arising on occasion. Nor do they regularly seriously injure people more generally. In fact, large numbers of encounters, which are probably benign or positive in nature,

[155] Sarjeant, *Submission*, 6.

[156] Jeanie Bell and Amanda Seed, *Dictionary of the Gubbi-Gubbi and Butchulla Languages* (Brisbane, 1994).

[157] Carter, 'Displacing Indigenous Cultural Landscapes', 199.

[158] See Section 3.5.4.

go unreported'.[159] It is clear that this kind of behaviour negatively affects the resilience of the dingoes, as individuals, family packs and as a species. All interactions between dingoes and people on the island have the potential to be interpreted as 'negative' by the people involved, even where the dingo behaviour is innocent or playful. Negative interactions can result in the dingo being 'destroyed'. The emotional connections fostered through positive experience and traditional forms of knowledge are valuable tools that could assist the process towards a positive human–dingo relationship on K'gari.

5.5.5 *Education*

A holistic transformative approach requires an appropriate analysis between institutions. This includes, for example, the role of education and the link between the law and governance policies and the visitor and stakeholder education. Public education is something that has been prioritised in the policies to date and that is reflective of the need for such in the human–wildlife conflict literature discussed in Chapter 3.[160] This included the advent of the 'Be Dingo Smart' awareness campaign in the 2001 policy[161] and has evolved to include increased ranger contact and a social media campaign in the 2013 policy.[162]

However, the educational messaging may require some tweaking to more closely align it with a vulnerability framework and close the gap between individual autonomy and the greater ecological impacts of one's action. Burns, MacBeth and Moore explain the need for a greater vulnerability approach (although note they describe it as an eco-centric approach) and outline several principles that need to be incorporated into the educational process.[163] These include an acknowledgement of the intrinsic value of dingoes, and what they call the 'Avatar' principle (an exciting and alternative term for the vulnerability principle). They define the Avatar principle as an acknowledgement of the interconnectedness of humans and nature that

[159] Appleby et al., 'Human–Dingo Interactions on Fraser Island', 153.

[160] See Section 3.5.5.

[161] This included distribution of brochures, on-site dingo interpretative display boards and information on toilet doors; Queensland Parks and Wildlife Service, *Fraser Island Dingo Management Strategy*, 8.

[162] Department of Environment and Heritage Protection, *Fraser Island Dingo Conservation and Risk Management Strategy*, 13.

[163] Georgette Leah Burns, Jim MacBeth and Susan Moore, 'Should Dingoes Die? Principles for Engaging Ecocentric Ethics in Wildlife Tourism Management' (2011) 10(3) *Journal of Ecotourism* 179, 185.

requires governance of both in a more holistic framework as part of shared ecosystems.[164] This type of acknowledgement needs to be introduced into education and awareness campaigns.

Finally, there is a lack of research concerning the effectiveness of the current awareness campaign and, given visitors continue to act in a way that is contrary to the policy and illegal, there is a strong implication that the education campaign is not as effective as it may otherwise be. Such a call for further research has been made before. Appleby and others recommend further investigations as to why visitors are ignoring or misunderstanding the educational material, such as warnings.[165] This type of sociological research may end up supporting the varying evidence that tourism at such a scale is inconsistent with conservation of the island and protection of the island's dingoes or that safe positive encounters with dingoes should be encouraged.

5.6 CONCLUSION

The primary cause of our ongoing poor relationship with dingoes on K'gari is the continued institutional promotion of liberal autonomy. The autonomy being promoted is not just that of the individual (in this case the tourist primarily) but the institutions that surround the decision-making process.

Within this particular conflict, autonomy has been shaped to fit the dominant paradigm and used as a tool in governance arrangements where it is useful to maintain conceptions of power. Autonomy is used to shape policies around 'naturalness' and separation of people from 'wild' dingoes, as well as being used to justify policies that are not based on equivocal science and contextual histories.

This promotion of autonomy defines the relationship between people and dingoes and K'gari and affects views of the conflict, tourism, the law, and Indigenous voices and the way those things are all connected. Not only do they define our relationship but they affect our ability to build resilience through mechanisms such as collaboration, equality and unity.

[164] Burns et al., 'Should Dingoes Die?'.
[165] Appleby et al., 'Human–Dingo Interactions on Fraser Island', 153.

6

Human–Elephant Conflict in Northern Botswana

6.1 INTRODUCTION

For some time, Botswana has been one of the last strongholds of African Elephant conservation.[1] Botswana has the largest and most sustainable elephant population in Africa, largely due to strong anti-poaching and conservation laws. However, apparent setbacks in conservation laws and policies in 2018 and 2019 have seen a worldwide debate over the governance of elephants and dismay from the conservation community and beyond. In May 2019 the President of Botswana, Mokgweetsi Masisi, reversed the total elephant hunting ban instigated by his predecessor, Ian Khama, in 2014.[2] The lifting of the ban was said to be necessary due to rising human–elephant conflict,[3] although the reality of this has been questioned,[4] especially as the number of

[1] The African elephant is a different species to the smaller Asian elephant. In addition, there are two genetic variations of African elephants – bush and forest elephants: Alfred L. Roca et al., 'Genetic Evidence for Two Species of Elephant in Africa' (2001) 293(5534) *Science* 1473. Asian and African elephants also have different social structures: Shermin de Silva and George Wittemyer, 'A Comparison of Social Organization in Asian Elephants and African Savannah Elephants' (2012) 33(5) *International Journal of Primatology* 1125.

[2] Rachael Bale, 'Botswana Lifts Ban on Elephant Hunting', *National Geographic*, 22 May 2019. Available at: www.nationalgeographic.com/animals/2019/05/botswana-lifts-ban-on-elephant-hunting/ (last accessed 23 March 2021); Robert Hitchcock, Nicholas Winer and Melinda Kelly, 'Hunter-Gatherers, Farmers, and Environmental Degradation in Botswana' (2020) 18(3) *Conservation and Society* 226, 229.

[3] Siobhán O'Grady, 'Botswana Overturns Ban on Elephant Hunting', *The Washington Post* (Washington), 23 May 2019. Available at: www.washingtonpost.com/world/2019/05/23/botswana-overturns-ban-elephant-hunting/?utm_term=.436bdfe621b6 (last accessed 23 March 2021).

[4] See for example the statements of Mike Chase and Cyril Taolo in Tendai Marima, 'In Botswana, Elephant Hunting Divides Opinion', *Al Jazeera News* (Rakops, Gumare Botswana), 6 August 2019. Available at: www.aljazeera.com/indepth/features/botswana-elephant-hunting-divides-opinion-190805214651490.html (last accessed 23 March 2021).

elephants that would have to be killed via way of legal hunting would have to be significant to have any real impact on human–elephant conflict in the country. Also, there is a concern that reinstatement of hunting will lead to an increase in the international ivory trade and a rapid decline of elephant numbers in Botswana,[5] which would have dire effects on the African elephant as a species. This concern is not surprising nor unfounded, given that the ivory trade as an international crime is a very real threat to the ongoing survival of elephant species.[6]

The announcement came off the back of two internationally newsworthy events. First, President Masisi's government had considered hunting elephants and using their meat as pet food.[7] The President had said that he would present the proposal to his cabinet,[8] with commercial utilisation of the elephant carcass thought to be preferable to letting it waste. Second, the charity organisation 'Elephants Without Borders' reported in September 2018 that 87 elephants had been found dead in the World Heritage Region of the Okavango Delta in Botswana, seemingly due to poachers.[9] The numbers were reported as a 'poaching frenzy', the likes of which had not been seen in the area since the hunting of elephants was banned in 2014.[10] Only days later, the claims made by Elephants Without Borders were disputed by scientists and the Government of Botswana.[11] It was pointed out that the scientists associated with the charity had not confirmed the causes of the deaths on the ground, instead only conducting an aerial survey. It was further claimed that the charity organisation had intentionally exaggerated the number to gain financial support and to influence the country's leaders to ensure the hunting ban was not reversed. Further

5 Jason Burke, 'Botswana Condemned for Lifting Ban on Hunting Elephants ', *The Guardian AU*, 23 May 2019. Available at: www.theguardian.com/world/2019/may/23/botswana-lifts-ban-on-hunting-elephants?CMP=share_btn (last accessed 23 March 2021).

6 Keith Lindsay et al., 'The Shared Nature of Africa's Elephants' (2017) 215 *Biological Conservation* 260, 260.

7 'Botswana Unveils Plan to Kill Elephants and Turn Them into Pet Food', *ABC News*, 23 February 2019, www.abc.net.au/news/2019-02-23/botswana-consider-culling-elephants-for-pet-food/10843450 (last accessed 23 March 2021).

8 'Botswana Unveils Plan to Kill Elephants and Turn Them into Pet Food'.

9 Kimon de Greef, 'Scores of Dead Elephants Found in Botswana "Poaching Frenzy"', The New York Times (New York), 4 September 2018. Available at: www.nytimes.com/2018/09/04/world/africa/elephants-botswana-poaching.html?module=inline (last accessed 23 March 2021).

10 de Greef, 'Scores of Dead Elephants'.

11 Kimon de Greef, 'Doubts Mount in Botswana Over Charity's Claim of Elephant "Poaching Frenzy"', The New York Times (New York), 28 September 2018. Available at: www.nytimes.com/2018/09/28/world/africa/botswana-elephants-poaching.html (last accessed 23 March 2021).

research is equivocal as to the cause of the deaths and Elephants Without Borders have not released their data.[12]

This conflict over poaching and conservation is indicative of the very complex and multi-faceted human–elephant relationship in Botswana. These recent developments show that the people–people side of human–elephant conflict is especially complex because of the very real problems posed by elephants, but also because of the domestic politics and international interest in such charismatic megafauna as the elephant. As stated in the *New York Times* '(t)he dispute has also revealed a deeper tension in conservation management, concerning how western advocacy groups can steer debates in developing countries, even without credible evidence'.[13] In this chapter, I will deconstruct the conflict and provide an eco-vulnerability critique, in an attempt to analyse the sociological and institutional influence of laws and policies on attitudes and values to elephants, both within Botswana and beyond. Vulnerability to neo-liberal conservation and politics and the influence of money as a whole is such that it can infiltrate even where there is a concerted effort to retract it. Further, attempts to establish collaborative governance systems do not achieve overall positive results when there is a lack of state devolution of power, and the process is not concentrated on mutual and interlinked vulnerability. This case study is also an important glimpse into Fineman's concept of 'the responsive state', particularly around welfare in areas where human–elephant conflict increases poverty and decreases human resilience.

6.2 HUMAN–ELEPHANT CONFLICT IN NORTHERN BOTSWANA

The Republic of Botswana is a landlocked country in Southern Africa with a dual legal system, combining a Roman–Dutch common law system with customary law.[14] The population of Botswana, of over 1.6 million people, is mainly Tswana. The common language spoken is Setswana, although English remains the official language.[15] The country is designated as an

[12] Hitchcock, Winer and Kelly, 'Hunter-Gatherers', 227.

[13] Hitchcock, Winer and Kelly, 'Hunter-Gatherers', 227.

[14] E. K. Quansah, *Introduction to the Botswana Legal System*, 3rd ed. (Pula Press, 2001).

[15] In Setswana, the official language of Botswana, one person from Botswana is referred to as a 'Motswana', multiple people are referred to as 'Batswana', and the adjective used to describe parts of the national culture is 'Setswana' (e.g., a 'Setswana way of life'). See Clare A. Gupta, 'Elephants, Safety Nets and Agrarian Culture: Understanding Human–Wildlife Conflict and Rural Livelihoods around Chobe National Park, Botswana' (2013) 20(1) *Journal of Political Ecology* 238.

'upper-middle-income country',[16] and Botswana is a wealthy country relative to other states in the area, due in large part to diamond mining.[17] While it is suggested that security and development in Botswana are some of the best across Africa,[18] there are large areas of ongoing and entrenched poverty.[19] Rural poverty and unemployment remain high.[20] In some areas, unemployment is as high as 90 per cent.[21] In 2018, then-President Masisi identified youth unemployment and poverty as the 'twin problems' that needed to be addressed by the state.[22] Poverty levels are particularly high (over 46 per cent) in the region of Ngamiland, which borders the Okavango Delta, and where human–elephant conflict is prevalent.[23] Sources of income in the regional areas of Botswana are mostly tourism, agriculture and subsistence farming.[24] While it is rare for a community to rely solely on hunting and gathering in Botswana today, many communities still rely on game for part of their diet.[25]

Botswana is home to almost 60 per cent of Africa's elephants and around a third of the global elephant population.[26] Although the Great Elephant Census suggested that population levels across the African continent continue to decline by 8 per cent per year,[27] the population in Botswana has not followed this trend, due to the conservation laws in place since 1968.[28] Recent estimates suggest the nationwide population to be more than 130,000, although that number is disputed, with some estimates at well over

[16] Piers Blaikie, 'Is Small Really Beautiful? Community-based Natural Resource Management in Malawi and Botswana' (2006) 34(11) *World Development* 1942, 1943; World Bank, 'The World Bank in Botswana'. Available at: www.worldbank.org/en/country/botswana/overview (last accessed 8 February 2022).

[17] Arnon Bar-On, 'On Elephants, Giraffes, and Social Development' (2006) 41(3) *Community Development Journal* 367, 370.

[18] Bar-On, 'On Elephants, Giraffes, and Social Development', 370.

[19] World Bank, 'The World Bank in Botswana'.

[20] Israel Blackie, 'The Impact of Wildlife Hunting Prohibition on the Rural Livelihoods of Local Communities in Ngamiland and Chobe District Areas, Botswana' (2019) 5(1) *Cogent Social Sciences* 1558716, 3.

[21] J. Salerno et al., 'Living in an Elephant Landscape' (2018) 106(1) *American Scientist* 34.

[22] His Excellency Eric K. Masisi, 5th President of the Republic of Botswana, State of the Nation Address, 5 November 2018, 1.

[23] Statistics Botswana, *Mapping Poverty in Botswana*, World Bank Group (2015). Available at: www.statsbots.org.bw/sites/default/files/publications/POVERTYpercent20Mappingper cent202010_Mayper cent2028per cent202015.pdf, 10 (last accessed 23 March 2021).

[24] Limpopo River Awareness Kit. Available at: www.limpopo.riverawarenesskit.org (last accessed 23 March 2021).

[25] Bar-On, 'On Elephants, Giraffes, and Social Development', 371.

[26] Michael J. Chase et al., 'Continent-Wide Survey Reveals Massive Decline in African Savannah Elephants' (2016) 8 *PeerJ* e2354.

[27] Chase et al., 'Continent-Wide Survey'.

[28] Chase et al., 'Continent-Wide Survey', 18.

200,000.[29] The geography of Botswana, especially Northern Botswana, is an ideal elephant habitat. Northern Botswana includes Ngamiland and the Okavango Delta, the Makgadikgadi Pans, and the world-renowned Chobe National Park. The Okavango Delta is the world's largest seasonal wetland and encompasses a network of seasonal channels and floodplains that empty into the Kalahari Desert.[30] Parts of the Delta also occur in Angola and Namibia.[31] The Okavango Delta is a habitat for about 1,300 identified plant species, 71 fish, 33 amphibians, 64 reptiles, 444 birds and 122 mammals, including the African Elephant. Together, the Okavango Delta and the Chobe area have the highest density of elephants in the world.[32]

However, the home range of most of these elephants is not limited to one area. African elephants can travel far, with some studies suggesting that they can have a home range of 24,000 km and higher.[33] As a result of their dispersal and significant home ranges, it is imperative that habitats are not significantly fragmented and that travel routes and connections are maintained.[34] This necessarily means that multi-state cooperation is required, especially around the Okavango Delta where borders intersect with significant elephant (and other species) habitats.[35]

The primary threat to Botswana's elephants is not dwindling numbers or loss of habitat but conflict with people. More than 70 per cent of Botswana's elephants are found outside of its protected areas and, as a result, they often enter 'human spaces'.[36] This conflict, including illicit poaching, is the greatest threat to the survival of elephants in Botswana. One of the reasons the conflict is such a threat is that it distils and fosters negative emotions, values and

[29] Louise De Waal, 'Confusion over Botswana's Elephant Population', *IOL*, 27 November 2018. Available at: www.iol.co.za/ios/opinion/confusion-over-botswanas-elephant-population-18283610 (last accessed 23 March 2021).

[30] Yurco et al., 'Human–Wildlife Interactions', 1114.

[31] Wildlife and Tourism Ministry of Environment and Botswana Department of Environmental Affairs, Botswana Department of Environmental Affairs, *Okavango Delta Management Plan* (January 2008), 11.

[32] Blackie, 'Impact of Wildlife Hunting Prohibition', 4.

[33] Michael J. Chase, *Home Ranges, Transboundary Movements and Harvest of Elephants in Northern Botswana and Factors Affecting Elephant Distribution and Abundance in the Lower Kwando River Basin* (ProQuest Dissertations Publishing, 2007), ch. 2.

[34] Lindsay et al., 'The Shared Nature of Africa's Elephants', 260.

[35] The legal mechanisms for this cooperation will be discussed in Section 6.3.1.

[36] Julian J. Blanc et al., *African Elephant Status Report 2007: An Update from the African Elephant Database*, IUCN Species Survival Commission, African Elephant Specialist Group, US Fish and Wildlife Service, European Commission (2007).

attitudes towards elephants, in those that live through the conflict regularly.[37] This then means that laws and policies are questioned or ignored as anger and resentment grows and any original conservation ethic is slowly diminished. As the conflict grows, so does this resentment, first at an individual level, then familial, then community and so on, until lawmakers and decision-makers can no longer ignore the voices of the local community. This appears to be the case in Botswana, with locals becoming resentful enough that politicians have used the conflict as a political platform, with the current President having been elected on that platform.[38]

The growing negativity around elephants has meant that there is a perception that the numbers of direct human–elephant conflict are growing. On the other hand, research has found that conflict may actually be reducing and that the local and political perception may be unsubstantiated.[39] In particular, the Eastern Okavango Panhandle is often singled out in attempts to substantiate the claim, an area where 16,000 people share living space with 11,000 elephants.[40] However, even if the evidence suggests that human–elephant conflict in Northern Botswana has not increased, local perceptions continue to differ.[41] This could be because the effects of the conflict are becoming more apparent or the social conflict surrounding the human–elephant conflict is increasing and causing further negative perceptions towards the elephant itself. Pozo and others also suggest that although conflict is reducing, the historical perception and its effects live on.[42]

What is clear is that the effects of human–elephant conflict on local people are many and often severe. The obvious hardships caused by elephants include threats to safety and lack of income due to crop-raiding. Crop loss is the most frequently cited example of elephant damage but they also sometimes damage boreholes, especially in times of drought or seasonal water shortages when humans and elephants are both seeking water sources.[43]

37 Lisa Naughton-Treves and Adrian Treves, 'Socio-Ecological Factors Shaping Local Support for Wildlife: Crop-Raiding by Elephants and Other Wildlife in Africa' in Rosie Woodroffe, Simon Thirgood and Alan Rabinowitz (eds.), *People and Wildlife: Conflict or Coexistence?* (Cambridge University Press, 2005) 253–77.

38 Nick Dall, 'Botswana, Where Elephants are Key Election Stakeholders', *Ozy*, 6 September 2019. Available at: www.ozy.com/fast-forward/botswana-where-elephants-are-key-election-stakeholders/96303/ (last accessed 23 March 2021).

39 R. A. Pozo et al., 'Determining Baselines for Human–Elephant Conflict: A Matter of Time' (2017) 12(6) *PLoS One* e0178840.

40 Pozo et al., 'Determining Baselines for Human–Elephant Conflict'.

41 See, for example, DeMotts and Hoon, 'Whose Elephants?', 842.

42 Pozo et al., 'Determining Baselines for Human–Elephant Conflict', 12.

43 DeMotts and Hoon, 'Whose Elephants?', 842.

Clare Gupta discusses areas where human–elephant conflict has led to an inability to farm and has documented the decline of farming in parts of Northern Botswana for this reason.[44]

Forced relocation from protected areas and elephant corridors is also still occurring in Northern Botswana.[45] Some insist such measures are necessary to ensure the strict protection of elephants.[46] At the most extreme end of conflict outcomes, elephants kill people and there are regular reports in this regard.[47] In 2019, the Government reported that elephants had killed 17 people in only 1 year (unlike on K'gari, the names and histories of these people is not clear from the English-language media, a fact which has its own connotations related to race and dominant hierarchies).[48]

But the complex problem goes much deeper than these evident and measurable threats. The hidden costs of human–elephant conflict are many and varied. The hunting ban has also had hidden impacts, including 'cultural decay'. Interviews with locals suggest that in some instances where subsistence living is more commonplace, the inability to hunt and provide has meant that many young people have nothing to do, adding to the unemployment and poverty levels.[49] In particular, the San people lost their social identity and aspects of their cultural heritage which were previously associated with hunting and the consumption of game meat.[50] Mayberry's interview participants discussed the impact of fear on free movement, impacted activities like visiting relatives, collecting firewood and water and undertaking social engagements.[51] These aspects of the conflict have a negative emotional effect that goes beyond the physical elephant threat. That emotional effect is significant: Mayberry's research found that 34 per cent of locals were not 'living good lives' as a result of elephants, specifically due to reduced feelings of safety and lost crops. Researchers cite locals who detail chronic fears and worries that

44 Gupta, 'Elephants, Safety Nets and Agrarian Culture', 244–45.

45 Hitchcock, Winer and Kelly, 'Hunter-Gatherers', 230.

46 See for example Salerno et al., 'Living in an Elephant Landscape'; Kent D. Messer, 'Protecting Endangered Species: When are Shoot-on-Sight Policies the Only Viable Option to Stop Poaching?' (2010) 69(12) *Ecological Economics* 2334.

47 Keamogetse Letsholo, 'Botswana – Man Trampled to Death by Elephant', *Africa Sustainable Conservation News* (Kasane), 5 August 2019. Available at: https://africasustainableconservation.com/2019/08/08/botswana-man-trampled-to-death-by-elephant/ (last accessed 23 March 2021); 'Elephant Kills Woman in Botswana', *Africa Geographic*, 18 April 2018. Available at: https://africageographic.com/blog/elephant-kills-woman-botswana/ (last accessed 23 March 2021).

48 Hitchcock, Winer and Kelly, 'Hunter-Gatherers', 234.

49 Blackie, 'Impact of Wildlife Hunting Prohibition', 9.

50 Blackie, 'Impact of Wildlife Hunting Prohibition', 9.

51 Mayberry, Hovorka and Evans, 'Well-Being Impacts of Human–Elephant Conflict in Khumaga, Botswana', 280.

elephants would raid crops and approach their property.[52] These worries and anxieties make human–elephant conflict a growing mental health concern in regional areas. As stated by DeMotts and Hoon: 'there is no accounting for the strain of waiting for devastation'.[53]

Traditional human–elephant conflict governance approaches in the area include separation via fencing, disturbance and chasing of elephants, translocation, bee-hives and chilli bombs.[54] These methods are of limited effect. Research suggests that bull elephants learn how to navigate fences and teach other elephants how to do the same.[55] Even after translocation, the culprit elephants teach elephants in their new area how to break and traverse fences.[56] Bee-hives and chilli bombs are effective temporarily until elephants learn to avoid them or become used to them.[57] Other policy measures, such as compensation programs and benefit programs, have been equally problematic. Something beyond the traditional methods is needed if the human–elephant relationship is to improve.

Human–elephant conflict in Botswana is also closely tied to the debate on the morality and appropriateness of a trophy and sport hunting industry in the country. Bans on hunting have been implemented at various stages in recent decades, and the most recent, in 2014, was stated to be because of a decline in population levels of several wildlife species,[58] and a general concern for the welfare of elephants abroad. This is despite evidence that elephant numbers had increased by 297 per cent between 1992 and 2012 in Botswana.[59] The effect of the ban on hunting has also been heavily debated. A recent study undertaken by Israel Blackie suggests that the ban negatively impacted on

52 Mayberry, Hovorka and Evans, 'Well-Being Impacts of Human–Elephant Conflict in Khumaga, Botswana'; Oitshepile MmaB Modise et al, 'Toward Sustainable Conservation and Management of Human–Wildlife Interactions in the Mmadinare Region of Botswana: Villagers' Perceptions on Challenges and Prospects' (2018) 12(2) *Human–Wildlife Interactions* 220.

53 DeMotts and Hoon, 'Whose Elephants?', 843.

54 Richard Hoare, 'Lessons From 20 Years of Human–Elephant Conflict Mitigation in Africa' (2015) 20(4) *Human Dimensions of Wildlife* 289, 289–90.

55 Hoare, 'Lessons From 20 Years'; Bridget Martin, *Survival or Extinction? How to Save Elephants and Rhinos* (Springer, 2019) 517–23.

56 Lauren A. Evans and William M. Adams, 'Elephants as Actors in the Political Ecology of Human–Elephant Conflict' (2018) 43(4) *Transactions of the Institute of British Geographers* 630, 640.

57 Evans and Adams, 'Elephants as Actors'; Hoare, 'Lessons From 20 Years'.

58 Blackie, 'Impact of Wildlife Hunting Prohibition'.

59 Department of Wildlife and National Parks, *Aerial Census of Animals in Botswana: 2012 Dry Season* (DWNP, 2012).

rural livelihoods, especially around employment and income.[60] A perceived rise in human–elephant conflict was also stated to be behind the most recent policy announcement to lift the ban. The reality of this as a reason is contentious, as it is unclear how trophy hunting will decrease human–wildlife conflict. Overall, the relationship between hunting, social welfare and human–elephant conflict has played heavily on the minds of many within Botswana.

6.3 THE LEGAL POSITION, AUTONOMY AND THE DOMINANT PARADIGM

The legal regime surrounding the governance of elephants and human–elephant conflict is complex and involves many actors and states. To give a holistic account of the legal regime it is necessary to understand the relationships it fosters, the autonomy it promotes, and the resilience it creates.

6.3.1 *International Law*

The Okavango Delta was listed as a Ramsar Wetland site in 1997 and was declared a World Heritage site in 2014. Hachileka writes that 'the Ramsar Convention promotes and supports the wildlife conservation policy of Botswana positively and effectively'.[61] This might be so as both prioritise the 'wise use' of natural resources within the Delta.[62] However, paradigms of wildlife governance that prioritise use and value are problematic for a variety of reasons that were discussed in Chapter 4, and specifically from a vulnerability point of view. Notwithstanding, the sustainable or wise use of resources continues to be promoted specifically because of the poverty of local people.[63]

60 Blackie, 'Impact of Wildlife Hunting Prohibition'.

61 E. Hachileka, 'Sustainability of Wildlife Utilisation in the Chobe District, Botswana' (2003) 85 (1) *South African Geographical Journal/Suid-Afrikaanse Geografiese Tydskrif* 50, 54.

62 See *Convention on Wetlands of International Importance especially as Waterfowl Habitat*, opened for signature 2 Feburary 1971, 11 ILM 963 (entered into force 21 December 1975), Art 3, and; Ministry of Environment, Wildlife and Tourism, Republic of Botswana, (2013) *Wildlife Policy*, Government Paper 2013; *Wildlife Conservation and National Parks Act (Botswana)* No.28 of 1992.

63 See, for example, Emily Hutchens, 'The Law Never Forgets: An Analysis of the Elephant Poaching Crisis, Failed Policies, and Potential Solutions' (2014) 31(4) *Wisconsin International Law Journal* 934; Sekondeko Ronnie Noga et al., "Wildlife Officials Only Care About Animals': Farmers' Perceptions of a Ministry-Based Extension Delivery System in Mitigating Human–Wildlife Conflicts in the Okavango Delta, Botswana' (2018) 61 *Journal of Rural Studies* 216.

The embedded vulnerability of the people in Northern Botswana is decidedly different to that of the people on K'gari involved in the human–dingo conflict, and it is a common argument that the level of local poverty engenders a different emphasis on state responsiveness. That is to say, a responsive state should promote the use of wildlife as a means of promoting economic development and increasing human resilience to vulnerability. However, such an argument, in reality, is based on the promotion of autonomy, over concerns of vulnerability. As discussed in Chapter 2, it is often a fallacy to state that economic development equates to a higher quality of living.[64] Responding to vulnerability does not require economic growth of a state, county or locality alone, but a response to the physical, emotional, social *and* economic needs of local people. All are interlinked so that one cannot be prioritised over the others. Yet the concepts of use and development, sustainable or otherwise, prioritise economic needs over others, suggesting that the other needs will be met once economic growth has been attained.

The premise of the Convention on the International Trade of Endangered Species (CITES) is also that of sustainable use, via regulation of international wildlife commerce. Species are listed in appendices based on their 'threatened' categorisation. Species listed in Appendix I are given the highest level of protection, and must be 'threatened with extinction'.[65] Trade is only allowed when it does not threaten the survival of the species and when the purpose of the trade is not primarily commercial.[66] Appendix II includes 'all species which although not necessarily now threatened with extinction may become so unless trade in specimens of such species is subject to strict regulation to avoid utilization incompatible with their survival'.[67] Trade is allowed only when it will not be detrimental to the species.[68] Finally, Appendix III includes any species which a state party has identified as being subject to conservation regulation under domestic laws and said state requires the cooperation of other state parties to control trade.[69]

African elephants have been 'split-listed' between Appendices I and II since 1997, based on national and regional populations. Botswana's population is listed under Appendix II, as are the populations in Namibia, South Africa and

64 See Section 2.4.1.

65 *Convention on International Trade in Endangered Species of Wild Fauna and Flora*, opened for signature 3 March 1973, 993 UNTS 234 (entered into force 1 July 1975), Art II(1).

66 Art III(3).

67 Art II(2).

68 IArt IV(2).

69 Art II(3).

Zimbabwe.[70] Elephants in every other African state are listed under Appendix I, as are all Asian Elephants.[71] Although there have been pushes to have the species united under an Appendix I listing, human–elephant conflict has been cited as a primary reason for not doing so.[72] This is said to be related to the economic cost to those at the forefront of human–elephant conflict and the need for elephants to 'pay their way' and compensate those losses, given that profits from the trade of wildlife components are one way for that to happen. Again though, the basis for this argument is the promotion of liberal autonomy, wherein it is considered that the locals will be capable of taking care of themselves and the conflict will resolve itself if only they had more money. This is a reflection of the conflict of values on which the Convention is based, as discussed in Chapter 4.[73] In this instance, the law imagines 'trade' in wildlife, which it regulates, while having a blind spot to the conflict which lies at the base of trade. Thereafter, the autonomy of locals is reduced to the potential for them to derive economic profit, while conflict-related vulnerability at all levels is ignored. As discussed in Section 6.2, the economic burden is only one facet of a very multi-dimensional conflict. CITES is not equipped to deal with these, because of its economic paradigm, but for other reasons as well.

First, the Convention does not seek to deal with ground-level conflict but instead imposes a top-down economic approach that was never going to be completely absorbed at the local level willingly, especially when one elephant kill can equal a year's worth of wages for poachers.[74] Second, CITES is not equipped to deal with the social conflict surrounding elephant governance and conflict, even at an international level. Instead, it appears to have increased social conflict at the international level, by ignoring the ecological reality of the species and focusing on political boundaries and national governance programs. When it comes to the governance of human–wildlife conflict, the state is an unrealistic autonomous agent. That is to say, the State cannot address conflict alone, and any expectation for them to do so is

[70] CITES. Available at: https://cites.org/eng/news/statement/international_trade_in_live_elephants (last accessed 23 March 2021). Although note that the listing in Botswana, Zimbabwe and Namibia was downgraded from Appendix I in June 1997, as elephant populations started to explode and there were concerns over their impact on the surrounding ecosystems; Hachileka, 'Sustainability of Wildlife Utilisation', 54.

[71] *Convention on International Trade in Endangered Species of Wild Fauna and Flora.*

[72] Lindsay et al., 'The Shared Nature of Africa's Elephants', 262.

[73] See Section 4.3.1.

[74] Messer, 'Protecting Endangered Species'.

unrealistic. Lindsay and others offer such an argument when discussing the efficacy of CITES:

> … some powerful parties within CITES remain preoccupied with sovereignty over wildlife within national borders and within nations' bilateral trading exchanges without reference to obligations to neighbours with whom populations of elephants and other species are shared. Through the influence of these groupings, the CITES process as a whole has yet to accept the 'big picture' transboundary thinking central to MEAs such as the Convention on Migratory Species …[75]

The split listing of elephants on the continent is evidence of the tension created by the nature of international regulation. The notion of state autonomy, in that states can create laws and governance practices independent of each other, does not fit the life history of an elephant herd and decreases their resilience to vulnerability through conflict.

Regional agreements are one potential way of encompassing the big picture thinking noted by Lindsay and others. Regional agreements are relevant in the Okavango Delta and Northern Botswana, particularly since Trans-Frontier Conservation Areas have been receiving international development assistance from high-income states such as the United States, Germany and the European Union.[76] In particular, the *Kavango-Zambezi Treaty* is a multilateral agreement between Angola, Botswana, Namibia, Zambia and Zimbabwe that establishes the Kavango-Zambezi Transfrontier Conservation Area (KAZA TFCA).[77] The purpose of the KAZA TFCA is to ensure that the natural resources the state parties share across their international boundaries along the Kavango and Zambezi River Basins are conserved and managed prudently for present and future generations within the context of sustainable economic development.[78] Half of Africa's elephants call the KAZA TFCA home.[79] Such cross-border collaboration is vital given it is impossible to determine the nationality of any particular elephant, noting that nationality is a human and political construct. However, it is noteworthy that KAZA's governance structures cannot make binding policy; decisions must come from member nations. Overall then, the agreement maintains the notion of

75 Lindsay et al., 'The Shared Nature of Africa's Elephants', 262.
76 Lindsay et al., 'The Shared Nature of Africa's Elephants', 261.
77 KAZA (2006) *Memorandum of Understanding Concerning the Establishment of the Kavango–Zambezi Transfrontier Conservation Area*, Gaborone, Signed 6th December, Victoria falls, Zimbabwe.
78 Preamble, Articles 4 & 5.
79 Lindsay et al., 'The Shared Nature of Africa's Elephants', 264.

autonomous states and sovereignty, and so has the potential to support systems that conflict with one another.[80] CITES Appendix listings may lead to systemic conflict between the parties to the KAZA TFCA, given that the different states of the KAZA TFCA have different elephant CITES listings. Botswana, Namibia and Zimbabwe all have elephants listed under Appendix II (although Namibia itself has a split listing), while Angola and Zambia have listed elephants under Appendix I.[81] As noted by Lindsay and others, it is also impossible to know if any given elephant in the KAZA TFCA is listed under Appendix I or II.[82]

That said, the KAZA TFCA has focused on human–wildlife conflict as a conservation issue in recent years. In 2016 the Secretariat commissioned a report on human–wildlife conflict mitigation measures, from Connected Conservation, an NGO concerned with biodiversity conservation.[83] The report addressed each member country and several specific species, including the elephant. The report noted the causes of human–elephant conflict in Botswana as 'human population growth, land-use transformation, habitat loss, degradation and fragmentation and growing elephant population as well as growing interest in ecotourism and increasing access to nature reserves, increasing livestock populations, climatic factors and stochastic (e.g. flooding) events'.[84] Institutional factors are once again missing from this list. The report acknowledged that further research is needed for a complete contextual analysis of human–wildlife conflict in Botswana, although research on institutional factors and human dimensions is also missing from that list.[85]

In addition to the issues already described, there are concerns that TFCAs and their agreements further the western neo-liberal autonomous paradigm by maintaining the dominant hierarchy. Ramutsindela notes that other global bodies such as the World Wildlife Fund (WWF), Conservation International (CI) and the Global Environment Facility (GEF), dominated by westerners, are active players in the creation of TFCAs in Africa (and indeed WWF and Peace Parks Foundation were instrumental in the creation of the KAZA

80 *Treaty on the Kavango Zambezi Transfrontier Conservation Area*, opened for signature 18 August 2011, Art 5.

81 CITES, 'African Elephant'. Available at: https://cites.org/eng/gallery/species/mammal/african_elephant.html (last accessed 9 February 2022).

82 Lindsay et al., 'The Shared Nature of Africa's Elephants', 264.

83 Karidozo, La Grange and Osborn, *Assessment of the Human Wildlife Conflict Mitigation Measures*.

84 Karidozo, La Grange and Osborn, *Assessment of the Human Wildlife Conflict Mitigation Measures*, 74.

85 Karidozo, La Grange and Osborn, *Assessment of the Human Wildlife Conflict Mitigation Measures*, 73.

TFCA).[86] Of course, such a TFCA institution cannot be separated from those surrounding it. With this in mind, Ramutsindela argues that 'TFCAs in Africa are by and large a product of ideas about ecological integrity while, at the same time, representing ways by which protected areas can be created and expanded through the merging of conservation and development ideals with the appropriate political and financial backing'.[87] When the underlying vulnerability of TFCAs and their creation to politics, economics, consumerism and western ideals is considered together with the top-down nature of the approach in instigating and implementing the TFCA,[88] the institution itself ends up pushing the autonomy hierarchy discussed in Chapter 4.

6.3.2 *National Laws and Strategies*

The Government of Botswana is the sole custodian of wildlife in the country, and it manages all wildlife through the Department of Wildlife and National Parks (DWNP).[89] *The Wildlife Conservation Policy* of 1986 initially established the wildlife governance structure, including Wildlife Management Areas (WMAs), which formed the basis for wildlife conservation and utilisation interventions for over two decades. It was succeeded in 2013 by a policy of the same name. The policy situates wildlife as a 'valuable development asset which needs to be conserved and carefully utilized and managed'.[90] It notes the importance of wildlife to the nation's tourism sector and economic diversification.[91] The policy closely ties wildlife to development, much more so than the dingo management policies on K'gari, and further states that the policy is not only about conservation of wildlife but also *about development* and poverty eradication.[92] This linking of the purpose of the policy is problematic for two key reasons. The first reason, as outlined in Chapter 4, is that the promotion of use-value creates an ideology that flows through to our attitudes and internal values towards wildlife.[93] The second reason is not

86 Maano Ramutsindela, *Transfrontier Conservation in Africa: At the Confluence of Capital, Politics, and Nature* (CABI, 2007), 3.
87 Ramutsindela, Transfrontier Conservation in Africa, 5.
88 William Wolmer, 'Transboundary Conservation: The Politics of Ecological Integrity in the Great Limpopo Transfrontier Park' (2003) 29(1) *Journal of Southern African Studies* 261.
89 Bar-On, 'On Elephants, Giraffes, and Social Development', 37.
90 Ministry of Environment, Wildlife and Tourism, Republic of Botswana, *Wildlife Policy*, 1.1.
91 Ministry of Environment, Wildlife and Tourism, Republic of Botswana, *Wildlife Policy*, 1.1.
92 Ministry of Environment, Wildlife and Tourism, Republic of Botswana, *Wildlife Policy*, 1.4.
93 See Section 4.4.

related directly to the linking of conservation and development but the oversight of key vulnerabilities that should factor into any decision concerning the conservation of wildlife. We know that to successfully protect, conserve and restore all aspects of the natural environment we have to integrate appropriate principles across all facets of governance and this has been the basis of recommendations on CBD implementation for some time. Therefore, integrating a policy on development with a wildlife conservation policy could be a positive move, but not where that policy simply shifts the focus from conservation to development. Although development is a relevant resilience-building technique in some circumstances, it does not address all vulnerabilities. As a result, the integration of development and conservation is not holistic and does not create resilience to *all* of our shared vulnerabilities, most notably, our shared environmental vulnerabilities.

While the policy does note that several wildlife species are threatened, and that it was necessary to create a system of national parks and protected areas to conserve them, the greater theoretical proposition is anthropocentric in a way that favours the short-term promotion of autonomy and development. It states: '(t)he commercial value of the wildlife resources provides an opportunity for the sector to contribute to the national development goals such as tourism development, economic diversification, poverty eradication, employment creation and improvement of rural livelihoods'.[94] Even the discussion on the elimination of hunting is discussed within these terms: '(w)hile hunting is recognised as a management tool, the future thinking is to move towards photographic tourism which provides more long term benefits for the local economy'.[95]

The policy is legislatively supported by the *Wildlife Conservation and National Parks Act* of 1992, which works as the regulatory model for the principles elucidated in the policy, as well as giving effect to the country's CITES obligations.[96] It enables the creation of National Parks protected areas and WMAs.[97] The Act categorises wildlife into protected game animals, partially protected game animals, animals that may be hunted with a license and animals that can be hunted without a license.[98] Elephants are partially protected under the Act,[99] meaning that they are not to be hunted or killed,

[94] Ministry of Environment, Wildlife and Tourism, Republic of Botswana, *Wildlife Policy*, 2.3.1.
[95] Ministry of Environment, Wildlife and Tourism, Republic of Botswana, *Wildlife Policy*, 2.3.2.
[96] *Wildlife Conservation and National Parks Act (Botswana).*
[97] *Wildlife Conservation and National Parks Act (Botswana)*, parts II and III.
[98] *Wildlife Conservation and National Parks Act (Botswana)*, ss 17–19.
[99] *Wildlife Conservation and National Parks Act (Botswana)*, schedule VII.

except with a license or permit.[100] The Act is enforced by way of the creation of offences. For example, it is an offence to kill, hunt, capture, injure or disturb any wildlife (unless under license), with a maximum prison sentence of seven years.[101]

The policy and Act also work together to detail the state's wildlife collaborative governance scheme. Botswana initially implemented a Community Based Natural Resource Management (CBNRM) policy in 1997 that was based on dividing the country into Controlled Hunting Areas (CHAs) and giving local communities access to leases over those areas to develop hunting and photographic tourism industries.[102] The policy has undergone various iterations since 1997, including moving revenue from communities to district councils and contracting out community managerial functions, to effectively take the collaboration out of the policy. The CBNRM policy and its effects on human–elephant conflict will be discussed in more detail in Section 6.5.1.

There are also soft legal instruments that attempt to address human–elephant conflict in Botswana and the KAZA TFCA. The DWNP has implemented various programs and policies that target specific conflict problems. The *Okavango Delta Management Plan* was drafted in January 2008, following *Ramsar Convention* requirements.[103] That management plan has several benefits, not least of which is its ecosystem approach orientation that includes acknowledgement of institutional and socio-economic aspects of ecosystem conservation.[104] This is certainly a more holistic approach than the ecosystem approach implemented by the CBD and discussed in Chapter 4, and goes some way towards an eco-vulnerability approach. However, the situation of the conflict within that approach is not as complete. Unfortunately, human–wildlife conflict is not listed as a 'potential threat to ODRS (Okavango Delta Ramsar Site) functioning', but is noted as a socio-economic planning issue.[105]

[100] *Wildlife Conservation and National Parks Act (Botswana)*, s 18.
[101] *Wildlife Conservation and National Parks Act (Botswana)*, s 11(1).
[102] Bar-On, 'On Elephants, Giraffes, and Social Development'; Blackie, 'Impact of Wildlife Hunting Prohibition', 3.
[103] Wildlife and Tourism Ministry of Environment and Botswana Department of Environmental Affairs, *Okavango Delta Management Plan*.
[104] Wildlife and Tourism Ministry of Environment and Botswana Department of Environmental Affairs, *Okavango Delta Management Plan*. See for example sections 3.1, 4.3.1, 4.3.3, 5.1.1.
[105] Wildlife and Tourism Ministry of Environment and Botswana Department of Environmental Affairs, *Okavango Delta Management Plan*, 112.

6.4 A WEB OF OPPRESSIONS; ELEPHANT CONSERVATION, AUTONOMY AND RACE

This conflict, perhaps more than any other, is influenced to a large extent by the promotion of autonomy of people who live outside of the state or who have never even visited. For example, the global ivory trade is considered to be responsible for the deaths of 100 elephants on the African continent every day.[106] China collectively has the highest consumption of ivory.[107] The relationships that locals have with elephants and with non-local poachers is premised on this backdrop.

At the other end of the spectrum of pro-elephant attitudes, the elephant is a charismatic species that is known to most people around the world and loved by perhaps almost as many. It is used as a conservation symbol and to raise funds for conservation efforts both within and outside of Africa. For the elephants and human–elephant conflict in Botswana, this has meant that the breadth of stakeholders concerned about policies and outcomes is much larger than it is for many other species and conflicts. These outside stakeholders have become embedded in the network of relationships and web of oppressions that surround conflict outcomes.

The vulnerability of the elephants, the locals and the ecosystems are all subject to this outside influence and the autonomy of external stakeholders for several reasons. The first is historical power and influence differentials in the making of international conservation laws. It is well established that African nations had little to do with the initial establishment of modern international law and the political/international relations system that affects their ability to resolve conflict with elephants.[108] There are specific critiques around the advent of the international agreements that specifically address wildlife and conservation. For example, Abensperg-Traun has stated that the original conception of CITES was a product of western cultural values and western conceptions of 'conservation'.[109] The Ramsar Convention was initially

[106] Monique C. Sosnowski, Toby G. Knowles, Taro Takahashi and Nicola J. Rooney, 'Global Ivory Market Prices Since the 1989 CITES Ban' (2019) 237 *Biological Conservation* 392.

[107] Achyut Aryal, Craig G. Morley and Ian G. McLean, 'Conserving Elephants Depend on a Total Ban of Ivory Trade Globally' (2018) 27 *Biodiversity Conservation* 2767.

[108] See, for example, Antony Anghie, *Imperialism, Sovereignty and the Making of International Law* (Cambridge University Press, 2005); John M. Hobson, *The Eurocentric Conception of World Politics: Western International Theory, 1760–2010* (Cambridge University Press, 2012).

[109] Max Abensperg-Traun, 'CITES, Sustainable Use of Wild Species and Incentive-Driven Conservation in Developing Countries, with an Emphasis on Southern Africa' (2009) 142(5) *Biological Conservation* 948.

criticised for having too few non-European parties, although this has now been addressed.[110]

The western influence via international environmental obligations appears to be changing somewhat, or at least being moderated by more regional agreements such as the KAZA TFCA, and a stronger voice within the international system. However, it is not enough. As noted earlier in this section, those regional agreements often result from outside influence.[111] The particular vulnerabilities of the people of nations such as Botswana are still not being accounted for within the international framework, and this affects their ability to deal with ground-level conflict in a way that is meaningful and works for them.

Another reason that Botswana's governance of elephants has deferred to the autonomy of international stakeholders is wealth and the neo-liberal tourist economy. Tourism is a factor in the network of influence on human–elephant conflict, just as it is on K'gari and its human–dingo conflict. In Botswana, tourism is meant to bring benefits to the local people, with community-based natural resource management plans designed to distribute income. In reality, the effect of tourism on the community is not as positive as intended. While tourism is a multi-billion-dollar industry in Botswana,[112] the locals live in poverty and struggle to find gainful employment in the tourism industry, or progress beyond menial levels once they are in. Those that are involved see the displays of wealth from international visitors, and this breeds resentment.[113] The community are of the view that the elephants belong to the visitors and white people in general.

The international and colonial origins of trophy hunting and compensation programs also influence the ongoing environmental colonisation discourse. De Motts and Hoon describe the following: 'Compensation originated under British administration, allowing landowners or occupiers to destroy damage-causing animals. Resulting trophies were the property of the colonial administration (or on tribal land, customary authorities), which gave farmers monetary compensation.'[114] The social aspect of local wildlife laws is also shaped by

[110] Bowman, Davies and Redgwell, Lyster's International Wildlife Law, 405.
[111] See Section 6.3.1.
[112] G. Mopelwa and J. Blignaut, 'The Okavango Delta: The Value of Tourism' (2014) 9(1) *South African Journal of Economic and Management Sciences* 113.
[113] Max Bearak, '"I Hate Elephants": Behind the Backlash Against Botswana's Giants', *The Washington Post* (Washington, USA), 7 June 2019. Available at: www.washingtonpost.com/world/2019/06/07/i-hate-elephants-behind-backlash-against-botswanas-giants/ (last accessed 23 March 2021).
[114] DeMotts and Hoon, 'Whose Elephants?', 841.

outside influence. A media analysis undertaken by Blackie in 2019 found that the conservation agenda continues to be shaped by the international community.[115] This was one reason for discontent amongst Batswana communities concerning the conservation policies of the former President, who they viewed as pandering to international conservationist perspectives.

The race issue is not limited to western international influence, as many within the affected communities suggest that white people within Botswana and the conservation community are given priority in the hierarchy of autonomy. A 2019 article in the Washington Post discussed this aspect:

> 'There's a sense among people across Botswana that Khama was a protector of the whites, the owners of many of our big farms and lodges, at the people's expense,' said Anthony Morima, a writer and political analyst. 'Masisi casts himself as a nationalist taking back control, which goes along with an increasing feeling here that we don't want white people or foreigners to tell us how to live.'[116]

Further, there is conflict around the wildlife policies between different tribes and ethnic groups. For example, Blackie details complaints of the San people around the hunting ban, who considered that it was a political decision undertaken by the Tswana speaking groups to assimilate into their community.[117] Assimilation is thought to be required because members of the main ethnic group are assisted via compensation to sustain their livelihood yet no similar compensation is provided to the San. Similarly, the state expects the assertion of a primary Motswana identity, not based on tribalism or ethnicity but as a member of the state.[118] As a result, CBNRM claims based on ethnic identity have been rejected, even though it was the areas of minority tribes where most CBNRM projects were initially implemented.[119] The State views local claims about CBNRM and living with wildlife as a resurgence of identity politics that challenges ethnically neutral citizenship.

Another interrelated oppression revolves around the issue of gender. Women are underrepresented in many facets of leadership in Botswana, including in decision-making in the wildlife and tourism sector.[120] Yet,

[115] Blackie, 'Impact of Wildlife Hunting Prohibition', 8.
[116] Bearak, 'I Hate Elephants'.
[117] Blackie, 'Impact of Wildlife Hunting Prohibition', 14.
[118] DeMotts and Hoon, 'Whose Elephants?', 847.
[119] Hoon, 'Elephants Are Like Our Diamonds', 62.
[120] Joseph E. Mbaiwa and Amanda L. Stronza, 'The Effects of Tourism Development on Rural Livelihoods in the Okavango Delta, Botswana' (2010) 18(5) *Journal of Sustainable Tourism* 635.

women are more likely to be in poverty.[121] Botswana's CBNRM and wildlife policies continue to face accusations of 'inequality associated with social and culturally constructed norms and rules that shape gender relations and lead to unequal power relationships between men and women'.[122] There continues to be unequal access to resources and control over wildlife policies, even where it has been found that a greater gender balance in decision-making would lead to fairer and more effective outcomes,[123] and as we saw in Chapter 3, better conservation outcomes.[124]

So how should the state respond to these embedded vulnerabilities and interlinked web of oppressions that reduces resilience to human–elephant conflict? Chapter 3 suggested that a responsive state needed to include individuals and communities via a collaborative governance framework, with institutional mechanisms to assess and respond to vulnerabilities.[125] Over the decades the state has attempted various iterations of a collaborative governance framework, with minimal effect on resilience to conflict.

6.5 BOTSWANA AS A RESPONSIVE STATE

Botswana's role as a 'responsive state' has been multi-faceted. There are three primary ways that the state has responded to the issue of human–elephant conflict; collaborative governance mechanisms with community members, compensation for crop damage, and direct approaches to welfare. All of these are consistent with a vulnerability approach to some extent, although as will be shown, are not being implemented to their full capability, and remain dependent on hierarchical ideologies.

6.5.1 *Community-Based Natural Resource Management (CBNRM)*

The historical circumstances of colonial rule over Botswana and the monopolisation of wildlife as a resource during that period have meant that, in large part, continued top-down governance of human–elephant conflict is not practical nor well-received by local people. Hunting was prohibited under

[121] Wildlife and Tourism Ministry of Environment and Botswana Department of Environmental Affairs, *Okavango Delta Management Plan*, 'Cross-Cutting Issues'.

[122] Blackie, 'Impact of Wildlife Hunting Prohibition', 6.

[123] Jon Anderson and Shreya Mehta, *A Global Assessment of Community Based Natural Resource Management: Addressing the Critical Challenges of the Rural Sector*, United States Agency for International Development (USAID), International Resource Group (May 2013).

[124] See Section 3.3.

[125] See Section 3.3.

colonial rule, except with permission from the state, and this created a divide between the traditional forms of land ethic and responsibility for wildlife and the Indigenous people of the country.[126] The ongoing issues of perception that come with top-down governance of this issue are well documented.[127]

CBNRM has been a feature of wildlife policy since 1997 when the first initiative was undertaken with assistance from USAID.[128] The collaborative management framework in Botswana involves community leases through the 'Controlled Hunting Areas' regime. Controlled Hunting Areas were leased to communities that had a registered 'Community-Based Organisation' to manage the enterprise. They would then obtain an annual wildlife off-take quota for hunting licenses if the scheme was to be that of hunting, and they could set up their own tourist operation or sub-lease to a tour operator. The community-based organisation could decide what to do with its revenue, minus 15 per cent for administrative costs.[129] The outcome thus resembled a collaborative scheme, however, the local communities did not have input into the design of the scheme itself, a necessary part of a collaborative governance structure. This is somewhat abnormal in Botswana, with the norm being genuine consultation of locals before a national policy is announced and implemented.[130] Indeed, the state has had four principles that have guided governance since independence, one of which is *therisanyo*, or the principle of consultation. This was traditionally done by community consultations with chiefs, often in front of their residence or in a *kgotla*, a traditional gathering point in a village.[131] However, even this traditional consultative process has seen a move towards debate on implementation, rather than consultation on the design of policies themselves.[132] It is increasingly used as a forum for informing of policies rather than genuine consultation.[133] As a result, the state

[126] Bar-On, 'On Elephants, Giraffes, and Social Development', 368. Bar-On also argues that this form of management led to the decline of control of village chiefs over wildlife, leading to democratisation of its use and over-utilisation.

[127] See, for example, Jill Zarestky and Leslie E. Ruyle, *Participatory Community Education to Mitigate Human–Elephant Conflict in Botswana* (Commission for International Adult Education, 2016); Mayberry, Hovorka and Evans, 'Well-Being Impacts of Human–Elephant Conflict in Khumaga, Botswana'; Modise et al., 'Toward Sustainable Conservation'; A. Taruvinga and A. Mushunje, 'Society's Perceptions of African Elephants and their Relative Influence towards the Conservation of Elephants' (2014) 10 *APCBEE Procedia* 299.

[128] Blaikie, 'Is Small Really Beautiful?', 1943.

[129] Bar-On, 'On Elephants, Giraffes, and Social Development'.

[130] Blackie, 'Impact of Wildlife Hunting Prohibition'.

[131] Blackie, 'Impact of Wildlife Hunting Prohibition'.

[132] Blackie, 'Impact of Wildlife Hunting Prohibition'; Noga et al., 'Wildlife Officials'.

[133] Blackie, 'Impact of Wildlife Hunting Prohibition', 7.

is not listening and responding to the needs of local communities but assuming needs and dictating approaches.

The *Wildlife Conservation Policy* gives further detail of the purpose of CBNRM in Botswana, stating that it will establish an 'institutional, regulatory and participatory framework for wildlife conservation and utilisation'.[134] It emphasises the 'devolution of wildlife management to landowners and communities to instil greater accountability for the resource'.[135] While the devolution process is admirable and needed, the practice of that institutional decentralisation and participation has not effectively worked to improve the human–elephant relationship in Botswana nor have the benefits been appropriately distributed. This may be because the purpose of CBNRM in Botswana, as stated in the *Wildlife Conservation Policy*, is not optimal. The purpose should not be to instil accountability to local people, because that assumes a particular level of autonomy and distance between the state and the local people. Bar-On explains that self-reliance can become an objective in its own right so that the goal becomes an economic one, rather than a response to human, animal and environmental vulnerability.[136] Instead, the purpose should be the sharing of responsibility and the costs and benefits of caring for wildlife and maintaining shared ecosystems.

Since 1998 the CBNRM program has seen several restructures to improve outcomes. The government virtually eliminated the programme in 2001, in all but its organisational form, by decreeing that district councils should manage the communities revenues in trust.[137] It was suggested that the revenues accrue from natural resources and so must benefit the entire nation. A huge 65 per cent of all revenue generated by local CBNRM projects had to be turned over to the state.[138] Part of this process involved having the communities contract out their managerial functions, which not only increased overheads by 25 per cent but minimised their role and decision-making power. The collaborative governance scheme became much less collaborative. This process further colonised the governance of wildlife as managers were substantially funded and organised by outside NGOs.[139] The program became more patriarchal and at odds with the purpose of a collaborative scheme. The benefits to be obtained from living with wildlife were not being evenly distributed to those who bore the greatest costs. Many suggested the scheme

[134] Ministry of Environment, Wildlife and Tourism, Republic of Botswana, *Wildlife Policy*.
[135] Ministry of Environment, Wildlife and Tourism, Republic of Botswana, *Wildlife Policy*.
[136] Bar-On, 'On Elephants, Giraffes, and Social Development', 378.
[137] Bar-On, 'On Elephants, Giraffes, and Social Development', 378.
[138] DeMotts and Hoon, 'Whose Elephants?', 848.
[139] Bar-On, 'On Elephants, Giraffes, and Social Development', 378.

had failed,[140] and that the central government was not interested in devolving authority or resources to the districts or in building capacity at the community level but sought to withhold revenues and strengthen upward accountability to the central government.[141]

Critiques of the scheme go further than the lack of real devolution of state power. Mismanagement claims are rife,[142] with the locals maintaining that they do not see any economic benefits since the CBOs had to outsource their management.[143] The necessity of involvement of private enterprise has also been argued by local people who suggest that the joint venture partnership model promotes private enterprise interests instead of empowering the local community to run tourist operations themselves.[144] This means the policies operate to achieve personal material enrichment instead of sustainable natural resource (or in this case wildlife) management.[145] When broken down, it is evident that personal enrichment operates as a goal of the CBNRM policies because the policies themselves are built around the dominant hierarchy, and promote the liberal autonomy of certain individuals who already hold power within the hierarchy. The result is a distrust between the local people and the state, and this contributes to the conflict. Mayberry states that local frustration stems originally from the fact that the community perceives the government as elephants 'owners' and thus considered them responsible for elephant management and accountable for mitigating conflict.[146] Indeed, it is the elites that are benefitting from the CBNRM policies, as tourists with access to elephants, and tour operators that are now effectively primarily responsible for the joint ventures with the community.

Further, the very ideology of CBNRM and collaborative governance techniques has been questioned because of the Botswana experience. Bar-On, for example, argues that CBNRM is 'typical top-down social engineering' and devolution is 'more about ensuring that the margins perform up to the centre's expectations than about their own welfare'.[147] There certainly appears to be a benefit in removing the neo-liberal paradigm from CBNRM policies,

[140] Blackie, 'Impact of Wildlife Hunting Prohibition'; Blaikie, 'Is Small Really Beautiful?'; Hoon, 'Elephants Are Like Our Diamonds'; Yurco et al., 'Human–Wildlife Interactions'.

[141] Hoon, 'Elephants Are Like Our Diamonds'.

[142] Hoon, 'Elephants Are Like Our Diamonds'.

[143] Blackie, 'Impact of Wildlife Hunting Prohibition', 11.

[144] Blackie, 'Impact of Wildlife Hunting Prohibition', 11.

[145] Bar-On, 'On Elephants, Giraffes, and Social Development', 369.

[146] Mayberry, Hovorka and Evans, 'Well-Being Impacts of Human–Elephant Conflict in Khumaga, Botswana'.

[147] Bar-On, 'On Elephants, Giraffes, and Social Development', 378.

however, that process is complicated by the very premise of CBNRM itself; that local people are more likely to conserve natural resources when there is a perceived benefit to their household or local community.[148] The benefit, as well as the perception of shared costs, is what drives community engagement, especially when they are battling with human–elephant conflict and its consequences routinely. However, the benefit does not necessarily have to be monetary. There are many costs to people as a result of conflicts with elephants, including emotional, social and cultural costs. It is possible, and even desirable, for a CBNRM policy to build resilience by responding to the vulnerabilities associated with these costs, rather than financial benefit.

CBNRM policies in Botswana also focus attention on the people who live with wildlife rather than wildlife as an entity itself, with its own vulnerabilities.[149] However, CBNRM and consideration of elephant agency and vulnerability are not mutually exclusive and Botswana's policies demonstrate this. The state, as the responsive agent, had set out clear boundaries for the inclusion of the conservation of the species and individual animals via the hunting bans that existed at the time the CBNRM mechanisms were developed. But again, this prioritisation sets out the difficulties in state dictation of the terms of engagement with CBNRM policies, compared to the need for devolution of power in some form. How does the devolved state then remain engaged insofar as to ensure primary conservation and human security goals are prioritised? They set a vulnerability framework and allow the many voices to discuss the best mechanisms for increasing resilience over the vast number of stakeholders, including the species and the ecosystems as stakeholders.

6.5.2 *Compensation and Welfare*

In Northern Botswana, where the greatest number of elephants live and human–elephant conflict is an everyday occurrence, over 50 per cent of locals are reliant on some form of welfare,[150] with some studies suggesting this figure to be as high as 65 per cent.[151] Notwithstanding this, Gupta argues that Botswana is a relatively well-functioning welfare state and that welfare can

148 Blackie, 'Impact of Wildlife Hunting Prohibition', 4; Konstantinos Andriotis, 'Community Groups' Perceptions of and Preferences for Tourism Development: Evidence from Crete' (2005) 29(1) *Journal of Hospitality & Tourism Research* 67.

149 Bar-On, 'On Elephants, Giraffes, and Social Development', 368.

150 Gupta, 'Elephants, Safety Nets and Agrarian Culture'.

151 Blackie, 'Impact of Wildlife Hunting Prohibition', 13.

mediate the effects of living near elephants.[152] Welfare in this instance includes subsidised farming programmes,[153] drought relief programmes[154] and old-age pensions and 'destitute allowances'.[155] This type of assistance is necessary where wildlife conservation has been prioritised over alternative land uses and local people have borne the cost of that prioritisation. Of course, welfare is a standard state response to vulnerability and has been discussed extensively by vulnerability scholars.[156] Welfare payments allow people to increase their resilience while being dependent on the state, rather than the state maintaining that they should strive to be autonomous from assistance.

However, the practical effects of a welfare policy around elephant conflict, where people can work or tend farms, have been mixed. Gupta describes the scenario for those near Chobe National Park as follows:

> For some households, state forms of assistance (entitlements or employment opportunities) augment income to the point that farmers who face high levels of wildlife disturbance can stop farming altogether, which I term the 'abandonment strategy'. Other households choose to continue farming, despite the fact that it is marginal in the area, because agricultural subsidies create incentives for people to continue to farm with low input and low risk, which I refer to as the 'low-level continuation strategy'.[157]

So while welfare may seem to be a response to vulnerability and increase resilience in the short-term, in these cases, it decreases resilience to vulnerability over the long-term. This is because the lack of farming, or the low-production farming, has an impact on the networks of people around those depending on the welfare and so there is a flow-on effect of decreased resilience that is not accounted for by the initial welfare payment. To determine if the policy is effective, we need to determine the desired effect of the policy. Within an eco-vulnerability framework, the goal should not be restricted to the short-term resilience of the recipient, but their long-term resilience, their

[152] At least in respect of those living near Chobe National Park in Botswana's North-East; Gupta, 'Elephants, Safety Nets and Agrarian Culture'.

[153] In 2002, the Ministry of Agriculture launched the National Masterplan for Arable Agriculture and Dairy Development; Gupta, 'Elephants, Safety Nets and Agrarian Culture', 241.

[154] Blackie, 'Impact of Wildlife Hunting Prohibition', 13.

[155] Gupta, 'Elephants, Safety Nets and Agrarian Culture', 241.

[156] See Helen Carr, 'Housing the Vulnerable Subject: The English Context', in Martha Albertson Fineman and Anna Grear (eds.), *Vulnerabilty: Reflections on a New Ethical Foundation for Law and Politics* (Routledge, 2016) 107; Rosemarie Tong, 'Vulnerability and Aging in the Context of Care', in Catriona MacKenzie, Wendy Rogers and Susan Dodds (eds.), *Vulnerability; New Essays in Ethics and Feminist Philosophy* (Oxford University Press, 2014) 288.

[157] Gupta, 'Elephants, Safety Nets and Agrarian Culture', 239.

relationships, and their environment. If the welfare payments perpetuate long-term poverty and substantiate a land-use payment via farming that exacerbates human–elephant conflict, the welfare policy is not meeting its goal.

Another form of 'welfare' in Botswana are the payments to locals under the various compensation schemes set up in response to human–elephant conflict and run by the DWNP. However, the compensation schemes are under-utilised and highly criticised for several reasons common to most compensation schemes and discussed in Chapter 3. First, potential recipients on the outskirts of the delta must travel to Seronga to file a report within seven days of when the damage occurs. Officials then must visit the site to verify the damage. The travel to Seronga can be time-consuming and difficult for locals, and illiteracy rates also add difficulty to the process. Some locals have suggested that the effort is not worth their time when the DWNP either fails to pay or the compensation does not adequately represent the losses sustained.[158] In addition, DeMotts and Hoon suggest that the compensation scheme symbolically reinforces the notion that elephants are owned by the state, rather than addressing local resilience and capacity to live with them, adding to the social conflict surrounding the issue.[159]

A further scheme that is heavily relied on is the *Ipelegeng* drought relief program. The *Ipelegeng* program is a labour-based public works programme, which provides temporary work to people, especially youth, who lack farming and formal employment opportunities.[160] This type of programme may build the long-term resilience of both the benefactor and the community at large, depending on the type of work done. It could also assist elephant vulnerability if the work was related to habitat conservation or assisting farmers with traditional conflict mitigation measures such as making chilli bombs.

6.6 A VULNERABILITY GOVERNANCE FRAMEWORK

The state of Botswana has attempted to respond to the issue of human–elephant conflict in various ways, some more successful than others. There are many aspects of the responses that are consistent with a vulnerability approach to the governance of the conflict, such as those noted in Sections 6.5.1 and 6.5.2. However, programs like the CBNRM and welfare payments are likely to continue to struggle to reduce negative interactions unless they can acknowledge their institutional vulnerability to other institutions and the

[158] DeMotts and Hoon, 'Whose Elephants?'.
[159] DeMotts and Hoon, 'Whose Elephants?'.
[160] Gupta, 'Elephants, Safety Nets and Agrarian Culture', 244.

dominant neo-liberal paradigm, and build further research around local and community vulnerability and resilience to human–elephant conflict. In this section, I will discuss the alternatives.

6.6.1 *State Autonomy or State Vulnerability; Is it a Necessary Choice?*

Constructs of nationalism based on State autonomy appear to be inconsistent with a vulnerability approach to human–elephant conflict given the multi-state home range of elephants and the international effort required to conserve them. The notion of institutional autonomy, in this case manifesting as state autonomy, is a myth because every state is vulnerable to the actions of other states, international organisations, global corporations, etc. As a result, state insistence on autonomy is detrimental to a vulnerability approach and an impediment to effective human–wildlife conflict governance. To respond to all interlinked vulnerabilities, a multi-lateral approach is required, and state vulnerability to other institutions, communities, and ecologies must be acknowledged.

Yet, autonomy remains a defining factor in all multilateral agreements, domestic policies and political discussions concerning the elephant. State autonomy can manifest as arguments of sovereignty or nationalism and in other ways, but the underlying motivation is the fallacy of autonomy. Examples commence with the signing of some of the multilateral agreements themselves. For example, it has been argued that Botswana's decision to become a party to the *Ramsar Convention* was nationalistic, especially given it had previously been reluctant to become a party due to fears that the requirements would interrupt development plans.[161] The national interest arose given that the delta flows from Namibia and Angola into Botswana, and there was planned abstraction of resources by those states. Botswana then became a party to attempt to situate the delta within a global framework and protect its own interests in it, including the tourism value.[162] Self-interest is often thought to involve the promotion of autonomy but, once the necessity of relational approaches to global problems becomes relevant, so does the fallacy of institutional autonomy.

[161] Larry A. Swatuk, 'State Interests and Multilateral Cooperation: Thinking Strategically about Achieving "Wise Use" of the Okavango Delta System' (2003) 28(20) *Physics and Chemistry of the Earth* 897, 901.

[162] It is estimated that 100,000 tourists pass through the delta every year, and tourism is the main economic activity in the area; Lapologang Magole and Lefatshe Innocent Magole, 'The Okavango: Whose Delta Is It?' (2009) 34(13) *Physics and Chemistry of the Earth* 874, 875.

This example is just one of many that highlight the difficulty of conceptions of autonomy in international law. In many ways, international law is a struggle between the creation and maintenance of institutional autonomy, via the principle of state sovereignty, and responses to vulnerability, via the rules that international law creates to moderate potentially harmful relationships between States.

The principle of state sovereignty in international law is unlikely to be abandoned, however sovereignty does not have to equal autonomy, just as autonomy is not the same as individual free will. States can remain free to make their own decisions about becoming part of international wildlife agreements, within a vulnerability framework. However, the decision-making process that lies behind whether or not to sign on to an environmental treaty, for example, should be based on the respective vulnerabilities of the state and its people, wildlife and ecologies, and the relationships that add to that embedded vulnerability or build resilience to it. State institutions must be moulded not for the pursuit of an abstract ideology such as autonomy, but upon responsiveness to their own, and their people's universal vulnerability. In this way, the issue is not one of sovereignty, but the continued political problematisation of state connectivity via international law. The connections are inherent and universal and representative of institutional vulnerability. As a result, separation via promotion of autonomy is not achievable and, instead, responding to that universal vulnerability is required.

In this case study, the issue is demonstrated via the ideological pull between the separation of African elephant conservation from western ideals of conservation, at the risk of local people, and the need for conservation approaches to be trans-boundary and a global effort, especially around the removal of trophy and sport hunting and the ivory market. Herein lies the conundrum. Botswana as a state institution is making decisions that are being influenced by other States and international and domestic organisations because the state of Botswana is inherently vulnerable to them. Global approaches and international law are increasingly important, yet Botswana is tightening around nationalistic conservation approaches and, in doing so, seeking to promote its institutional autonomy. While nationalism may appear important in rallying and paying attention to local vulnerability, over and above the interests of the far away, the pull away from an international response is counter-productive because we know that the drivers of human–elephant conflict are both national *and* international. By promoting State autonomy, Botswana is unable to respond to the vulnerability of the State institution and instead is taking an 'ignore it and hope it goes away' approach. Yet, international influence and relationships are not going away. They are universal to the condition of humanity and Earth systems.

6.6.2 *Vulnerability in a Welfare State*

At first instance, the nature of Botswana as a 'welfare state' is consistent with a vulnerability approach.[163] The State is responding to the decrease in the resilience of its people by providing welfare payments to those who are directly affected by human–elephant conflict. However, rarely are such processes so simplistic. An eco-vulnerability analysis could improve the welfare process to make sure that resilience is increased and all relevant interconnected vulnerabilities are addressed.

First, the welfare process requires an ecological perspective. Some might question the benefit of Botswana shifting from an anthropocentric view to an eco-centric one. Local communities clearly have a great need when it comes to human security and face struggles that many in the western world never need to consider. There is a reason that they are focused on sustainable use and development: poverty. But the purpose of this book is to show the universality of an eco-vulnerability approach to human–wildlife conflict and so this section will show that an eco-vulnerability approach could be more beneficial to people, as well as elephants and other biodiversity in the Delta.

The KAZA TFCA Assessment report proposed several legislative and policy changes that are consistent with an eco-vulnerability approach. The first was that each state party should include recognition of wildlife within their constitution (albeit on their basis as a national resource to be conserved for present and future generations, which, as discussed in Chapter 4, is *not* consistent with a vulnerability approach).[164] Constitutional recognition of the inherent value of wildlife could be an important step in the process towards an eco-vulnerability framework. The intrinsic value of nature has been represented in other national Constitutions, and these could provide a basis for inclusion in Botswana's own Constitution.[165] Constitutional recognition of wildlife itself though would not encompass a holistic account of our relationship with

163 Botswana has been described as a 'welfare state' in Gupta, 'Elephants, Safety Nets and Agrarian Culture', 241.

164 Karidozo, La Grange and Osborn, *Assessment of the Human Wildlife Conflict Mitigation Measures*, 57.

165 For example, Article 71 of the *Constitution of Ecuador* states: 'Nature, or Pacha Mama, where life is reproduced and occurs, has the right to integral respect for its existence and for the maintenance and regeneration of its life cycles, structure, functions and evolutionary processes.'

wildlife. A statement on the interlinked and individual vulnerabilities of wildlife, biodiversity, ecosystems and people would help to guarantee consideration of all those vulnerabilities in every facet of decision-making, including in issues of human–wildlife conflict. There is a risk that a constitutional representation like this is at risk of being an empty symbolic platitude, particularly if the institutional arrangements did not support its implementation. However, such a shift would help to ensure that all welfare issues were also superimposed over a whole-of-ecosystem ethic. Further, the value of constitutional recognition also lies in the ability to shift public perception, values and attitudes towards wildlife and all environmental components towards a vulnerability approach.

The second proposal in the KAZA TFCA assessment report was that all compensation schemes should be phased out and replaced with conditional payments, whereby farmers would receive compensation for the loss of crops and farm animals only where they comply with conservation farming principles and implement common forms of crop and farm animal protective measures.[166] Such a compensation scheme remains consistent with the provision of welfare and assistance payments in a responsive state while attending to the vulnerability of wildlife, ecosystems and the farmers themselves. Such an approach has also been recommended by researchers who suggest that the moral hazard of compensation schemes (wherein farmers may not adopt new or revise current practices to reduce crop raiding: when they know they will be compensated) is high in Northern Botswana.[167] Further, the bureaucratic costs far outweigh the compensation provided.[168] As a result, performance payments would not only benefit farmers and elephants but also the state, by reducing overhead costs. Jackson, for example, outlines the cost-benefit to be obtained and states that a more direct performance payment approach may benefit both the Botswana Government and local farmers.[169] These payments need to be matched with the relevant support needed to achieve the desired goal. People not involved in farming should be provided with training and financial incentives to become involved in collaborative projects, the focus of Section 6.6.3.

[166] It recommends such a move as a first step towards a community-based insurance scheme. See Karidozo, La Grange and Osborn, *Assessment of the Human Wildlife Conflict Mitigation Measures*, 62–63.
[167] Tim P. Jackson et al., 'Solutions for Elephant Loxodonta Africana Crop Raiding in Northern Botswana: Moving Away from Symptomatic Approaches' (2008) 42(1) *ORYX* 83, 88–89.
[168] Jackson et al., 'Solutions for Elephant Loxodonta Africana Crop Raiding'.
[169] Jackson et al., 'Solutions for Elephant Loxodonta Africana Crop Raiding', 89.

6.6.3 *Collaboration in a Responsive State*

Many of the instruments that promote collaboration in Botswana have prima facie resulted from the State responding to vulnerability. Whilst this is necessary and the goal of Fineman's theory, the end result in Botswana shows that the process matters. For example, the creation of the KAZA TFCA resulted from a top-down process[170] and, arguably, it would not have been created without the State parties implementing that process. Linnell suggests that a previous version driven primarily by NGOs was unsuccessful because the States would not agree when *they* had no control over the process.[171] Thereafter, the KAZA TFCA was able to succeed because it fulfilled an existing desire of the main political actors. We have seen that long-lasting collaborative agreements require State support and integration into the existing institutional structures. But we have also seen that the process that such integration takes requires collaboration to reduce conflict over the long-term. The process itself can create resentment and animosity that only grows as conflicts become more apparent. This seems to have been the case with the KAZA TFCA too, where the structure was forced on locals, with no discussion.[172] Similarly, the 2014 introduction of the hunting ban was not the result of community discussion and collaboration, with most locals (over 90 per cent) stating they were not consulted or were 'merely informed'.[173]

As a result, improvement of the process is imperative to improve outcomes. A move away from the patriarchal structure is necessary. Studies have demonstrated that African CBNRM requires less state imposition and more shaping of the social–environmental relationship by locals.[174] So how does a collaborative program strike the balance between local directions and institutional support and implementation?

A beneficial collaborative model should start and finish with local mobilisation. Modise and others discuss the benefit of letting community members set the goals of a CBNRM policy.[175] They state that community goal-setting can work because the community still believe in 'coexistence' and understand that

[170] Amanda Linell, Martin Sjöstedt and Aksel Sundström, 'Governing Transboundary Commons in Africa: The Emergence and Challenges of the Kavango–Zambezi Treaty' (2019) 19(1) *International Environmental Agreements: Politics, Law and Economics* 53, 60.

[171] Linell, Sjöstedt and Sundström, 'Governing Transboundary Commons in Africa', 60.

[172] Linell, Sjöstedt and Sundström, 'Governing Transboundary Commons in Africa', 60.

[173] Blackie, 'Impact of Wildlife Hunting Prohibition', 6.

[174] Blaikie, 'Is Small Really Beautiful?', 1946.

[175] Modise et al., 'Toward Sustainable Conservation', 227.

collaboration is essential in that respect.[176] However, goal-setting should be paired with educational programming concerning the deeper vulnerabilities surrounding the human–elephant relationship, so that participants are educated on the benefits of such an approach.[177] The role of the state is to respond to the community needs by way of providing institutional support in achieving the goals set. This might entail financial assistance or incentives, on-the-ground support, and alterations to local laws and policies.

Some local politicians have suggested that a CBNRM policy is a threat to national cohesiveness, where CBNRM provides different benefits to different people.[178] However, people bear the cost of living with wildlife differently and want to obtain different benefits. Additionally, we know that no conflict is the same, and no community will have the same issues and ideas to resolve them. The state needs to allow participants to form their own relationships within their community and beyond to feel part of the larger state, including the choice of partners and support networks.

6.6.4 *Elephant Vulnerability*

The focus of this chapter on the human impacts of human–elephant conflict may implicitly suggest that the expansion of vulnerability to the non-human is not desirable in this situation. This is not the case. Elephant vulnerability is a factor that must still be considered when framing laws and policies around conflict governance. Elephants, of course, have their own inherent vulnerability, and their sentience, intelligence and emotional connections to others have long been understood.[179] They have extensive spatial-temporal and social memory when compared with great apes and humans[180] and extensive vocal recognition.[181] They show compassionate behaviour to other elephants in distress and have a general awareness and curiosity about death.[182] Further, they can distinguish between ethnic communities that persecute them and

[176] Modise et al., 'Toward Sustainable Conservation', 227.

[177] A similar educational programme is suggested in Suzanne Katherine Hamel, *A Participatory Approach to Community-Based Curriculum Development for the Living with Elephants Outreach Program in Botswana* (Lakehead University, 2003).

[178] DeMotts and Hoon, 'Whose Elephants?', 847.

[179] Evans and Adams, 'Elephants as Actors', 635.

[180] Benjamin L. Hart, Lynette A. Hart and Noa Pinter-Wollman, 'Large Brains and Cognition: Where do Elephants Fit In?' (2008) 32(1) *Neuroscience and Biobehavioral Reviews* 86.

[181] C. Moss and M. Colbeck, *Echo of the Elephants: The Story of an Elephant Family* (William Morrow & Co, 1993).

[182] Iain Douglas-Hamilton et al., 'Behavioural Reactions of Elephants towards a Dying and Deceased Matriarch' (2006) 100(1–2) *Applied Animal Behaviour Science* 87.

those that do not and are quick to learn and avoid traditional management techniques.[183] In addition to this, elephant agency is a topic often discussed, as with dingoes. For example, Evans and Adams state: 'Elephants impose cost and risk on smallholder farmers, and do so in a way that minimises risk and maximises opportunity for themselves. This is straightforward elephant behaviour – hunger, group collaboration, dexterity, awareness and avoidance of risk – but it is also an exercise of agency over human actors. In particular, elephants hold the balance of power at night.'[184] Their agency means that elephants in Botswana have been able to adapt to anthropogenic conditions and become 'dynamic and powerful actors in the heterogeneous networks that constitute the political ecology of conservation and land use in rural Africa'.[185] Their resilience to vulnerability thus depends on their ability to exercise agency.

However, unlike the case study in Chapter 5, here the elephant vulnerability has been given priority in the decision-making hierarchy in recent decades and so their resilience has increased to the detriment of the resilience of local people, or that is at least the perception of most locals who deal with the costs of the conflict. For example, a study undertaken by DeMotts and Hoon reports one respondent stating the following: 'I also can testify that when damage to my crops was reported to the DWNP office, my wife was told to leave the elephants to continue the destruction.'[186] Allowing space for vulnerability then does not mean reversing the hierarchy and prioritising human vulnerability once again but assessing all vulnerabilities and taking appropriate action that considers all of them. Here, the conflict is a manifestation of the unaccounted vulnerability and the insistence on liberal autonomy.

6.6.5 *Is Trophy Hunting an Appropriate Eco-Vulnerability Response?*

Whether or not trophy hunting is an appropriate eco-vulnerability policy proposal is relevant given the current political climate around hunting and the social conflict it presents. Botswana has had some form of elephant hunting ban on and off between 1968 and 2019 when commercial elephant hunting was banned, but hunting for bushmeat and individual or community needs was legal.[187] Elephant hunting was stopped altogether in 1983 due to

[183] Evans and Adams, 'Elephants as Actors', 637.
[184] Evans and Adams, 'Elephants as Actors', 637.
[185] Evans and Adams, 'Elephants as Actors', 632.
[186] DeMotts and Hoon, 'Whose Elephants?', 845.
[187] Blackie, 'Impact of Wildlife Hunting Prohibition', 3.

concerns that tusk weights were declining and hunting was causing unusually high concentrations of elephants in protected areas. The Government of Botswana reinstated sport-hunting of elephants in 1996. Since then hunting was prohibited again in 2014 for a period of 12 months, with extensions every year until 2019.[188] Yet the call to lift the ban has become a political catch cry. Botswana's general elections were set to take place less than five months after President Masisi's announcement, and the hunting ban had become a campaign issue, especially in the North and rural areas where conflicts with elephants are prominent.[189]

Considering the complex issues and the apparent local desire to reinstate trophy hunting, is it an appropriate response within an eco-vulnerability framework? There are certainly those who argue so. For example, there are various lines of argument around the value of trophy hunting lying in its potential to have a related conservation effort, and so hunting can, paradoxically, increase the resilience of the species, as well as the local people if the benefits are distributed appropriately.[190] The voices of the local community are overwhelmingly in favour of the reinstatement of hunting.[191] As a result, reinstatement of hunting may reduce conflict via reduction of social conflict at the ground level, at least in the short-term (although the social conflict will likely return in the long-term when the policy does not result in a reduction of negative interactions). There is evidence to suggest that the removal of legal hunting reduced the income from wildlife tourism to local communities.[192] The hunting ban also led to a scarcity of game meat, not only in their ability to hunt elephants but through their agreement with hunting safari companies where all animal carcasses would be given to local communities through their trusts. In this way, elephant meat was often available for free, and often sold on

[188] Note that the relevant legislation allows for a hunting ban for a period of 12 months only, with the possibility of yearly extensions; *Department of Wildlife and National Parks Act of 1992*, Botswana (Cap38:01), s 45.

[189] O'Grady, 'Botswana Overturns Ban on Elephant Hunting'.

[190] Andrew J. Loveridge, Jonathon C. Reynolds and E. J. Milner-Gulland, 'Does Sport Hunting Benefit Conservation', in David W. MacDonald and Katrina Service (eds.), *Key Topics in Conservation Biology* (Blackwell Publishing, 2007); Enrico Di Minin, Nigel Leader-Williams and Corey J. A. Bradshaw, 'Banning Trophy Hunting Will Exacerbate Biodiversity Loss' (2016) 31(2) *Trends in Ecology & Evolution* 99; Peter A. Lindsey et al., 'Trophy Hunting and Conservation in Africa: Problems and One Potential Solution' (2007) 21(3) *Conservation Biology* 880.

[191] For example, one study found that almost 92 per cent of respondents were in favour of the reinstatement of hunting in Northern Botswana: Blackie, 'Impact of Wildlife Hunting Prohibition', 14.

[192] Salerno et al., 'Living in an Elephant Landscape'.

for community profit. It has been suggested that the removal of this income and source of food severely affected some families, especially those that were already experiencing very high levels of poverty.[193] On the other hand, and as discussed in Sections 6.5.1 and 6.5.2, the actual revenue streams, outside of the animal carcass, making it to individuals within local communities has been challenged.

However, an eco-vulnerability analysis moves beyond the politics or the economics of the policy to a recognition of and analysis of the actual conflict. An appropriate eco-vulnerability analysis needs to consider not just the academic and economic arguments but the realities of the lived experiences of the people involved, the historical and societal context and the alternatives, and how all of those things together can promote resilience to vulnerability associated with human–elephant conflict. That is to say, the appropriate question should be whether trophy hunting promotes autonomy (the underlying driver of conflict) or resilience to conflict vulnerability? To answer this question we need to examine not only how trophy hunting reduces the embodied nature of the human–elephant conflict in Northern Botswana but also how it reduces the embedded nature of the conflict.

There is unlikely to be a rational argument that trophy hunting reduces the embedded nature of human–elephant conflict and its related social conflict. First, trophy hunting *is* human–elephant conflict. It involves people negatively impacting the needs and security of elephants. Reinstatement of hunting is an escalation of the conflict, at least in the embodied sense. Responding to conflict with further conflict is not an appropriate eco-vulnerability response. Further, there is a complete denial of elephant vulnerability. Eco-vulnerability requires a voice to be given to wildlife because they have their own vulnerability, and also because our vulnerability is intertwined with theirs.[194]

An analysis of how trophy hunting further embeds autonomy into the conflict response also demonstrates its likely ineffectiveness. In reality, the policy gives priority to the autonomy of westerners who pay money to shoot elephants and can dictate the terms of their conservation because they hold the money and power. The policy itself is a manifestation of this power – they, and people like them, have power over conceptions of power and development, and have used that to convince the State and locals that such a policy is the best way to respond to conflict because it benefits them and furthers their autonomy. This is evident from the first auction of hunting licenses, where it

[193] Blackie, 'Impact of Wildlife Hunting Prohibition', 10.

[194] See Section 2.5.3.

has been reported that participants paid $18,000 each, just for a seat at the auction.[195]

So, what would an eco-vulnerability response require? Although the locals state that legal hunting is the better option for them, it is possible that the resentment they feel is a result of the top-down nature of the decision process. We know from Chapter 3 that top-down decisions can have effects that lead to conflicts over the laws and policies themselves.[196] Additionally, the choices presented to the local people appear to be limited and they may view hunting as their only viable option, as so far the alternatives have not worked. What if they did work? What if a truly collaborative scheme based on non-use tourism could provide benefits to locals that mitigate the high levels of human–elephant conflict? As discussed in Chapter 3, educational programmes should accompany the design and implementation of collaborative mechanisms, so that alternative options could be discussed.[197] What if the state then made structured institutions that helped and delivered, without claiming ownership and a larger percentage of the profits? Unfortunately, it seems the question will not be answered when the state focuses on neo-liberal incarnations of collaborative governance that promotes the autonomy of those at the top of the dominant paradigm. This is supported by local commentators such as Swatuk, who have stated that the government actively works against empowering people to become more actively involved in the collaborative governance regimes because 'a population with choice particularly in an ethnically divided society, is a potential political problem'.[198]

Further, a return to a hunting policy is unlikely to affect direct human–elephant conflict numbers, and this is something that should also be communicated to locals. Botswana's government has said that it plans to issue no more than 400 permits annually.[199] At the time of writing, seven hunting packages had been sold, providing licenses for the hunting of 10 elephants per package.[200] Removal of such a low number of elephants nationally per year is not likely to result in a significant reduction of the elephant population and so will not reduce conflicts. The main purpose then seems to be political, as with most action on human–wildlife conflict at a national level, to appease the farmers on whose side the President is said to be and to be seen to be taking action. There is limited evidence that the money made from the permits will increase the resilience of the local

195 Bearak, 'I Hate Elephants'.
196 See Section 3.5.2.
197 See Section 3.5.5.
198 Swatuk, 'State Interests and Multilateral Cooperation', 903.
199 Bearak, 'I Hate Elephants'.
200 Bearak, 'I Hate Elephants'.

communities to the vulnerabilities associated with deep poverty, especially not with the current CBNRM regime. The effect of the hunting ban on reducing human–elephant conflict will be negligible. As noted by a local: 'Will they come from America in time to shoot an elephant in my field?'[201]

6.7 CONCLUSION

Chapter 5 was focused on a case study that included a relatively small number of animals within a small area dominated by humans. Within that case study, it was the vulnerability of the dingo species that was being neglected in law and policy. In Chapter 5 I explained why that was so and how it might be rectified.

This chapter is focused on a case study that has a comparatively smaller number of people with a very large number of animals over a much larger space. Arguably, elephant conservation programmes in Botswana have been a resounding success. Elephant numbers in Botswana have risen while numbers in other parts of Africa have drastically fallen. However, the result is that human–elephant conflict is intense, regular, and threatening to life and food/income security. This case study focuses on the human side of the conflict and how people can be overlooked when they do not fit within the dominant paradigm. However, it also analyses the effect of institutional vulnerability and State attempts to circumnavigate it by promoting autonomy and separation. The relevant relationships within this conflict are many and vast and include conflicts between cultures and states, and these broader influences cannot be ignored in a governance framework. As a result, the promotion of institutional autonomy can perpetuate human–wildlife conflict to the same extent, if not more so, than individual autonomy.

Yet, the bones of a vulnerability approach to the governance of human–elephant conflict in Northern Botswana are present in the current framework. The recognition of institutional vulnerability and the need to respond to it to increase resilience in conflict has been noted in some way in two key policy documents; the Okavango Delta Management Plan and the KAZA TFCA. Further, State responsiveness to individual vulnerabilities associated with the conflict has been prioritised in the past, via compensation and welfare programmes. Although they were not effective in many ways and the State has moved away from them in the interests of 'national cohesiveness', the evidence shows that such programmes can become effective if combined with a vulnerability ideology.

[201] Bearak, 'I Hate Elephants'.

7

Pandemic Vulnerability and Resilience

Wildlife and COVID-19

7.1 INTRODUCTION

At no time in recent history have we, as a global people, seen the effect of our use and abuse of wildlife in such a direct, immediate and catastrophic way as we have with COVID-19. Contraction of a virus is a very real demonstration of our universal embodied vulnerability, and it arises because COVID-19 and all other pandemics in recent history are zoonoses, meaning that they originate in microbes found in biodiversity and become an infectious disease that can be passed between animals and people via human–wildlife interactions.

Despite the suspected Chinese origin of this disease, a pandemic such as this could have originated anywhere in the world because governance at global and local levels does not adequately respond to the vulnerability that humanity shares with the environment. International and domestic wildlife and environmental laws continue to allow for the same exploitation that resulted in the initial disease transmission. Global economic systems, as a symptom of our vulnerability, affect our ability to stem the biodiversity loss that drives pandemics. These things, together with the human relationship with wildlife and their habitat, has led to an increase in zoonotic 'spill-over' (that is, the passing from a non-human species to a human). Our shared vulnerability has never been more evident.

The embedded nature of vulnerability is also clear within the COVID-19 crisis. For example, both COVID-19 and another recent disease, Ebola, can be connected to poverty as wildlife hunting is often connected to a basic need for food. Culture, politics, issues of gender and racial equality and economics (to name a few) are all connected to human–wildlife conflicts as well. Some people and communities are inherently less resilient to COVID-19 because of their socially defined and constructed vulnerability.

While the pandemic has had devastating human and societal consequences, there is promise in the worldwide collaborative efforts to combat the disease and prevent future pandemics. Communities all over the world recognise that COVID-19 disruptions are leading to a 'new normal', and many are calling for deep institutional change. A vulnerability approach is clearly emerging from the rubble of the immediate response. In this chapter, I will demonstrate how COVID-19 demonstrates the Fineman concept of vulnerability (both embedded and embodied, at the individual and institutional level) and analyse several responses to the pandemic that are examples of a move towards building resilience to vulnerability and away from the promotion of individual and institutional autonomy.

7.2 COVID-19 AS A DEMONSTRATION OF ECO-VULNERABILITY

Just as other forms of human–wildlife conflict are not solely environmental, COVID-19 is not solely a public health crisis, despite various commentaries to the contrary.[1] It is also economic, technological and environmental and encompasses aspects of animal health, race and gender relations, as well as social inequality. The currently available evidence indicates that COVID-19 was first transmitted in a wildlife market in Wuhan where products are derived from both legal and illegal wildlife trades in China and beyond.[2] COVID-19, as a symptom of human–wildlife conflict, amply demonstrates the traditional mode of dealing with conflict; the conflict itself is only considered a problem worthy of consideration when wildlife disease threatens human populations. This was illustrated throughout 2020 by the worldwide reaction to COVID-19 and the resonating calls for a Chinese ban on 'wet markets'[3] and the

[1] See, for example, Steve Matthewman and Kate Huppatz, 'A Sociology of Covid-19' (2020) 56(4) *Journal of Sociology* 675.

[2] World Health Organization, 'Virus Origin/Origins of the SARS-CoV-2 Virus'. Available at: www.who.int/health-topics/coronavirus/origins-of-the-virus (last accessed 25 March 2021); A. Alonso Aguirre et al., 'Opportunities for Transdisciplinary Science to Mitigate Biosecurity Risks from the Intersectionality of Illegal Wildlife Trade with Emerging Zoonotic Pathogens' (2021) 9 *Frontiers in Ecology and Evolution*.

[3] The term 'wet market' is not largely understood in the western world. It is not necessarily a market that sells wildlife or wildlife products but a broader category of markets that sell products 'such as meat, poultry, seafood, vegetables and fruits'. From here in this chapter I will refer to markets that sell live wildlife and wildlife products as 'live wildlife markets'. See M. Cheng, 'The Case Against Wet Markets', *The Atlantic* (Washington, DC, 10 April 2020). Available at: www.theatlantic.com/culture/archive/2020/04/ban-wet-markets/609781/ (last accessed 25 March 2021).

consumption of wildlife.[4] The response is focused on what many consider to be the problem wildlife and their handlers, rather than the institutional and societal factors that led to that particular conflict. Conservationists have known for decades that live wildlife markets and the wildlife trade impact negatively on the welfare of species and their ecosystems, yet the calls for a ban on these activities have only really been given a global voice since it became clear that their associated impact on the general human population can be long-term, substantial and, in many cases, devastating.

But wildlife trade is not the only driver of pandemics. Research shows environmental destruction is also leading to an increase in zoonotic diseases. The United Nations Intergovernmental Science-Policy Platform on Biodiversity and Ecosystem Services (IPBES), in their report titled 'Biodiversity and Pandemics', has confirmed that the 'underlying causes of pandemics are the same global environmental changes that drive biodiversity loss and climate change'.[5] Land-use change, agricultural intensification, climate change and wildlife trade are all key drivers of pandemics. For example, clearing forests and destroying habitats can force animals to move closer to urban areas, creating more opportunities for zoonose spill-over. As IPBES has noted, the human–environment relationship has been linked empirically to the emergence of dozens of zoonose diseases, and almost all pandemics of the modern era.[6] To list a few examples; Hendra virus is linked to land-use change,[7] Nipah virus is linked to agricultural intensification,[8] Ebola and

4 See, for example, J. Northam, 'Calls Grow to Ban Wet Markets Amid Concerns over Disease Spread' (WYSO, 16 April 2020). Available at: www.wyso.org/2020-04-16/calls-grow-to-ban-wet-markets-amid-concerns-over-disease-spread (last accessed 25 March 2021); *The Straits Times*, 'Australia Calls on G-20 Nations to End Wet Wildlife Markets over Coronavirus Concerns' (*The Straits Times*, 23 April 2020). Available at: www.straitstimes.com/asia/australianz/australia-calls-on-g-20-nations-to-end-wet-wildlife-markets-over-coronavirus (last accessed 25 March 2021); 'On World Health Day, Governments around the World Are Urged to Heed the Coronavirus "Tipping Point" and Ban Wildlife Trade to Reduce Risk of Future Pandemics' (*Humane Society International*, 7 April 2020). Available at: www.hsi.org/news-media/world-health-day-ban-wildlife-trade-to-reduce-pandemics/ (last accessed 25 March 2021); H. Briggs, 'WHO Developing Guidance on Wet Markets', BBC News (London, 21 April 2020).

5 Intergovernmental Science-Policy Platform on Biodiversity and Ecosystem Services (IPBES) et al., *Workshop Report on Biodiversity and Pandemics of the Intergovernmental Platform on Biodiversity and Ecosystem Services* (Zenodo, 29 October 2020). Available at: https://zenodo.org/record/4147317 (last accessed 25 March 2021).

6 IPBES et al., *Workshop Report on Biodiversity*, 5.

7 IPBES et al., *Workshop Report on Biodiversity*, 13.

8 Juliet R. C. Pulliam et al., 'Agricultural Intensification, Priming for Persistence and the Emergence of Nipah Virus: A Lethal Bat-Borne Zoonosis' (2012) 9(66) *Journal of The Royal Society Interface* 89.

Marburg viruses are linked to wildlife hunting and butchering,[9] vector-borne diseases related to ticks have been linked to climate change[10] and the other raft of coronaviruses are linked variously to wildlife trade and contact with wild birds.[11]

In essence, the human–environment relationship is responsible for the circumstances that cause spill-over events and these events are increasing. As seen in the preceding chapters, this relationship is built on the promotion of neo-liberal autonomy that benefits the already powerful and wealthy.

The other dominations encompassed in eco-vulnerability, and described in Chapter 2, also play a role in the spread of zoonotic diseases. IPBES suggests that diseases with pandemic potential tend to originate in rural areas that are also biodiversity hotspots, and where human populations are growing, rapidly driving land-use change and closer contact between people and wildlife.[12] Diseases are originating in expanding rural communities in developing countries, where there is less capacity to contain an initial outbreak. From there, the global emergence of a zoonotic virus is tied to urbanization, domestic and international trade networks and international travel.[13] Essentially, resource-rich, dominating countries with high consumption patterns and the ability to travel increase the rapid virus spread. In turn, it is these consumption patterns that are one of the drivers of rural encroachment into habitat in the first place.

Thereafter, ongoing social inequalities have played out in the response to COVID-19, as they have during past pandemics.[14] Indigenous peoples have been disproportionally affected both historically and currently. The 1918 influenza pandemic killed Māori at seven-times the rate of Europeans in New Zealand, and the 2009 H1N1 influenza pandemic caused four-times greater mortality in Native Americans than the general United States population.[15] Aboriginal people in central Australia experienced COVID-19 rates five-times higher than the non-Indigenous population.[16] Additionally, Indigenous

9 Maria Cristina Rulli et al., 'The Nexus between Forest Fragmentation in Africa and Ebola Virus Disease Outbreaks' (2017) 7(1) *Scientific Reports* 41613.

10 Milan Daniel et al., 'Increased Relative Risk of Tick-Borne Encephalitis in Warmer Weather' (2018) 8 *Frontiers in Cellular and Infection Microbiology*.

11 Andrés Gómez and A. Alonso Aguirre, 'Infectious Diseases and the Illegal Wildlife Trade' (2009) 1149 *Annals of the New York Academy of Sciences* 16.

12 IPBES et al., *Workshop Report on Biodiversity*, 8.

13 IPBES et al., *Workshop Report on Biodiversity*, 8.

14 See, for example, Lorenzo Cotula, 'Towards a Political Economy of the COVID-19 Crisis: Reflections on an Agenda for Research and Action' (2021) 138 *World Development* 105235, 2.

15 IPBES et al., *Workshop Report on Biodiversity*, 39.

16 Tamara Power et al., 'COVID-19 and Indigenous Peoples: An Imperative for Action' (2020) 29 (15–16) *Journal of Clinical Nursing* 2737.

communities suffer a raft of other disadvantages during pandemics that are not the case for non-Indigenous communities.[17]

Women have also been disproportionally disadvantaged. Around the world, sexual and reproductive health services were closed as they were not considered an essential service.[18] UNFPA predicted up to seven million unintended pregnancies worldwide during the pandemic, with potentially thousands of deaths from unsafe abortion and complicated births due to inadequate access to emergency care.[19] Domestic violence rates have increased.[20] The extra domestic workload associated with lockdown, such as home-schooling, seems to have mostly fallen on women, and this is evidenced by the reduced productivity of working women, particularly in academia. Various journals have reported a drop in article submission by women authors and a simultaneous increase from men.[21]

The same dominations are seen in the realm of vaccine development and distribution. High-income countries have been able to spearhead vaccine development and distribution, leaving the lower- and middle-income countries without viable short-term access to vaccines or the genetic information required to develop one (assuming the sufficient financial and human resources to do so). What this means is that high-income countries will have likely vaccinated their populations by 2022, but the poorest and most disadvantaged nations will have to wait until 2023 before vaccines are even available to them.[22]

Additionally, and like the previous case studies, vulnerability is not limited to humans. Zoonotic diseases can become 'anthroponosis', or reverse

[17] See for example Power et al., 'COVID-19 and Indigenous Peoples'; Sergio Meneses-Navarro et al., 'The Challenges Facing Indigenous Communities in Latin America as They Confront the COVID-19 Pandemic' (2020) 19(1) *International Journal for Equity in Health* 63.

[18] Sophie Cousins, 'COVID-19 Has "Devastating" Effect on Women and Girls' (2020) 396(10247) *The Lancet* 301, 301.

[19] Cousins, 'COVID-19 Has "Devastating" Effect'.

[20] Audrey Lebret, 'COVID-19 Pandemic and Derogation to Human Rights' (2020) 7 *Journal of Law and the Biosciences*.

[21] Michelle L. Bell and Kelvin C. Fong, 'Gender Differences in First and Corresponding Authorship in Public Health Research Submissions during the COVID-19 Pandemic' (2021) 111 (1) *American Journal of Public Health* 159; Wietske Van Osch, Dorothy E. Leidner and Cynthia M. Beath, 'Does a Societal Lockdown Treat Gender the Same? Submission and Reviewing Patterns at JAIS During Spring 2020' (2020) 21 *Journal of the Association for Information Systems* 1370; Laura Inno, Alessandra Rotundi and Arianna Piccialli, 'COVID-19 Lockdown Effects on Gender Inequality' (2020) 4(12) *Nature Astronomy* 1114.

[22] 'More than 85 Poor Countries Will Not Have Widespread Access to Coronavirus Vaccines before 2023', *Economist Intelligence Unit* (27 January 2021). Available at: www.eiu.com/n/85-poor-countries-will-not-have-access-to-coronavirus-vaccines/ (last accessed 25 March 2021).

zoonoses, wherein the disease is passed back to an animal species, often with devastating consequences. In Hawaii, over one-third of native bird species have been driven to extinction or have become highly endangered because of introduced avian malaria and pox.[23] COVID-19 has been transmitted to lions and tigers, cats and dogs, and minks in fur farms, and millions of these animals have subsequently been killed as a result.[24]

Every aspect of the development, the spread of, and response to COVID-19 demonstrates humanity's shared vulnerability with wildlife and the environment, and how embedded vulnerability continues to be tied to race, gender, environmental destruction, and other societal structures that privilege the 'autonomous few' over the vulnerable whole.

The increasing risk of spill-over events and the high ability of transmission between communities and across borders means that the risk of further pandemics is increasing, and COVID-19 is unlikely to be the last significant spill-over event we see if a transformative change is not undertaken. IPBES has deemed 2020 to be the start of the era of pandemics.[25] They suggest that avoiding the era of pandemics requires a seismic shift in how we deal with pandemics, moving from a focus on reacting to pandemics after the fact, to a focus on pandemic prevention, that is, preventing the spill-over events that can lead to large scale transmission. What is left unsaid is that such a seismic shift is underpinned by an inherent acknowledgement that we need to shift from an autonomy approach to one of resilience to vulnerability.

7.3 INTERNATIONAL VULNERABILITY RESPONSES

Disasters arising from human–wildlife conflict are socio-political events.[26] The resilience of people and communities before, during and after instances of conflict is certainly political and institutionally embedded. COVID-19 has highlighted that international institutions have been built on a foundation of autonomy and that such a structure has not been able to adequately address the vulnerabilities that are associated with this and other pandemics. First,

[23] P. Daszak et al., 'Collaborative Research Approaches to the Role of Wildlife in Zoonotic Disease Emergence' (2007) 315 *Current Topics in Microbiology and Immunology* 463.

[24] Piers Beirne, 'Wildlife Trade and COVID-19: Towards a Criminology of Anthropogenic Pathogen Spillover' [2020] *The British Journal of Criminology*; 'Denmark to Cull up to 17 Million Mink amid Coronavirus Fears', *BBC News* (online, 5 November 2020). Available at: www.bbc.com/news/world-europe-54818615 (last accessed 25 March 2021); Aguirre et al., 'Opportunities for Transdisciplinary Science'.

[25] IPBES et al., *Workshop Report on Biodiversity*, 6.

[26] Matthewman and Huppatz, 'A Sociology of Covid-19'.

international institutions have mandates related to response, monitoring, and management of wildlife disease spill-over events, and not on prevention before they occur. Likewise, international law that directly concerns zoonose spill-over prevention is minimal, with most relevant international law also being on the subject of pandemic response. Even then, there is no one treaty or binding legal instrument; much of the work is done via soft law (through non-binding agreements) and international organisations, making this not exactly a matter of law but more of voluntary and haphazard international collaboration. Yet, that collaboration is also lacking at times, with the traditional mandate of international organisations falling within their autonomous objectives and structures.

The primary source of international law on pandemic response is the World Health Organisation's (WHO) 2005 *International Health Regulations* (IHR).[27] The IHR was passed after the 2003 SARS outbreak, as a means of giving the WHO greater authority to combat diseases of pandemic potential.[28] The purpose of the IHR is 'to prevent, protect against, control and provide a public health response to the international spread of disease in ways that are commensurate with and restricted to public health risks, and which avoid unnecessary interference with international traffic and trade'.[29] However, prevention has not been the focus of WHO in terms of disease spill-over. As Childs notes, the WHO focus instead lies on tracking, regulating genome sequencing and sharing of the virus and data and regulating human activity and movement around viruses.[30]

The health and welfare of wildlife and farm animals also fall within the responsibility of the World Organisation on Animal Health (often known as the OIE, due to its original French name, Office International des Epizooties). The OIE is tasked with monitoring and preventing animal disease, including zoonoses, and maintains a list of 'notifiable animal diseases'.[31] Member countries are required to conduct surveillance of farmed and

[27] World Health Organization, *International Health Regulations* (2005), 3rd ed. (World Health Organization, 2016).

[28] Eric Mack, 'The World Health Organization's New International Health Regulations: Incursion on State Sovereignty and Ill-Fated Response to Global Health Issues Developments' (2006) 7(1) *Chicago Journal of International Law* 365, 366.

[29] WHO, *International Health Regulations*, Article 2.

[30] James E. Childs, 'Pre-Spillover Prevention of Emerging Zoonotic Diseases: What Are the Targets and What Are the Tools?', in James E. Childs, John S. Mackenzie and Jürgen A. Richt (eds.), *Wildlife and Emerging Zoonotic Diseases: The Biology, Circumstances and Consequences of Cross-Species Transmission* (Springer, 2007) 389, 394.

[31] 'OIE-Listed Diseases 2021: OIE – World Organisation for Animal Health'. Available at: www.oie.int/animal-health-in-the-world/oie-listed-diseases-2021/ (last accessed 25 March 2021).

wild animals and must notify the OIE of newly detected or re-occurring OIE-listed diseases. Thereafter member countries must also provide weekly reports on the evolution of the disease and internal control measures. The OIE uses this information to maintain the World Animal Health Information System (WAHIS) which is publicly accessible.[32] They also produce policy documents such as the Terrestrial Animal Health Code. Initially, the OIE was created to address contagious diseases in farmed animals, not wild animals, and that aspect of the OIE's role is still developing. The OIE does have a wildlife working group but the outputs are not the same as for farmed animals, and as Childs discusses at length, are limited by State's ability to adequately detect and monitor diseases in wildlife, a difficult task.[33] The other issue with policies produced by the OIE is that they are not law, and so not binding. In essence, any Codes or policies released by the OIE are 'best practice' guidelines with no requirement for compliance or uptake. While it is encouraging that the OIE has 182 member countries, suggesting that there would be large-scale compliance, without any reporting or regulatory requirements the true level of compliance cannot be known.

In addition to the OIE and the WHO, the Food and Agriculture Organisation, the Secretariats of the *Convention on Biological Diversity* and CITES, the World Bank, and a wide diversity of civil society organisations have all been engaged in disease monitoring and risk in similar, limited ways.[34] Additionally, and given the anthropogenic environmental drivers of disease spill-over, international environmental governance is relevant on a broader scale. Yet, as discussed in Chapter 4, environmental governance is also fragmented and limited to a specific environmental problem or area. This fragmentation poses a problem when governing complex issues that require multi-dimensional consideration, such as in the case of human–wildlife conflict broadly or zoonoses specifically, where land clearing and habitat destruction, poverty, natural and cultural rights, trade, development, animal welfare and disease control must all be factored into a governance paradigm. Moreover, pandemic prevention has not factored heavily in environmental governance thus far, it remains mostly within the public/animal health domain. Some instruments seem, prima facie, able to encompass zoonose

[32] See 'The World Animal Health Information System: OIE – World Organisation for Animal Health'. Available at: www.oie.int/en/animal-health-in-the-world/the-world-animal-health-information-system/the-world-animal-health-information-system/ (last accessed 25 March 2021).

[33] Childs, 'Pre-Spillover Prevention', 417.

[34] IPBES et al., *Workshop Report on Biodiversity*, 22.

spill-over in their ambit, but do not, or at least do not specifically and, because of this, they have limits.

Neither zoonoses nor the broader types of human–wildlife conflict are mentioned in any of the main international wildlife treaties. Let us examine the area of wildlife trade specifically. At the international level, the *Convention on International Trade in Endangered Species* (CITES) is the only treaty that deals directly with the issue of wildlife trade. However, as the name suggests, the treaty is limited to regulation of the trade in endangered species, and even there it has severe limits in terms of its ability to stem the spread of zoonoses. The treaty seeks to protect highly traded wildlife from extinction and is therefore not equipped to deal with the issue of wildlife disease. It is also ultimately a trade treaty, which means that it does allow trade of wildlife with some controls, which largely revolve around the Treaty's permit system and the classification of species into categories.[35] The treaty has no power to list species that should not be traded due to their zoonose risk, although there have been recent calls for the Treaty to take this approach.[36]

From a domestic point of view, the treaty has little real effect as it only places limits on the import/export of endangered species. It does not regulate the trade of species that originate inside state territory. For example, the Asian pangolin is a critically endangered species listed in Appendix 1 of CITES, which means that import/export of pangolins or their products is prohibited. However, the Treaty does not, and cannot, prohibit China (or any other Asian range-state) from trading them domestically. It is up to the laws of the State to regulate that trade and those laws, together with monitoring and enforcement, are often lacking. It also allows the trade of captive-bred animals and so allows farming of wild animal species (although some suggest sustainable farming as a way of controlling spill-over risk, while others argue that legal and illegal wildlife trade are inextricably linked).[37] Further, and despite the listing of the Asian pangolins, it is still legal to import African pangolin species and the scales into China, continuing the cultural practice and creating further unsustainable demand.[38]

[35] For a more detailed account of the mechanisms of CITES, see Section 6.3.1; and chapter 15 of Bowman, Davies and Redgwell, *Lyster's International Wildlife Law*.

[36] B. Weissgold et al., 'How We Can Use the CITES Wildlife Trade Agreement to Help Prevent Pandemics', *Scientific American*, 24 August 2020.

[37] IPBES et al., *Workshop Report on Biodiversity*; Jeffrey A. McNeely, 'Nature and COVID-19: The Pandemic, the Environment, and the Way Ahead' (2021) 50(4) *Ambio* 767, 777. Although note the contrasting position in Neil D'Cruze et al., 'Trading Tactics: Time to Rethink the Global Trade in Wildlife' (2020) 10(12) *Animals* 2456.

[38] Beirne, 'Wildlife Trade and COVID-19', 12.

What the OIE and CITES also highlight is that there remain gaps around disease surveillance and monitoring because of the 'list' frameworks that exist. Regular monitoring of species only occurs once they are on a list. The way that species get on a list is problematic too, because it is only those that are important for social/conservation reasons that are regularly researched (and those research projects funded) and not those that need to be monitored for disease.[39] They are also largely terrestrial mammals[40] and, even when they are on a list, there are still deeply embedded impediments to disease surveillance and research.[41] The aspects of wildlife ecology that need to be monitored are also generally lacking when it comes to legal requirements. In short, the legal mechanisms for protection/conservation, are not congruent with human and animal health and could go further to encourage and even mandate a base level of environmental monitoring (and thereafter a base standard of conservation and animal health).

In addition to treaties that have direct relevance to pandemic prevention, but lack the mandate to address it, there are areas of international law that, at first glance, seem outside of the ambit of zoonose prevention but fit squarely within it. For example, trade law and, in particular, free trade agreements and their housed institutions, need to be considered as a relevant, connected institutional framework. What we have seen is that trade is not free, despite the claims to the contrary. It is not free for those that are exploited in sourcing and preparing the product, and it can have wider societal implications, as we have seen with COVID-19. Some costs are not dispersed evenly. However, the nature of 'free trade' has not been widely questioned, even concerning wildlife and wildlife products such as fur. This is despite evidence that trade itself can increase the risk of spill-over events that result in uneven cost allocation and distribution.[42]

But it is not all bad news, and the particular universal vulnerability that has been made evident by pandemic risk has united international organisations in the past, and those collaborations have progressed an approach to pandemics that could be considered a resilience approach to vulnerability. One of the

[39] McNeely, 'Nature and COVID-19', 777.

[40] IUCN, 'Summary Statistics'. Available at: www.iucnredlist.org/about/barometer-of-life (last accessed 25 March 2021); Nico Eisenhauer, Aletta Bonn and Carlos A. Guerra, 'Recognizing the Quiet Extinction of Invertebrates' (2019) 10(1) *Nature Communications* 50, 51.

[41] See for example Childs, 'Pre-Spillover Prevention'; D. E. Stallknecht, 'Impediments to Wildlife Disease Surveillance, Research, and Diagnostics', in James E. Childs, John S. Mackenzie and Jürgen A. Richt (eds.), *Wildlife and Emerging Zoonotic Diseases: The Biology, Circumstances and Consequences of Cross-Species Transmission* (Springer, 2007) 445.

[42] Daszak et al., 'Collaborative Research Approaches'.

more promising resilience measures is the framing and uptake of the 'One Health' approach. The One Health approach to public health governance recognises that human, animal, and environmental health are systematically entwined and need to be considered simultaneously in health decision-making (as the eco-vulnerability suggests).[43] Although the definition of the approach differs between institutions and users, WHO defines it as: '… an approach to designing and implementing programmes, policies, legislation and research in which multiple sectors communicate and work together to achieve better public health outcomes …'[44]

The One Health approach, in theory, acknowledges mutual vulnerabilities and allows a focus on universal resilience. It gained prominence in direct response to the threat of emerging infectious diseases and zoonoses and the recognition that greater interdisciplinary collaboration was required to combat the threat.[45] The basis of the approach is established in 12 principles drafted in 2004 and known as the 'Manhattan Principles'.[46] The principles include (emphasis added):

2. Recognize that decisions regarding land and water use have real implications for health. Alterations in the *resilience* of ecosystems and shifts in patterns of disease emergence and spread manifest themselves when we fail to recognize this relationship …
4. Recognize that human health programmes can greatly contribute to conservation efforts …
10. Form collaborative relationships among governments, local people and the private and public (i.e., non-profit) sectors to meet the challenges of global health and biodiversity conservation …
12. Invest in educating and raising awareness among the world's people and in influencing the policy process to increase recognition that we must better understand the relationships between health and ecosystem integrity to succeed in improving prospects for a healthier planet.

43 Alicia Davis and Jo Sharp, 'Rethinking One Health: Emergent Human, Animal and Environmental Assemblages' (2020) 258 *Social Science & Medicine* 113093, 1.

44 WHO, 'One Health; What Is "One Health"?' (2017). Available at: www.who.int/features/qa/One Health/en/ (last accessed 25 March 2021).

45 For a discussion of the history of the development of the One Health approach, see E. Paul J. Gibbs, 'The Evolution of One Health: A Decade of Progress and Challenges for the Future' (2014) 174(4) *Veterinary Record* 85.

46 The draft principles were termed the Manhatten Principles by the organisers of the 'One World, One Health' event in 2004, and can be accessed at www.oneworldOne Health.org/ (last accessed 25 March 2021).

Additionally, the principles seek to reduce the demand for wildlife trade and bushmeat, restrict the mass-culling of wild animals to control a disease threat and seek investment in animal health infrastructure, amongst other things. Versions of the One Health approach have since been adopted by the World Health Organisation, the Food and Agriculture Organisation and the OIE.

As the approach also recognises institutional vulnerability, it has had some success in encouraging institutional collaboration. For example, in 2008, a resolution by the *Convention on Migratory Species* Conference of the Parties (CoP) asked its Secretariat and the FAO Animal Health Service to jointly convene a Task Force on Wildlife Disease and to integrate the One Health approach.[47] Also in 2008, the FAO, OIE, UNICEF, World Bank, WHO and UN System Influenza Coordination drafted a Strategic Framework for Reducing Risks of Infectious Diseases, called 'Contributing to One World One Health'.[48] In 2013, the OIE and the CBD signed a cooperation agreement that promotes a One Health approach to managing the risks of animal diseases at the animal–human–ecosystem interface.[49] The approach has also been acknowledged by both the Ramsar and CITES CoP[50] and the UN Convention to Combat Desertification CoP considered that the One Health approach could help deal with the drivers of desertification.[51]

The COVID-19 pandemic has only increased this collaboration between and within international institutions and those same institutions are striving to publicly highlight the interconnected vulnerabilities we face through the One Health approach. For example, the IPBES Workshop Report on Biodiversity and Pandemics recommended the creation of an intergovernmental panel with a specific mandate on pandemic prevention, rather than the haphazard institutions tasked with various aspects of pandemic response. The international community responded with the World Health Organisation

47 *Convention on Migratory Species*, CoP 10, 2011, Resolution 10.22, Wildlife disease and migratory species, Preamble and §1. Available at: www.cms.int/en/meeting/tenth-meeting-conference-parties-cms (last accessed 25 March 2021).

48 Claire Lajaunie and Pierre Mazzega, 'One Health and Biodiversity Convention; The Emergence of Health Issues in Biodiversity Conventions' 7 *IUCNAEL EJournal* 105, 117.

49 *Cooperation Agreement between the Secretariat of the Convention on Biological Diversity and the World Health Organisation for Animal Health (OIE)*, 15 February 2013. Available at: www.oie.int/fileadmin/Home/eng/About_us/docs/pdf/accords/CBD_accord_ANG.pdf (last accessed 25 March 2021).

50 *Convention on Biodiversity*, COP XII, 2014, Decision XII/18 Sustainable Use of Biodiversity: Bushmeat and Sustainable Wildlife Management, §4; *Ramsar Convention*, COP XI, 2012, Resolution XI.12 Wetlands and Health: Taking an Ecosystem Approach, Preamble and §7.

51 *United Nations Convention to Combat Desertification*, COP 11, 2013, Final outcome of the UNCCD 2nd Scientific Conference, ICCD/COP (11)/CST/INF.3, §29.

supporting the establishment of a One Health High-Level Expert Council and offering to host its secretariat, in collaboration with the FAO, OIE, and UNEP.[52] This support arose as a result of an initiative instigated by some authors of the IPBES report and the French Government, called PREZODE (PREventing ZOonotic Disease Emergence). It already has support from the UN Environment Programme, the World Bank, the European Commission, and partner countries. It was prepared through a series of online workshops that convened nearly 400 researchers and public health authorities from 50 countries. At the time of writing, the supporting institutions had called for experts to apply to be appointed to the Council and it seems as though this initiative will proceed, although the full mandate of the Council along with its governance arrangements and State support remains to be clarified.

Similarly, there have been global leaders that have called for a 'pandemic treaty'. Boris Johnson, the Prime Minister of the United Kingdom, has suggested the objective of the treaty would be to 'foster an all of government and all of society approach, strengthening national, regional and global capacities and resilience to future pandemics. This includes greatly enhancing international co-operation to improve, for example, alert systems, data-sharing, research and local, regional and global production and distribution of medical and public health counter-measures such as vaccines, medicines, diagnostics and personal protective equipment'.[53] The treaty would also utilise a One Health approach. However, genuine questions have been raised about the nature of any such treaty, including its overlap with the already existing IHR, and the difficulty in having a wide range of nations concede the sovereignty necessary for further legal measures, especially given some states returned to a more 'nationalist' approach following the pandemic.[54]

On this note, and while a vulnerability approach to international governance of the issue is moving forward, there remain some detractors. It is often

[52] 'WHO Director-General's Speech at the Paris Peace Forum "Strengthening the Multilateral Health Architecture and Fighting against Infodemics" – 12 November 2020'. Available at: www.who.int/director-general/speeches/detail/who-director-general-s-speech-at-the-paris-peace-forum-strengthening-the-multilateral-health-architecture-and-fighting-against-infodemics—12-november-2020 (last accessed 25 March 2021).

[53] 'No Government Can Address the Threat of Pandemics Alone – We Must Come Together', *GOV.UK* (29 March 2021). Available at: www.gov.uk/government/speeches/no-government-can-address-the-threat-of-pandemics-alone-we-must-come-together (last accessed 25 March 2021).

[54] Clare Wenham, 'A Global Pandemic Treaty Won't Work until Leaders Realise the Benefits of Solidarity | Coronavirus | The Guardian', *The Guardian* (Online), 2 April 2021. Available at: www.theguardian.com/commentisfree/2021/apr/01/global-pandemic-treaty-covid-disease-control?CMP=fb_cif (last accessed 25 March 2021).

argued, for example, that the WHO's response mandate already infringes on state sovereignty,[55] a principle that, as discussed in Chapter 4, remains an impediment to an effective vulnerability response. Mack argues that the WHO is seeking to become a supranational organization capable of side-stepping states' rights irrespective of geopolitical boundaries and that public international health concerns appear to have superseded all notions of state sovereignty as a matter of customary international law.[56] This argument will only be amplified by the creation of a further panel tasked with prevention. Yet, this argument is to be contrasted with the worldwide call for greater compliance and transparency by the Chinese administration, following the spread of COVID-19. In such a situation, it appears that states are willing to prioritise public health over state sovereignty, although perhaps only where the state sovereignty being compromised is lower in the dominant hierarchy (in this case, not a western state). This is to be considered in the context of state-based dissidence surrounding the role of WHO. While the SARS outbreak seems to have united states to give WHO more power to address and respond to international public health emergencies, COVID-19 seems to have had the opposite effect in some instances, where people have not been able to see that the WHO had any effect in minimising the spread of COVID-19.[57]

Finally, and although this section has focused on the laws and institutions that are directly relevant to pandemic prevention, a vulnerability approach is required elsewhere as well. Our environmental and health institutions are not in this alone, nor are they solely responsible for increasing resilience to pandemics and other environment-related health and well-being issues, such as climate change, biodiversity loss and ocean acidification, to name a few. Consider the vast number of institutions that have been concerned with the COVID-19 response. Alternatively, consider whether any institutions are not concerned with the COVID-19 response. This pandemic has shown not only that no institution is an island, but that a connective and relational institutional response is not only desirable but possible. Several States have embraced a holistic response to the reduced levels of resilience that individuals have experienced as a result of the pandemic, and they will be the focus of Section 7.4.

[55] Mack, 'New International Health Regulations'.

[56] Mack, 'New International Health Regulations'.

[57] For example, the US withdrew WHO funding. See Tong Wu, 'The Socioeconomic and Environmental Drivers of the COVID-19 Pandemic: A Review' (2021) 50(4) *Ambio* 822; Javier C. Hernández, 'Trump Slammed the W.H.O. Over Coronavirus. He's Not Alone', *The New York Times* (Online), 8 April 2020. Available at: www.nytimes.com/2020/04/08/world/asia/trump-who-coronavirus-china.html (last accessed 25 March 2021).

7.4 EXAMPLES OF LOCAL AND NATIONAL VULNERABILITY RESPONSES

Like international responses, national and local responses to COVID-19 have been a mixed bag of business-as-usual policies that perpetuate the existing hierarchies and dominations evident in the promotion of autonomy, with a spattering of innovative and transformative approaches that recognise the role of interconnections between people, wildlife and society in preventing future pandemics.

In the short-term, control responses, such as lockdowns and travel restrictions, appear to have eased some environmental pressures. There has been a reduced demand for production and so less extractive resource mining.[58] The great 'anthropause', as it has been described, has allowed wildlife to move freely through metropolitan areas.[59] In the early months of lockdown and travel restrictions, environmental air pollution was reduced by up to 30 per cent, worldwide.[60] However, it is important to note that these effects were temporary and need to be balanced with the negative effects of lockdown and restrictions. On balance, COVID-19 policy responses may be more harmful to wildlife than they are beneficial.[61] For example, elephant and rhinoceros poachers have been able to expand into areas where there are usually too many tourists to effectively poach.[62] A reduction in nature tourism has affected conservation fundraising and outcomes.[63] The OECD has suggested that the clearest example of a biodiversity-harmful response measure to date is the loosening of environmental regulation.[64] The Australian Government, for example, has sought to lead an environmentally harmful 'gas-led recovery'

[58] Daniel Rondeau, Brianna Perry and Franque Grimard, 'The Consequences of COVID-19 and Other Disasters for Wildlife and Biodiversity' (2020) 76(4) *Environmental and Resource Economics* 945, 946.

[59] Christian Rutz et al., 'COVID-19 Lockdown Allows Researchers to Quantify the Effects of Human Activity on Wildlife' (2020) 4(9) *Nature Ecology & Evolution* 1156.

[60] Sulaman Muhammad, Xingle Long and Muhammad Salman, 'COVID-19 Pandemic and Environmental Pollution: A Blessing in Disguise?' (2020) 728 *Science of the Total Environment* 138820, 1.

[61] OECD, 'Biodiversity and the Economic Response to COVID-19: Ensuring a Green and Resilient Recovery', *OECD* (28 September 2020) 9. Available at: www.oecd.org/coronavirus/policy-responses/biodiversity-and-the-economic-response-to-covid-19-ensuring-a-green-and-resilient-recovery-d98b5a09/ (last accessed 25 March 2021).

[62] Siyabonga Sishi and Tim Cocks, 'South Africa Dehorns Dozens of Rhinos to Prevent Lockdown Poaching Surge, Reuters 5 June 2020. Available at: www.reuters.com/article/us-world-environmentday-safrica-rhinos-idUSKBN23C00B (last accessed 25 March 2021).

[63] Rondeau, Perry and Grimard, 'Consequences of COVID-19', 948.

[64] OECD, 'Biodiversity and the Economic Response', 9.

and has attempted to introduce changes to its national environmental legislation that 'cuts green tape' in major development applications.[65]

Some countries though have followed the OECD's suggestion of a 'green recovery' and have tightened environmental regulation or promoted economic and social policies that promote conservation. In their report 'Biodiversity and the Economic Response to COVID-19: Ensuring a Green and Resilient Recovery', the OECD lists several examples.[66] These include China and Vietnam, which have introduced measures to regulate wildlife trade to reduce the associated human health risks. Canada is spending CAD $1.7 billion to clean up orphaned or inactive oil and gas wells, providing thousands of jobs while achieving lasting environmental benefits. The Finnish government adopted a package of economic recovery measures that includes EUR $53 million for protections that involve green areas, water services and forest conservation and EUR $13.1 million to rehabilitate nature sites and develop nature tourism. The New Zealand government has launched a 'jobs for nature' programme worth NZD $1.3 billion.

Other, non-environmental examples of recovery packages also fall within the 'resilience to vulnerability' type responses already described in this section and in Section 7.3. For example, the European Commission invested 37 billion euros to help small companies and the healthcare sector and support short-term work.[67] The Australian Federal Government, despite their failures in the environmental sector, invested AUD $198 billion in welfare payments, ensuring that people in work who were at risk of unemployment and the already unemployed received AUD $750 per week as a safeguard.[68] Afghanistan provided bread to the poor and waived electricity bills.[69] In Malaysia, RM 6 billion was spent on stimulus measures such as social security relief and rural infrastructure spending.[70]

65 The Hon Scott Morrison MP, 'Gas-Fired Recovery | Prime Minister of Australia', 15 September 2020. Available at: www.pm.gov.au/media/gas-fired-recovery (last accessed 25 March 2021); Lisa Cox, 'Coalition Is Aiming to Change Australia's Environment Laws before Review Is Finished', *The Guardian* (Online), 23 April 2020. Available at: www.theguardian.com/australia-news/2020/apr/23/coalition-is-aiming-to-change-australias-environment-laws-before-review-is-finished (last accessed 25 March 2021).

66 OECD, 'Biodiversity and the Economic Response', 10–11.

67 Lebret, 'COVID-19 Pandemic and Derogation to Human Rights', 1.

68 Australian Federal Government, Budget 2020/21; COVID-19 Response, Supporting Australians through the crisis. Available at: https://budget.gov.au/2020-21/content/covid-19.html (last accessed 25 March 2021).

69 International Monetary Fund, 'Policy Responses to COVID19'. Available at: www.imf.org/en/Topics/imf-and-covid19/Policy-Responses-to-COVID-19 (last accessed 25 March 2021).

70 International Monetary Fund, 'Policy Responses to COVID19'.

In contrast, states that have not led a holistic response have struggled to reduce the impact of COVID-19, particularly states that have focused on economic stability over public health, such as the United States and Indonesia.[71] Further, and at a deeper level, prevention and response to this pandemic were hindered by the perceived autonomy of States and their continued reliance on the principle of State sovereignty, as noted in Section 7.3. Various commentators have pointed out that the pandemic is an example of a disaster that can disrupt governance arrangements.[72] Indeed, the pandemic has seen a rise in nationalism, away from globalisation and the international order, because of the severe negative effects on their economies, the need to control access to certain goods and manufacture within the State and the retaliatory actions this has prompted.[73] International institutions have not been excluded from this process. As already noted, the International Health Regulations have been considered ineffective, despite the expanded mandate post-2005, as it was still concerned with balancing state sovereignty and requiring and fostering support for wildlife disease monitoring and notification protocols. In particular, the critiques include that WHO acted too slowly and that it was too trusting of and should have taken further action against China (an incursion into state sovereignty that would unlikely be tolerated by any of the heads of nations that called for such action).[74] This, combined with States' non-compliance with requirements and recommendations, such as mandatory mask-wearing, made the Regulations look ineffective according to some commentators.[75]

71 David P. Carter and Peter J. May, 'Making Sense of the U.S. COVID-19 Pandemic Response: A Policy Regime Perspective' (2020) 42(2) *Administrative Theory & Praxis* 265; Muhammad Zulfikar Rakhmat, 'Indonesia's Poor COVID-19 Responses Take a Toll on Its Global Image', *The Conversation*. Available at: http://theconversation.com/indonesias-poor-covid-19-responses-take-a-toll-on-its-global-image-150939 (last accessed 25 March 2021).

72 Cotula, 'Towards a Political Economy of the COVID-19 Crisis', 1.

73 Michael A. Hitt, R. Michael Holmes and Jean-Luc Arregle, 'The (COVID-19) Pandemic and the New World (Dis)Order' (2021) 56(4) *Journal of World Business* 101210, 2–3.

74 Hernández, 'Trump Slammed the W.H.O.'; Stephen Buranyi, 'The WHO v Coronavirus: Why It Can't Handle the Pandemic', *The Guardian* (Online), 10 April 2020. Available at: www.theguardian.com/news/2020/apr/10/world-health-organization-who-v-coronavirus-why-it-cant-handle-pandemic (last accessed 25 March 2021).

75 Amy Maxmen, 'Why Did the World's Pandemic Warning System Fail When COVID Hit?' (2021) 589(7843) *Nature* 499; Lawrence O. Gostin, Roojin Habibi and Benjamin Mason Meier, 'Has Global Health Law Risen to Meet the COVID-19 Challenge? Revisiting the International Health Regulations to Prepare for Future Threats' (2020) 48(2) *Journal of Law, Medicine & Ethics* 376.

7.5 CONTINUING THE MARCH TOWARD RESILIENCE POLICY; ADDRESSING ISSUES WITH THE ONE HEALTH APPROACH AND INTERNATIONAL RESPONSES TO COVID-19

While the global response to COVID-19 has seen a push towards resilience-based policies and practices, there is still work to be done at both the international and local levels. One Health, for example, has unfortunately not been as holistic in practice as it is in definition and the institutional support at a State level and in some cases at the international level was unsurprisingly lacking before the spread of COVID-19. But, at a broader scale, there remain various aspects of the One Health approach that require improvement,[76] as it suffers many of the same institutional critiques covered in Chapters 2 and 3 and has the potential to maintain the dominant hierarchy.

First, and despite its ambitious framing, One Health, in practice, remains largely a process of collaboration between human health and veterinary health experts, focused on preventing contact between people and possibly diseased wildlife and farm animals.[77] The environmental pinnacle of the people–animal–environment triangle is largely neglected and, instead, the approach remains a scientific endeavour primarily falling within the field of epidemiology. In other words, it remains, even at a base level, highly anthropocentric. Some commentators suggest that this was an inevitable outcome from the start of the development of One Health. For example, the initial concept of 'bringing together' three separate research areas assumed that they were previously three separate conceptual areas.[78] As this book and many others have demonstrated, this separation is and always was a myth. By starting with such a premise, however, the dominant hierarchy of humans at the top and environment and individual non-human animals at the bottom remains embedded in the approach. That said, this dominant approach to One Health has not been without its benefits, as it has worked well in terms of coordinating detection of spill-over and response,[79] but it

[76] See for example, the discussion in Aguirre et al., 'Opportunities for Transdisciplinary Science'.

[77] See, for example, Susan Craddock and Steve Hinchliffe, 'One World, One Health? Social Science Engagements with the One Health Agenda' (2015) 129 *Social Science & Medicine* (1982) 1; Sara Woldehanna and Susan Zimicki, 'An Expanded One Health Model: Integrating Social Science and One Health to Inform Study of the Human–Animal Interface' (2015) 129 *Social Science & Medicine* 87.

[78] Davis and Sharp, 'Rethinking One Health', 2; Alex M. Nading, 'Humans, Animals, and Health: From Ecology to Entanglement' (2013) 4(1) *Environment and Society* 60.

[79] Woldehanna and Zimicki, 'Expanded One Health Model', 88; Belinda Crawford, Ian Roth and Tiggy Grillo, 'One Health and Hendra Virus: A Collaborative Approach in Action' (2012) 23(7–8) NSW *Public Health Bulletin* 160.

does not assist with the complex web of factors relevant to wildlife conflict and pandemic prevention.

A subset of this critique is that the approach universalises western health and ideas of development[80] and, in this way, as in other conflict governance regimes, places only some humans at the top of the hierarchy following a western modernist epistemology.[81] Social behaviours, cultures and contexts at the local level are not a focus in this universalised approach,[82] nor are the political and economic processes surrounding spill-over prevention and pandemic events.[83] Woldehanna and Zimicki list the social determinants that contribute to human–wildlife interactions that are not considered in current iterations of One Health, including biological and household characteristics, location and resilience of a community, levels of poverty, access to resources, norms and livelihood patterns and governance and political systems (all of which have been discussed as interrelated and relevant to human–wildlife conflict elsewhere in this book).[84]

This dominant perspective can also be seen through the lack of engagement with the environmental realm in general and the lack of a non-human perspective (as with all other international approaches discussed in Chapter 4).[85] Rock argues that the problem arises due to the primary collaboration being between the 'health' industries, wherein the goal is to protect 'public health'.[86] The 'public' is defined very narrowly. Rock suggests instead that communities can be multispecies in composition and gives dog parks as an example. We too have seen examples of multispecies communities, where multispecies interactions define communities, in Chapters 5 and 6. To look solely then at the minimalisation of contact in these communities is erroneous.

With a lack of consideration of wildlife welfare, reverse zoonoses are not considered problematic, nor is the mass killing that can be a response to pandemics and more general spill-over events. Further, non-humans are as

80 For further discussion of the universalisation of development, see Section 4.4.2.
81 Davis and Sharp, 'Rethinking One Health', 2.
82 Woldehanna and Zimicki, 'Expanded One Health Model'.
83 Davis and Sharp, 'Rethinking One Health', 1.
84 Woldehanna and Zimicki, 'Expanded One Health Model', 90.
85 Melanie J. Rock, 'Who or What Is "the Public" in Critical Public Health? Reflections on Posthumanism and Anthropological Engagements with One Health' (2017) 27(3) *Critical Public Health* 314.
86 Rock, 'Who or What Is "the Public"'.

integral to the remedies and prevention methods as they are to the formation of the problem.[87]

Fortunately, an expanded One Health model, that better accommodates environment and social drivers of pandemics, as well as local context, has been called for by various authors in recent years.[88] What is needed then is institutional guidance and support from an international level, and within States, to support a reinvigorated, inclusive One Health approach to the governance of the human–wildlife–environment relationship. Any international, intergovernmental One Health panel should include researchers and practitioners from many disciplines, including the social sciences, law, philosophy, and animal studies to ensure that these gaps are filled.

Complete recognition of the One Health approach would see it used as a tool to ensure political, social, and expert drive behind the drivers of pandemics and the inequalities it produced, both between and within human groups and between humans and non-humans. A complete environmental framing of One Health may result in local policies that protect, restore and regenerate tropical forests, wetlands and other biodiversity hotspots and appropriately respond to the threat of climate change, both as a matter of urgency. At a more localised level, such an approach would see potential spill-over risk as a consideration in local planning laws,[89] dedicated funding to stay on top of wildlife research and monitoring, prohibition of tourists in high-risk areas and in high-income countries, a dedicated effort to reduce wildlife consumption and cease land-clearing.

7.6 CONCLUSION

As responses to COVID-19 continue to develop and evolve, we need to ensure that the underlying drivers of this and other pandemics are not lost in the chaos. This disaster has confirmed the interrelated vulnerability arising from the pandemic and its effect on human, animal and environmental health and social inequalities, and this is clearly a matter of human–wildlife conflict.

Laws that can help to prevent disease spill-over are not focused on zoonoses as such, but the connection with zoonoses and the vulnerabilities associated with them (from all aspects, not just human health) need to be made clearer

87 Rock, 'Who or What Is "the Public"', 320.

88 Steve Hinchliffe, 'More than One World, More than One Health: Re-Configuring Interspecies Health' (2015) 129 *Social Science & Medicine* 28; Craddock and Hinchliffe, 'One World, One Health?'; Woldehanna and Zimicki, 'Expanded One Health Model'.

89 Rebecca Lipman, 'Zoonotic Diseases: Using Environmental Law to Reduce the Odds of a Future Pandemic' (2015) 33(1) *Virginia Environmental Law Journal* 153, 166.

to allow proper collaboration and deliberations around implementation, compliance and monitoring. A piecemeal approach that props up individual and institutional autonomy, the current power over conceptions of power and the dominant hierarchy facilitated this worldwide event. As many ecofeminists have noted over the decades, the factors responsible for the oppression of women, the global south, racial minorities, the LGBTIA+ community and the domination of wildlife and the environment are one and the same and are detrimental to the global resilience of individuals and communities and the ecological health of the planet itself.

While this pandemic was created through institutional promotion and maintenance of hierarchical autonomy, resilience should be the answer and policies seem to implicitly be moving towards that. This pandemic has the potential, more than any other issue of human–wildlife conflict in recent decades, to change values and attitudes towards wildlife conservation and ecosystem protection. We have seen this change already in the sense of community being built. A 2020 survey of 1,000 people in New Zealand found that 81 per cent of respondents thought the pandemic had made people learn about 'being in it together and being kind', and 88 per cent believed this attitude would continue or grow post-lockdown period.[90] This period of time, then, appears to be a unique opportunity to revisit our self-professed autonomous structures and legal promotion of individual autonomy, and undertake the 'transformative approach noted by IPBES, to embed a connected resilience approach throughout society.

90 'Coronavirus: How NZ's Covid-19 Lockdown Has Changed Our Lives', *Stuff*, 18 April 2020. Available at: www.stuff.co.nz/national/health/coronavirus/121087682/coronavirus-revealed–how-lockdown-has-changed-our-lives (last accessed 25 March 2021).

8

Conclusion

8.1 THE HUMAN–WILDLIFE RELATIONSHIP

What is the nature of the human–wildlife relationship? I've asked many people what they consider their relationship with wildlife to be. Many people often look fondly at their experiences with wildlife and consider their relationship with wildlife to be a positive, beneficial one and do not consider the negative impacts that we have on them and vice versa. Others have a more moderate response, getting annoyed at the birds that wake them up before sunrise or the animals that eat their crops, while still having some affinity for wild animals that don't have any negative impact on them directly. We know that positive experiences with wildlife can create positive emotions and increase our sense of place and community and many of us support wildlife and their habitat through charities. We also often think we are supporting wildlife through our actions. For example, we might visit a wildlife sanctuary and donate time or money, we might learn about wildlife habitat and what we can do to help at zoos, we might take a selfie with the wildlife we encounter and share it on social media to show our friends/followers their value. But is this positive feeling actually reflective of the totality of the human–wildlife relationship? For example, while wildlife volunteer tourism has positive psychological benefits for the human volunteers[1] and, in some cases, can create an increased conservation ethic,[2] it can have devastating negative effects on

1 Susanna Curtin, 'Wildlife Tourism: The Intangible, Psychological Benefits of Human–Wildlife Encounters' (2009) 12(5–6) *Current Issues in Tourism* 451.

2 Roy Ballantyne, Jan Packer and John Falk, 'Visitors' Learning for Environmental Sustainability: Testing Short- and Long-Term Impacts of Wildlife Tourism Experiences Using Structural Equation Modelling' (2011) 32(6) *Tourism Management* 1243.

the wildlife.[3] Selfies with wildlife can be more damaging than we suspect.[4] We also know that not all interactions with wildlife are positive and negative interactions have consequences that reach far beyond one encounter. Yet, much of the human governance of the relationship remains anthropocentric, involves managing 'problematic' animals, and does not entail a deep look into the true nature of our actions.

Questions must necessarily be raised about behaviour, attitudes and values towards wildlife and whether they are congruent with the human–wildlife relationship, in terms of how we view it, how it is in reality and how it should be. The current human–wildlife relationship is not positive on balance and certainly not mutually beneficial to both people and wildlife. It is founded on a web of interrelated dominations that serves to promote the autonomy of certain people within society, usually those that already have power and seek to maintain it. In this book, I have demonstrated this by analysing negative wildlife interactions, often called *human–wildlife conflict*. The way we attempt to manage instances of conflict reflects on the overall relationship we have with wildlife because it involves a wide range of stakeholder perspectives, is representative of how we create a hierarchy of interests around wildlife and habitat protection and demonstrates how we believe ourselves to be autonomous from wildlife.

8.2 THE NATURE OF HUMAN–WILDLIFE CONFLICT: WHAT IT IS

Human–wildlife conflict is a manifestation of human use and abuse of wildlife habitats and degradation of the human relationship with wildlife and with each other. Conflict arises because of, and is exacerbated by, notions of individual and institutional autonomy. Fineman's theory of vulnerability describes the promotion of autonomy as a fundamental flaw in the human way of thinking about our place in society and in the world.[5] Autonomy is the belief that we are free from interference, from the State, from people around us, and the environment. An autonomous legal subject is a person who contributes to society by, for example, paying taxes, and is not viewed as dependent on society, for example, by depending on welfare payments.

3 Ronda Green and Melissa Giese, 'Negative Effects of Wildlife Tourism on Wildlife', in Karen Higginbottom (ed.), *Wildlife Tourism; Impacts, Management and Planning* (Common Ground Publishing Pty Ltd, 2004) 81.

4 Aini Hasanah Abd Mutalib, 'The Photo Frenzy Phenomenon: How a Single Snap Can Affect Wildlife Populations' (2018) 19(3–4) *Biodiversity* 237.

5 See Chapter 2.

Western institutions promote this concept of autonomy as the goal of the individual; to provide for and support yourself and your private family unit.

However, no one is truly autonomous and, in this sense, the promotion of autonomy is a fallacy. We are all reliant on society's structures, the people around us, and the environment in which we live. We are especially dependent at various stages of our lives, such as during infancy and childhood and old age. It is these dependencies that demonstrate the universal nature of human vulnerability but, while autonomy is a flawed concept, it continues to be promoted in a way that is unattainable for all people and damaging for most. The promotion of autonomy as a desirable state benefits only a few members of society, those that already fit the mould and have power over what an autonomous legal subject looks like. It segregates those that are dependent from those that are viewed as autonomous and creates conflict and inequality.

Similarly, autonomy drives conflict because people and wildlife are held to be separate and distinct entities, autonomous from each other and ecosystems. There is no bridge over which relationships are formed and encouraged. Throughout this book I have demonstrated that methods of governance of human–wildlife conflict are informed by several differently named ideologies, depending on the context and laws governing the process. The three main theoretical positions that are stated to inform conflict governance are anthropocentrism, ecological holism, and welfare individualism. However, a critical analysis of all three theoretical positions shows a commonality – that they actually drive conflict. This is because the ideologies are largely inconsistent with one another and are the underlying origins of differing value positions held by conflict stakeholders. As human–wildlife conflict is largely a social conflict, it is these differences in value positions that maintain and exacerbate the conflict. In addition, the theoretical positions actually work to promote individual autonomy in practice and so autonomy is the common denominator in conflict governance.

For example, in Chapter 6, we saw all three held value positions as drivers of the conflict. The people that maintain that elephants must 'pay their own way' (by allowing people to act on their economic value) and seek to value elephants in economic terms alone, are acting consistently with an anthropocentric ideology. They argue that elephants must show human-defined value to have the right to continue to exist. Some argue that elephant numbers must be reduced because of their impact on the ecosystems; that such high numbers of elephants are turning forest areas into grasslands.[6]

[6] Christina Skarpe, Johan T. Du Toit and Stein R. Moe, *Elephants and Savanna Woodland Ecosystems: A Study from Chobe National Park, Botswana* (Wiley-Blackwell, 2014).

This is consistent with the ideology of ecological holism, where the good of the ecosystem must take priority over individuals. Having said that, the health of an ecosystem is defined by human constructions of conservation and a nostalgic view of the natural state and, therefore, even an ecological ideology is anthropocentric in some sense. This was also demonstrated in Chapter 4 when the ecosystem approach in the *Convention on Biological Diversity* was deconstructed as a model of anthropocentric governance. Finally, some take an individualistic welfare ideology; they consider the welfare of each individual to have priority over the health of their habitats and human-centred interests. In the context of Botswana, such views are largely informed by people who do not live with the conflict and it is this ideology that drives occurrences of conservation displacement. Each of the ideologies fails to consider the necessity of all components of the relationships involved. Anthropocentrism promotes individual autonomy by separating people from wildlife. Ecological holism promotes individual and institutional autonomy by separating ecosystems from people, the individual organisms that rely on them, and the human constructions of an ecosystem upon which the institutions rely. Welfare individualism promotes individual autonomy because it separates individual animals from their habitat, their ecological effects and the impact they can have on human security.

It is the promotion of individual and institutional autonomy then that is the central ideology that drives conflict and the human–wildlife relationship as a whole. It also informs conflict governance. Herein lies an essential paradox; attempts to resolve the conflict are informed by the very cause of the conflict. Autonomy drives conflict governance because most methods of governance rely on the separation between wildlife and people that comes from the promotion of autonomy (such as fencing and wildlife relocation) or the promotion of neo-liberal autonomy (such as promoting individual autonomy in a capitalistic sense by using financial incentives to 'get along' with wildlife or to understand the human 'value' of wildlife). However, these common methods of governance are ineffective because autonomy is a false idea that cannot be achieved. For example, animals that are deemed to be problematic from a human perspective are often separated via fencing and relocation. People kill wild animals because their sense of autonomy means that they deem wild animals unnecessary. State institutions may pay individual people who are affected by conflict to promote their neo-liberal autonomy, essentially overruling the inherent conflict with money. However, such governance 'techniques' do not reduce negative interactions; instead, in many cases, they prolong or exacerbate the conflict.[7]

The eco-vulnerability theory developed throughout this book differs from other methodologies that have been used to analyse the problem due to its focus on autonomy and the placement of autonomy within the web of domination. It provides a starting point for analysing conflict wherein it is recognised that conflict occurs because of autonomy, but also autonomy is placed in a web of domination that creates a very particular hierarchy that is detrimental to effective conflict governance. For example, several societal factors contribute to ongoing conflict, such as patriarchal institutions, the domination of the environment, the oppression of women and minorities, power over conceptions of power, capitalism and the attainment of western notions of personal wealth. Yet, eco-vulnerability links all of these factors back to the promotion of the individual autonomy of a select few, to maintain the hierarchies that support their power and wealth and continue the use of wildlife in a way that suits them. The promotion of autonomy is not equal across all groups of people, but instead creates another hierarchy, with those already in power at the top, and those who currently bear the greatest costs associated with the conflict at the bottom. Neo-liberal markets prioritise consumptive users of wildlife over non-consumptive users and the pull of the market often overrides strict conservation, as shown by the recent lift of the hunting ban in Botswana and the continued wildlife trade as a whole, which is largely driven by western consumption. Conservation displacement is also a result of this hierarchy, as people lower in the hierarchy are subject to removal as a result of the conservation interests of those higher in the hierarchy.

Not only is the conflict defined by these factors and more, but these factors also interact with each other differently in every instance of conflict. All of the different oppressions and dominations, values and attitudes that surround conflict are connected in a web with the conflict in the centre, similar to Plumwood's 'Web of Domination'.[8] All aspects of the ecological and social conflict are vulnerable to small shifts in the others. The relationships, views, attitudes, structures, rules and processes surrounding the conflict cannot be viewed in isolation from one another.

By way of example, the held values and attitudes of people towards wildlife and wildlife governance practices are defined by the attempted promotion of autonomy. The stakeholders vary in every situation of conflict, as do their values and attitudes towards wildlife. But those values are influenced by the

[7] See Chapter 3.
[8] Plumwood, 'The Ecopolitics Debate and the Politics of Nature', 64.

dominant hierarchy and web of oppressions, whether the values are aligned with that hierarchy or not. Values held by both the Butchulla and the Batswana have been dismissed due to the dominant hierarchy, aggravating the conflict as the communities doubled down on their views, making social resolution nearly impossible.

All of these interrelated dominations are embedded into our institutional structures and, in this book, I demonstrated this by analysis of the law and governance structures surrounding instances of conflict.

8.3 THE INSTITUTIONAL RESPONSE: LAW AS A SOURCE OF CONFLICT

As a regulator of behaviour, the law has been a part of conflict resolution for centuries. Yet, human–wildlife conflict, and autonomy within that conflict, are not explicitly contained within the overt discourse of law and policy. Indeed, the conflict itself is rarely found in law and policy except at the very local level, such as in the original Fraser Island Dingo Management Policy (as discussed in Chapter 5).[9] What does this mean for the way that conflict is dealt with? If the ideologies behind the conflict are not accounted for in law and policy, the conflict is prone to exacerbation *as a result of* the application of law and policy. Law and policy promote the underlying drivers of conflict without addressing conflict itself.

The conflict is also influenced by the values promoted by law and governance institutions. The institutional settings of a place can also define the extent of the conflict. Previously, the institutional influence over human–wildlife conflict was not a consideration in the research and practice around conflict governance. Instead, governance tended to remain focused on managing wildlife behaviour or assessing the attitudes of people toward wildlife, to determine what practice is most acceptable to the greatest number of people. In this book, I suggested that such an approach misses an important defining factor that can inform both wildlife behaviour and human attitudes – institutions that govern our everyday lives and moderate our interactions with wildlife. Both people and wildlife are *vulnerable* to society's governing institutions, such as the economy and markets, religion, education, and the law. For example, Chapter 5 demonstrated the institutional influence through analysis of an international treaty, the *World Heritage Convention* (WHC) and its effect on the ground-level governance of human–dingo conflict. The

9 Queensland Parks and Wildlife Service Environmental Protection Agency, *Fraser Island Dingo Management Strategy*.

WHC's requirement to maintain a 'natural' space defines the current human–dingo relationship on K'gari, and promotes separation. Chapter 6 demonstrated the influence of both international law and the state as institutions. International laws such as CITES have dictated strict conservation of elephants, in an attempt to place a westernised form of conservation ethic over local values, needs and interests. The state community-based management schemes then attempted to neo-liberalise elephants to provide economic benefit, further dictating that elephants do have value, but it is in monetary form.

The intrinsic value of wildlife is rarely espoused by law and policies as an overriding factor. It is noted in some legal documents and, arguably, this is evidence of a small shift towards disassembly of the hierarchy. However, it is rare for intrinsic value to be contained within substantive or hard laws; instead, it is usually mentioned in the objectives or soft law provisions, and even where it is mentioned it is still contained within a list of other values that have been implemented for decades longer. The result is that intrinsic value is not considered as a factor in decision-making as it does not have to be, nor has it historically been. The hierarchy, therefore, emerges in decision-making as an application of the hard laws and a multi-species perspective cannot be accommodated.

Eco-vulnerability also demonstrates how laws and policies create and perpetuate hierarchies *between people* in situations of human–wildlife conflict, so that individual autonomy becomes something that is viewed as attainable to the already elites; those that create and maintain the systems from which they benefit and maintain the power over conceptions of power and privilege. For example, the westernisation of environmental protection through the influence of international law in Botswana represents the continued colonisation of the global south that has not traditionally 'developed' in a western capitalist way. The structural promotion of westernised versions of liberal autonomy has meant that individuals in Botswana, and the state itself, are striving for an autonomy ideology that affects the relationship that people have with wildlife. Unsurprisingly, the promotion of autonomy and ignorance of vital relationships that support and sustain the planet and human security are not only detrimental to the low-income states but high-income states as well. This is a paradigm in which what shores up our legal subjectivity is autonomy, via the power to freely enter into agreements, transactions, etc., with other autonomous individuals, the condition of being individually responsible for one's infractions, etc. This remains in place regardless of whether the law itself acknowledges particular economic goals; but the economic goals are only possible through it. This institutionalisation operates in the same way that human rights law, while denouncing the effects of power, shores up the very structure of that power.[10] Wildlife laws also shore up an underlying structure that promotes autonomy the more it claims to be rectifying its deficiencies.

The COVID-19 pandemic has demonstrated the way that these hierarchies play out when human–wildlife conflict turns into a global crisis. International law is used as a tool to exert power over those not in the dominant hierarchy (such as China) while, at the same time, those exerting power deny international law's ability to compromise their own. This has been very evident with the rhetoric surrounding the *International Health Regulations* (IHR). Western states such as the United States and Australia have used the IHR as a tool to infringe on China's sovereignty, to send teams to investigate the origin of the COVID-19 virus. At the same time, they fight against the power of its overarching body, the World Health Organisation, so that the IHR has no power over their sovereignty. For example, States have rebelled against the WHO by withdrawing funding from the Organisation itself.

8.4 THE NATURE OF THE HUMAN–WILDLIFE RELATIONSHIP: WHAT IT SHOULD BE

So, what should the human–wildlife relationship look like? It would be remiss of me not to say that some level of human–wildlife conflict is inevitable. Conflict will ensue as long as humans and wildlife continue to co-occupy spaces and seek the same resources (water and food as examples). Some aggressive wildlife behaviour cannot be moderated through human manipulation or by creating wildlife safe-havens. However, the burgeoning global spread and increase in rates of human–wildlife conflicts are indicative of a change in the nature of most conflicts, not all of which are inevitable.

But how should we manage the avoidable conflicts? To start, an acknowledgement that they are avoidable is important. And not just avoidable in the sense that we can kill the culprit species or fence them off. Most conflicts will be avoided if there is transformative change in how we view and treat wildlife and how we look at the conflict as a societal and institutional problem and not a problem solely for the individual or conservationists.

Eco-vulnerability theory is a useful, holistic methodology for analysing the problem of human–wildlife conflict and offering a perspective on the transformative change required. It can draw together various human values and respond to conflict while emphasising relationality and community.

[10] See Section 4.4.1.

Eco-vulnerability takes Fineman's vulnerability theory and uses principles of eco-feminism to extend it to include environmental, ecological, and multi-species vulnerability. The theory of eco-vulnerability analyses conflicts with the starting premise that vulnerability is an inherent condition, not only for humans, but for the vast range of life on Earth, as well as the ecosystems and environments that house them. It acknowledges that human vulnerabilities are interconnected with those of the environment, including wildlife. It is our shared vulnerability with each other, wildlife and the environment that should form the basis for our institutional response to conflict and the inequalities surrounding it, not a continued focus on the liberal notions of autonomy. Just as autonomy from other people and society is a myth, so too is autonomy from the wild animals with which we share space.

First, an eco-vulnerability methodology can be used to address the theoretical gap that arises around the issue of 'coexistence' as an appropriate governance outcome. As demonstrated by both situational case studies, the conflict is not able to be entirely eliminated where humans and wildlife occupy shared spaces. Instead, it is vital to understand that whilst the human condition is one of vulnerability, the environmental condition has also been one of vulnerability. Yet, the Earth and its creatures have been resilient to changes for billions of years. Now though that resilience is being threatened by the promotion of liberal human autonomy. Autonomy is not only decreasing our resilience to inherent vulnerability but also that of the environment and wildlife. As a result of this premise and combined with the fact that some level of conflict is inevitable, coexistence is not an appropriate conflict governance goal. Instead, governance should be focused on building the *resilience* of all stakeholders involved in the conflict.

Fineman writes that resilience is not something we are born with, it is 'accumulated over the course of our lifetimes within social structures or institutions over which individuals may have little control'.[11] These social structures not only affect our resilience but the resilience of wildlife and their habitats as well. As a result, responses to conflict that work to build resilience need to promote the resilience of both people and wildlife. In addition to building individual resilience, responses to the conflict need to focus on building relationship resilience, that is to say, increasing the ability of the human–wildlife relationship to 'bounce back' after negative interactions. A resilient relationship survives and this requires the survival of all involved in the relationship. Institutional governance of conflict needs to respond to

[11] Fineman, 'Vulnerability, Resilience, and LGBT Youth', 320.

vulnerability by fostering individual and relationship resilience of and between all people, wildlife, ecosystems, and the planet as a whole.

A vulnerability response requires a State that is *responsive to vulnerability*, instead of one that actively promotes autonomy. This means that resilience to vulnerability has to be promoted institutionally; that is, vulnerability should be considered by all institutions in decision-making processes, but also institutions should consider and respond to their own vulnerability as well. Through analysis of the conflict literature, this book has demonstrated several legal pathways to conflict resilience.

First, it has become clear that the law ignores the conflict and its social drivers whilst simultaneously embedding values that are detrimental to the effective governance of the conflict. For example, the Fraser Island Dingo Management Policy does not acknowledge the inherent conflict contained within the document; that to completely remove negative interactions there need to be fewer people or fewer dingoes. Although many people know this and discuss it within the policy context, the policy itself needs to acknowledge that it operates to embed the conflict further, before setting out the ways that it attempts to minimise that conflict. There needs to be an acknowledgement at least that some of the objectives are seemingly inconsistent, and they require balancing, so that achievement of the objectives is unlikely to ever fully be realised, as one will always need to make leeway for others. For example, the need to naturalise dingoes and keep them separate from people does not allow a natural fear of dingoes to develop. The provisions around animal welfare and restrictions on hazing do not allow an appropriate level of fear of humans to develop in the dingoes and so contradicts the policy of separation.

The next law reform option is to alter the autonomy-based values that are present in wildlife laws and replace them with values that reflect a more accurate representation of the real relationship between people and wildlife, that of intertwined vulnerability. As discussed in Chapter 4, the representation of values in law further embeds those values into society and prevents deviation from them during decision-making processes. Anthropocentrism, individual autonomy and the prioritisation of economic value are concepts that can be removed from many wildlife laws and replaced with descriptions of eco-vulnerability. For example, a slight amendment in the wording of *the Convention on Biological Diversity* preamble could shift the focus from singular human vulnerability to the vulnerability of wildlife and the human relationship with it; from 'Affirming that the conservation of biological diversity is a common concern of *humankind*' to 'Affirming that the conservation of biological diversity is a common concern of *all of Earth and its species*'. Of course, such notional changes may be viewed as meaningless, and hard law provisions and amendments are also undoubtedly required. However, we have seen the value-making potential of soft legal provisions and a cultural shift must start somewhere.

Next, there are avenues to include the concepts of holism and relationality within legal institutions. Just as ecofeminism asserts that all oppressions are related, we have seen that the domination of wildlife, the environment and many minorities are connected in the different conflict scenarios that have been examined in this book. There is an 'oppressive conceptual framework' into which human–wildlife conflict is embedded. As a result, a responsive State must address the oppressions that are related to any one instance of conflict. Chapter 5 demonstrated the relevance of the historical treatment of Indigenous Australians on K'gari and beyond, to the point where their collective voice and knowledge were systematically oppressed. The result was a type of 'blame game' that occurs after each instance of human–dingo conflict on K'gari, where the Butchulla can naturally distance themselves from the governance of the conflict and place the blame on the State Government and QPWS. This results in an exacerbation of the social conflict, which requires redirection of resources away from dingo governance to social conflict management. To their credit, the State Government and QPWS have recognised the relationship and have sought to be more inclusive of the Butchulla. They now have an Indigenous ranger and have funds to hire an Indigenous communications officer.[12] A Butchulla spokesperson has been involved in the latest review of the Management Strategy. Yet, the State remains committed to the promotion of the autonomy of the Butchulla people, the island's locals and visitors and the dingoes. There is little legal requirement to go beyond tokenisation of these positions and the reversal of such systemic oppressions needs to be more deeply embedded in the legal system. One potential law reform solution involves institutionalisation of the Butchulla voice by making mandatory their involvement as *leaders* in the policy review process (where they desire it as they do on K'gari), not a mere voice that may or may not be heard.

Embedding the intrinsic value of wildlife and their habitats is required for a response to acknowledge multispecies vulnerability. Haraway suggests that any instance of flourishing must inevitably be multispecies in nature.[13] The welfare of animals is not trivial, and can start a chain reaction that leads to a

[12] Queensland Government, 'Indigenous Land and Sea Ranger program – ranger locations'. Available at: https://apps.des.qld.gov.au/land-sea-rangers/?ranger=kgari-fraser-island (last accessed 9 February 2022).

[13] Donna Haraway, *When Species Meet* (University of Minnesota Press, 2008) 134–35.

worldwide crisis, as we have seen with COVID-19. The intrinsic value of all species cannot be accommodated in practice while the primary ideology is concerned with autonomy and anthropocentrism. Again, a focus on shared and mutual vulnerabilities in our legal institutions can facilitate this shift.

8.5 CONCLUDING THOUGHTS; MOVING FORWARD WITH ECOLOGICAL VULNERABILITY

With a focus on the interconnected vulnerabilities of people and wildlife, the issue of human–wildlife conflict is viewed as a historical, social and institutional phenomenon, rather than stand-alone interactions between a species and individual people. As a result, the area of human–wildlife conflict needs a fundamental shift in culture and theory, away from the sole assessment of individual negative interactions and human values to particular governance approaches, and to a holistic and multi-disciplinary account of all societal and institutional factors that lead to negative interactions between humans and wildlife.

This book has set out the need for and viability of an eco-vulnerability approach to the legal governance of human–wildlife conflict on a theoretical basis. Future research directions involve assessing the approach empirically. For example, there is a need for research around the most appropriate mechanism for developing long-lasting collaborative governance schemes, from a vulnerability perspective. That is to say, what is the best way to build vulnerability and resilience into an existing collaborative mechanism? Francine Madden facilitates conflict transformation and her method of peace-building with a human–wildlife conflict scenario may be a good starting point for a vulnerability collaborative approach.[14]

Additional and continual research also needs to be conducted on the social and ecological nature of human–wildlife conflict to ensure that the governance of each conflict is holistic. Research around the social aspect of the conflict is also still needed in the majority of conflicts and the law as a player in those conflicts. For example, why do people continue to avoid compliance with the policy of separation on K'gari? How exactly do the Butchulla people want to be involved in the governance of the island and the conflict, so that we

[14] See Francine Madden, 'Can Traditions of Tolerance Help Minimise Conflict? An Exploration of Cultural Factors Supporting Human–Wildlife Coexistence' (2004) 13 *Policy Matters* 234–41; Madden and McQuinn, 'Conservation's Blind Spot'; Madden 'Growing Conflict Between Humans and Wildlife'; Center for Conservation Peacebuilding. Available at: https://cpeace.ngo/ (last accessed 14 April 2021).

can ensure involvement is on their terms and does not antagonise a major stakeholder, furthering the social conflict in the area? Are there initiatives that could assist a move away from trophy hunting towards a shared vulnerability approach to the governance of human–elephant conflict in Northern Botswana? How can we make people aware of the underlying drivers of pandemics such as COVID-19 and their impact on biodiversity? Why is there a continued difference between local perceptions and conflict numbers in most major human–wildlife conflicts around the world?

Finally, the societal and institutional influence on the human–wildlife relationship is much broader than law and governance. Questions remain about how autonomy and the dominant hierarchy are promoted in the other institutions that maintain social orders. How do the family, education, religion, the economy and work, government, and healthcare promote autonomy in individuals and amongst themselves, and what are the long-term effects on the human–wildlife relationship? Can an eco-vulnerability approach be embedded in them? I believe it can, but that is a question for another book.

Index

Printed in the United Kingdom by TJ Clays Ltd.